Events and Urban Regeneration

In recent years, major sporting and cultural events such as the Olympic Games have emerged as significant elements of public policy, particularly in efforts to achieve urban regeneration. As well as opportunities arising from new venues, these events are viewed as a way to stimulate investment, gain civic engagement and publicise progress to assist the urban regeneration process more generally. However, the pursuit of regeneration involving events is a practice that is poorly understood, controversial and risky.

Events and Urban Regeneration is the first book dedicated to the use of events in regeneration. It explores the relationship between events and regeneration by analysing a range of cities and a range of sporting and cultural event projects. It considers various theoretical perspectives to provide insight into why major events are important to contemporary cities. It examines the different ways that events can assist regeneration, as well as problems and issues associated with this unconventional form of public policy. It identifies key issues faced by those tasked with using events to assist regeneration and suggests how practices could be improved in the future.

The book adopts a multi-disciplinary perspective, drawing together ideas from the geography, urban planning and tourism literatures, as well as from the emerging events and regeneration fields. It illustrates arguments with a range of international case studies placed within and at the end of chapters to show positive outcomes that have been achieved and examples of high-profile failures.

This timely book is essential reading for students and practitioners who are interested in events, urban planning, urban geography and tourism.

Andrew Smith is a Senior Lecturer in the School of Architecture and the Built Environment at the University of Westminster, UK.

D1056796

Events and Urban Regeneration

The strategic use of events to revitalise cities

Andrew Smith

Routledge
Taylor & Francis Group

LONDON AND NEW YORK

First published 2012
by Routledge
2 Park Square, Milton Park, Abingdon, Oxon OX14 4RN

Simultaneously published in the USA and Canada
by Routledge
711 Third Avenue, New York, NY 10017

Routledge is an imprint of the Taylor & Francis Group, an informa business

British Library Cataloguing in Publication Data
A catalogue record for this book is available from the British Library

Library of Congress Cataloging-in-Publication Data

Smith, Andrew, 1975 June 25-
    Events and urban regeneration / Andrew Smith.
        p. cm.
    Includes bibliographical references and index.
    1. Urban renewal. 2. City promotion. 3. Festivals. I. Title.
HT170.S547 2011

                                                              307.3´416–dc23

ISBN: 978-0-415-58147-9 (hbk)
ISBN: 978-0-415-58148-6 (pbk)
ISBN: 978-0-203-13699-7 (ebk)

Typeset in Times New Roman
by Cenveo Publisher Services

Printed and bound in Great Britain by
TJ International Ltd, Padstow, Cornwall

Contents

Figures

Tables

Boxes

Extended case studies

Preface

Events and Urban Regeneration has been written mainly for the growing number of students and researchers interested in events who want to know more about urban regeneration. Since the urban crisis of the 1970s, approaches to urban regeneration have evolved considerably and there have been some impressive achievements. This book has been written in the context of a new crisis that has undermined some of the progress made in post-industrial cities. The specific effects of the latest recession are not dealt with in this book, but the difficult circumstances currently faced by many post-industrial cities suggest that there is a strong case for refocusing attention on urban regeneration

This book explores the use of major events within urban regeneration. My personal involvement in this field of study dates back to research into the efforts of Birmingham, Manchester and Sheffield in the 1990s. A series of field trips to Barcelona around the turn of the century helped to reaffirm my interest in urban event projects. After relocating to London in 2003, any thoughts of moving away from this research topic were effectively ended by London's successful bid for the Olympic Games.

It is hoped that the book will provide a useful resource for a wide audience, not merely those specifically interested in events. Major events should not be considered as merely specialised phenomena. They can illustrate wider urban issues and they provide useful lenses through which to explore cities in general.

Andrew Smith
June 2011

Acknowledgements

This book would not have been possible without support from family and friends, in particular my wife Jo Thornhill. I would also like to acknowledge the contributions of my colleagues at the University of Westminster. Whilst they were unable to give me any dedicated time to write the book, the reorganisation of my workload in the latter stages of the project helped enormously. I would also like to thank the individuals and organisations I have worked with over the past few years. Related research conducted in association with Tim Fox, Nancy Stevenson, the Royal Institution of Chartered Surveyors, Manchester City Council and ECOTEC Consulting helped to inspire, develop and refine the ideas contained in this book. Tim Fox of ECOTEC co-produced the Manchester Case and some of the good practice principles in the conclusion.

I would also like to credit the following people/agencies for several images that are reproduced in this book.

Figure 2.1: Gerhard Bissell/RIBA Library Photographs Collection.
Figure 3.2: RIBA Library Photographs Collection.
Figure 3.4: Colin Westwood/RIBA Library Photographs Collection.
Figures 4.6 and 8.4: Richard Dyson.
Figure 4.9: Ben Crewe.
Figure 4.10: Andrea Pavoni.
Figures 5.2 and 5.3: Peter Colman.
Figure 5.4: Danielle Tinero/RIBA Library Photographs Collection.
Figures 8.6 and 9.6 were produced by MasonEdwards Design.

All other illustrations were produced by the author.

Abbreviations and acronyms

ACOG   Atlanta Committee for the Olympic Games
ANZ   Australia and New Zealand Banking Group
ATP   Association of Tennis Professionals
BBC   British Broadcasting Corporation
BC   British Columbia
BCA   Business Club Australia
BIE   Bureau International des Expositions
CODA   Corporation for Olympic Development in Atlanta
CPC   Canadian Paralympic Committee
DoE   UK Department for the Environment
EU   European Union
FIFA   Fédération Internationale de Football Associations
GLLaB   Greenwich Local Labour and Business
HLC   Healthy Living Centre
IOC   International Olympic Committee
LOC   Local Organising Committee
LOCOG   London Organising Committee for the Olympic and Paralympic
          Games
LTA   Lawn Tennis Association
MAOGA   Metropolitan Atlanta Olympic Games Authority
NBA   National Basketball Association
NGF   National Garden Festival
OCA   Olympic Co-ordination Authority
ODA   Olympic Delivery Authority
PR   Public Relations
PVP   Pre Volunteer Programme

PwD   Persons with Disability
UDC   Urban Development Corporation
UEFA   Union of European Football Associations
UEL   University of East London
VANOC   Vancouver Organising Committee for the Olympic and Paralympic
           Games

An introduction to events and urban regeneration

1

INTRODUCTION

Major events are staged for many reasons. They are opportunities for socialising, celebrations of achievement, markers of time and vehicles for political posturing. In the contemporary era, events have become platforms to sell a variety of products, including the host city itself. Major events are also increasingly associated with urban regeneration. This book explores this relationship. The aim is neither to justify the use of events as regeneration tools, nor to denigrate this practice. Instead, the principal objectives are to identify and evaluate different ways that events have been used within urban regeneration policy. As it would appear that cities are increasingly keen to link events to urban regeneration objectives, a subsidiary aim is to suggest how organisers and other stakeholders can optimise the regeneration outcomes of event strategies. The intention is not merely to explore the use of events within urban regeneration, but to use the analysis of this specialised practice to enhance understanding of urban regeneration generally.

In this chapter the two key concepts – events and regeneration – are introduced; initially as separate phenomena, and then as related ideas. The synergies between the concepts are discussed and the introductory section also maps out how the concept of event regeneration is addressed within the book. In later sections of the Introduction, the relationship between events and policy is discussed. This introductory chapter culminates in several shorter sections that cover the key stakeholders involved in event regeneration, the focus of the book, the sources used and the structure of subsequent chapters.

EVENTS

This book focuses on official, public events: themed occasions that take place at a stipulated time. These are different from everyday occasions or those which are not advertised publicly. Official events usually adopt a set of rituals that help to mark their start and end; and they have always been important markers of time. This is most obvious in celebrations associated with certain dates such as Midsummer's Day and New Year's Eve. But major sport events and cultural festivals also allow years to be differentiated and they are ways that people remember certain moments in their lives. People participate in events because of the opportunities for entertainment, but also because of their sociability, festivity and the way that they allow people to break with normal routines. Packard and Ballantyne (2010) call these dimensions the social experience, the festival experience and the separation experience. The popularity of events, and the positive associations attached to them, mean they are also coveted by governments and private companies who are keen to harness the power of events. This 'power' is derived from the public's awareness of, identification with, and participation in, events. Participation can take different forms: the public can be part of the spectacle; or they can consume events via mediated output. Events are social tools and forms of leisure activity, but they also have a more profound role: they communicate a society's values.

The events focus of the book

This book focuses on major events – in particular leisure events that are not tied to one particular location. Various attempts have been made to categorise events according to their scale, content, location and the regularity with which they are staged. In this book, the discussion of major events includes consideration of mega-events – occasions that can defined as those with global reputations that generate significant economic impacts and attract sustained media attention (Roche, 2000). There is a notion in the literature that, to match the metric definition of mega, mega-events should be defined as those that attract over a million visitors (Getz, 1997). Visitors are difficult to define, but it would be useful to confine the term mega-event to those events that sell over a million tickets. There are only three events that really deserve the title 'mega': the Olympic Games, the Football World Cup and World Expos (see Table 1.1). The world's major religious festivals would perhaps satisfy many of the criteria of mega-events but because of the nuanced characteristics of these events, they are not addressed here. This book does address major events that do not quite reach the thresholds seemingly required for mega status (see Table 1.1). Major events are those which attract international visitors and international media coverage. They exist at a scale that could justify investment in new venues built especially to stage the event (although as will be discussed in Chapter 4 this isn't always sensible). The focus on major events is not meant to denigrate the power of smaller events. Small events, either alone or in combination with other events, can be significant urban phenomena. However, to provide focus, and because this book is about urban regeneration, the discussion is limited to major events.

Table 1.1 An indicative list of the type of events considered in this book

	Sport	Non-sport
Mega events	Olympic Games, Football World Cup	World Expo
Major multi-purpose events	Commonwealth Games, Pan American Games, Asian Games, Universiade World Police and Fire Games, International Gay Games, World Medical and Health Games	European Capital of Culture
Events dedicated to specific sports/themes	African Nations Cup (football), UEFA European Football Championships, IAAF World Athletics Championships, European Athletics Championships, ICC Cricket World Cup, Formula 1 Grand Prix, America's Cup (sailing), World Ice Hockey Championships, Superbowl (American football), Rugby World Cup+ Other world championships+ Dislocated events	National Garden Festivals, MTV Music Awards, Eurovision Song Contest

Location

The book focuses on major events that do not have a fixed location. There are a large number of major events that cities compete to host – these are sometimes referred to as footloose events, or peripatetic events in the literature. Footloose events are staged in any city (e.g. the Olympic Games), whereas peripatetic events move between an established circuit of cities (e.g. the Open Golf Championship). These mobile events are the opposite of hallmark events – events that are indelibly associated with their host location.

In terms of location, whilst most events are staged by one city, others are staged in several cities or a combination of locations. Most events are static, but others move through a city (carnivals, marathons) or travel to different cities (cycle and sailing races). Just to add to the confusion, there is a recent trend for the geographical diffusion of event franchises that had previously been geographically rooted. Some major events used to happen in the same locations at regular intervals, but they are now staged in unexpected locations. This means we now have regular season US NBA (basketball) fixtures in the UK (see Figure 1.1), European Tour golf events in Asia, and Tour de France stages outside France. Other events are being exported to new audiences via the creation of new editions in new locations. Examples include the Spoleto Festival (now also staged in Melbourne, Charleston), and various iterations of the Trinidad Carnival (Rio, London, Toronto). Events are valuable assets; and in our increasingly commercialised world, this means that organisations who own the rights to them are keen to exploit their value by offering them to different destinations. The emerging market for footloose events is an interesting trend. In this marketplace the bargaining power tends to rest with the rights holders of major events because there are a limited number of valuable event franchises but a large number of cities vying to host major events.

Content

Alongside identifying hallmark and mega-events, a common way of categorising events is by their content. This usually means differentiating between sport

Figure 1.1 Dislocated events. The Toronto Raptors play the New Jersey Nets at the O$_2$ Arena, London, in 2011. This was the first ever regular season NBA game in Europe

Ways of categorising events	Focus of this book		Not addressed
Size	Mega	Major	Minor
Content	Sport	Culture	Business
Location	Footloose	Peripatetic	Fixed

Figure 1.2 *The type of events that provide the focus of this book*

events, cultural events and business events. To provide more focus, this book is confined to sport events and cultural events. Of course, all events are cultural, but this distinction is made to differentiate between sport and non-sport events. Business events such as conferences, conventions and other meetings are not addressed (see Figure 1.2).

Timing

Major events also vary according to the frequency with which they are staged and their duration. Some events take place in the same place every two weeks (sporting fixtures) or every year (cultural festivals). Others move about and are staged every year (European Capital of Culture), every two years (European Athletics Championships), every four years (FIFA World Cup, Olympic Games) or every five years (Universal Exhibitions). Some events last for a whole year (European Capital of Culture), six months (World Expos), a few weeks (Olympic Games, Football World Cups) or just one night (Eurovision Song Contest). Many events are themselves made up of a series of events. In the cultural sphere this is what differentiates festivals from individual events. Festivals and individual events are also different from what is known as the 'season': a regular programme of events staged over an extended period. Most major sport events are also made up of multiple events.

This book addresses a range of events that last for between a day and a year. However, as outlined above, events staged regularly in the same location are not considered in depth.

Key events covered in this book

The focus of this book is major events that cities stage on a one-off basis, in particular major sport events, World Expos and cultural festivals. The Olympic Games are used as a key reference point; not merely because they are the world's most significant event, but because the rites and rituals have been used as the template for other events (Roche, 2000). The modern Olympic Games were re-established in 1896 and summer and winter editions are co-ordinated by the International Olympic Committee. The world's other global mega-event, the Football World Cup, is also featured extensively in this book. Like the Summer Olympic Games, the World Cup is staged every four years, but it is staged by several different host cities. The event was established in 1930 and it is co-ordinated by FIFA – football's world governing body.

The rise of these sport mega-events occurred in the twentieth century, but in the late nineteenth and early twentieth centuries World Expos were the most significant world events. These events remain important today and they also feature heavily in the following chapters. World Expos fall into different categories: Universal Exhibitions (staged every five years) and International Exhibitions (smaller editions staged in between Universal Exhibitions). To add to the confusion, in the USA, these events are often referred to as World's Fairs. For the purposes of clarity, the generic term 'World Expos' is used in this book for these events. Since 1928, World Expos have been co-ordinated by the Bureau International des Expositions (BIE).

Other sport events are also addressed in the book, including the Commonwealth Games, a multi-sport event contested by nations belonging to the Commonwealth of Nations (it was formerly called the British Empire Games). A series of cultur-ally-oriented events also features, most notably the European Capital of Culture event. This annual event was instigated by the European Union in 1985 when it was known as the European City of Culture event. The event was conceived as way of developing closer cultural ties between member states. Several other major events are also considered where appropriate. As mentioned previously, the main focus is on one-off events, rather than events that are staged by the same city on a regular basis. However, it should be noted that some cities have staged more than one mega-event. Indeed, there are a number of cities that have used a major event to assist urban objectives on more than one occasion. These 'event cities' are listed in Table 1.2.

REGENERATION

The word regeneration has become a very widely used term and it is used to refer to a variety of processes. It is hard to separate regeneration from general urban policy, but its distinctive characteristic is that it involves attempts to reverse decline in cities (or in certain parts of cities). Initially the term was used to refer to housing renewal and other property-led initiatives (Oatley, 1998) but in recent years, a more holistic conceptualisation has emerged in which 'partnership, spatial targeting, integration, competition, empowerment and sustainability have

Table 1.2 A tale of twelve cities: a dozen cities that have used major events extensively within urban development and regeneration

City	World Expos	Olympic Games	Capital of Culture	Other
1 Paris	1855, 1867, 1878, 1889, 1900	1900, 1924	1989	1998 FIFA World Cup Final
2 London	1851, 1862, 1951*	1908, 1948, 2012		1966 FIFA World Cup Final, 1996 UEFA European Championships Final
3 Barcelona	1888, 1929, 2004*	1992		Venue for 1982 FIFA World Cup
4 Melbourne		1956	N/A	2006 Commonwealth Games
5 Glasgow	1938		1990	2014 Commonwealth Games, 1988 National Garden Festival
6 Lisbon	1998		1994	2004 UEFA European Championships Final
7 Montreal	1967	1976	N/A	
8 Vancouver	1986	2010	N/A	1954 Commonwealth Games
9 Amsterdam		1928	1987	2000 UEFA European Championships Final
10 Genoa	1992		2004	Venue for 1990 FIFA World Cup
11 Rio de Janeiro		2016	N/A	2014 FIFA World Cup Final, 2007 Pan American Games
12 Liverpool			2008	1984 National Garden Festival

Note: * Not an official BIE registered event

assumed increasing importance' (Jones and Gripaios, 2000: 218–219). This fits with Furbey's (1999: 428) comment that: 'the distinguishing mark of recent regeneration is its broad stretch'. The emergence of a more holistic approach to regeneration is reaffirmed by other contemporary definitions which describe regeneration as 'comprehensive and integrated vision and action which leads to the resolution of urban problems and which seeks to bring about a lasting improvement in the economic, social and environmental conditions of an area that has been subject to change' (Roberts, 2000: 17). As well as reaffirming the points made above, Roberts's definition highlights the importance of sustaining any improvements made to urban districts.

Regeneration is also often used in conjunction with, or in the place of, other terms such as renewal and revitalisation. Exploring the different nuances of these terms seems pedantic, but it helps to shed light on different objectives. The term regeneration implies that efforts are being made to recover the position that a city once held. The term derives from the notion of rebirth and this suggests that regeneration involves more than simply restoring or replenishing cities. Of course, urbanism is not the only field of study where the term is commonly used. In the natural sciences, regeneration is very widely used to refer to the re-creation of organic life. Regeneration also has a religious meaning; a sphere where to be 'born again' has great significance. These wider uses of the term are not irrelevant to the study of urbanism. Indeed, Furbey (1999) suggests that Darwinian natural selection has parallels with the ways urban regeneration involves competitive strategies to outperform rivals. Biblical derivations imply that people can be transformed and this is relevant to contemporary urban regeneration, which now usually includes attention to social objectives.

In the sphere of urban policy, 'regeneration' suggests the achievement of certain goals in a certain context. In terms of context, for somewhere to have been regenerated it must, at some point, have suffered from some sort of degeneration. This highlights an important difference between regeneration and change classed merely as development. The latter could presumably take place in areas that have not suffered in the past. In terms of what is achieved, regeneration also seems to suggest more than minor change – it implies transformation; and it suggests that any transformation will last (rather than merely existing in the short term). Ultimately, regeneration implies impressive and progressive outcomes. However, reflecting the use and abuse of other terms (e.g. sustainability, accessibility), the popularity of the term means that it has been appropriated by a range of interests. Regeneration is now not only a policy term, but one which is used within everyday language as well as within the discourses of place marketing and property speculation. This means that there is a distinction between academic definitions of the term, the way it infuses policy discourses and popular representations of regeneration.

The term regeneration is also one used at different geographical scales. At the urban policy level regeneration is usually a concept that refers to policies enacted at the neighbourhood level. These are often termed area-based initiatives (ABIs). For example, most UK government-funded regeneration schemes aim to assist neighbourhoods of no more than 4,000 households. However, outside official policy circles the term is used more loosely to refer both to specific schemes, and wider programmes that aim to enhance the fortunes of a city as a whole.

In this book, a very broad definition of regeneration will be used. The term is largely used in the following chapters to refer to an aim, rather than an outcome. This is not merely an expedient decision; it is one that reflects contemporary usage. Regeneration is best understood as a laudable, but a normative concept. Understanding regeneration requires knowledge about what should happen, but also what does happen, and this explains why this book covers examples of regeneration that many would argue are not worthy of this classification. For this reason, it is tempting to always use the term with the prefix 'so-called' attached. When regeneration is cited by key stakeholders as an outcome of events, the term is often used in its broadest sense. Therefore, in this book, it makes sense to analyse these examples, whilst recognising that only in a very few examples would the ambitions match academic definitions of regeneration.

EVENTS AND REGENERATION

The preceding discussion implies some important links between events and regeneration. These links go beyond the increasing use of events as tools or themes within regeneration. Both events and regeneration are concepts that can be understood only with reference to time. Events take place at particular times, and they can compartmentalise time (e.g. into periods before, during and after the event). As Roche (2000) and others have argued, major events of the past helped to formalise the modern notion of time and they continue to mark time. Regeneration is also a concept that can be understood only with reference to temporal considerations. Periods before, during and after regeneration are often noted. Major regeneration initiatives are often allocated a specific time frame, something that gives the process a sense of urgency. For example, many UK regeneration projects have to be completed in a certain period to qualify for funding. This is also a noted characteristic of event projects – event deadlines provide useful drivers of action – something explored in Chapter 5. Major events are very much associated with bidding processes, and this is also a characteristic of regeneration policy. In many regeneration schemes, funding is awarded by governments after a competitive bidding process in which cities or urban districts bid to secure regeneration funding from a limited central fund.

Events and regeneration are concepts which occur in specific places, but they are also both important mechanisms through which places are made. They are both agents of territorialisation. Designating spaces as event sites or regeneration projects marks them and reclaims them as official spaces, rather than informal, vague spaces (see Chapter 2). In a more abstract sense, the two concepts are synonymous. Regeneration can be viewed as an event – a planned spectacle which takes place at a certain time. Some authors have suggested that monumental regeneration projects (e.g. Bilbao's recent redevelopment) act like an event (e.g. van Vrijaldenhoven, 2007), whilst others suggest that events act like physical monuments. For example, one commentator suggests that a major event 'functions like a monument, supporting and reinforcing the image of established power' (Bonnemaison cited in Quinn, 2005: 929). Other similarities are also apparent. Regeneration involves demolitions, launches and other ways of marking the start and finish of the process (breaking ground, topping off, cutting the ribbon): in other words, events. Furthermore, the architecture of regenerated spaces often provides spaces in which events can take place, or which are designed to evoke the spirit of events – as in festival malls. There is even a style of architecture used in regenerated spaces that is associated with events – the canopy roof (famously deployed at Sheffield's Don Valley Stadium and London's Lord's Cricket Ground) that mimics the marquees traditionally seen at outdoor events. Major events have become associated with urban structures and urban space and so it is no coincidence that we call the period before an event the 'build-up'. Events spawn new spatial relations and new architectures. And events have always been associated with social transformations. For example medieval fairs were times when people and places were transformed and reborn.

Whilst it is possible to make interesting connections between events and regeneration, there are also some fundamental problems uniting these concepts. Regeneration is a long-term ambition that involves attempts to rectify problems in disadvantaged urban places. Events are short-term occasions that, according to some authors, have little to do with the pressing problems faced by de-industrialising cities. In this context, event regeneration projects can be seen as either desperate attempts to compensate for the failure of more conventional urban policy, or spurious efforts to justify inappropriate levels of expenditure on events. Chapter 2 of this book argues that event projects are often viewed suspiciously by academic analysts, and one of the main tasks in the rest of the book is to explore whether this is fair and what – if anything – host cities could do to secure more regeneration benefits from events.

EVENT REGENERATION

Event regeneration is now considered a subsidiary form of regeneration in its own right. It is usually regarded as a form of culture-led regeneration or as an example of the emerging trend for regeneration that is themed (Tallon, 2010). In this book, the term 'event regeneration' is used as shorthand for instances when events and urban regeneration are linked. But it should be acknowledged that this phenomenon takes several forms. An obvious distinction is between projects that are directly related to staging an event, and those which a city voluntarily chooses to pursue in conjunction with an event. For the purposes of clarity, in this book the former is termed event-led regeneration, whilst the latter is referred to as 'event-themed' regeneration. These basic categories can be further subdivided as illustrated in Figure 1.3. *Event-led* projects involve either the development of new facilities, or the upgrading of existing facilities. In event-led regeneration, the process of change is driven by the event. *Event-themed* regeneration uses an event within a broader strategy driven by goals that exist over and above the event. In event-themed regeneration, parallel initiatives are bolted on to events in order to lever wider effects. Parallel physical regeneration involves changes to the built environment made in association with events, but which are not necessarily required to stage an event. These projects are underpinned by the rationale that an event provides a good opportunity to fund, accelerate or showcase urban development (see Chapter 5). In recent years, host cities have also pursued parallel social regeneration in association with events. As Figure 1.3 illustrates, events can also assist in more abstract ways. Events can instigate institutional reconfiguration – providing the basis for future regeneration work – and they can

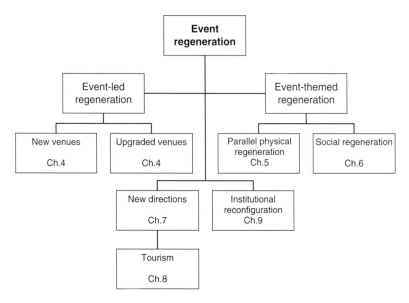

Figure 1.3 *A model representing the different elements of event regeneration and the chapters in this book that focus on these different elements*

provide the focus for efforts to point a city in a new direction, including the development of a viable tourism sector.

The physical, social and economic dimensions of event regeneration highlighted in Figure 1.3 fit well with the notion that urban regeneration involves a combination of place-based changes plus initiatives that focus on the needs of people and businesses. Figure 1.3 also demonstrates that event regeneration can take place at different scales. Whilst the effects of new venues may be felt only locally, parallel projects may result in city-wide outcomes. Indeed, social regeneration effects may extend even further into the city region and beyond (see Chapter 6). Acknowledging social regeneration also highlights that event regeneration involves tangible and intangible effects.

There are other dimensions of event regeneration not apparent in Figure 1.3 that need to be highlighted. An obvious distinction is between short-term and long-term effects. The word regeneration implies sustained effects, but these long-term effects may be stimulated by short-term 'impacts' or short-term investors. Preuss (2007) acknowledges that event legacies can be intended and unintended. Many of the most important effects of events may not be deliberately planned. They may also be negative. Indeed, some commentators think that events distract and disrupt long-term efforts to regenerate cities. It is also slightly mistaken to think of event regeneration as merely encompassing outcomes. Many of the changes made to cities are a prerequisite for staging these events rather than something that magically changes once an event has finished. Figure 1.3 omits the counterfactual – what would have happened if the event had not been staged at all (in other words the opportunity cost of staging the event). As Pitts and Liao (2009) recognise, some regeneration projects never happen because of the redistribution of funds/priorities associated with staging an event, whilst others are downscaled. These effects are also part of event regeneration.

EVENTS AND POLICY

A useful way of understanding event regeneration is as a form of policy. In a sometimes desperate search for solutions to urban problems, governments – often in partnership with other organisations – have deployed events as interventions. These are either made in isolation from, or in conjunction with, other policies. These interventions and their evolution are explored in the sections below. The discussion makes the distinction between policy on events, events as public policy and, finally, where policy is formulated to complement events.

Policy on events

Traditionally, governments have acted to regulate events – to ensure the safety of those involved, but also to promote the values of ruling regimes. These two motives are very much interconnected. Many events have been cancelled or discontinued by municipal authorities because of fears for public safety. But in these instances there is also concern that overly riotous, radical or violent events portray a negative image of places (and their governments) and encourage resistance to dominant elites. Thus public safety and public relations are mutually compatible reasons for 'clamping down' on unruly events. History is strewn with examples of governments shutting down urban festivals because of moral panics regarding their effects. The UK's 1871 Act of Parliament allowed central and local government to suppress fairs in England and this legislation was used to close 700 over the next decade (Harcup, 2000). By the twentieth century, the great carnivals of Europe – including the famous Venice carnival – had been driven out of the continent's cities to creole peripheries – New Orleans, Trinidad and Brazil (Davis and Marvin, 2004). Therefore, concerted efforts in recent years to (re)introduce major cultural and sporting events to cities can be understood as attempts to recover some of the festivity of medieval cities, albeit in a more regulated fashion.

The highly regulated nature of contemporary urban events is indirectly related to urban regeneration projects. Government interventions to ensure the safety of event participants and spectators have provided opportunities to use events to regenerate brownfield sites. In 1989, ninety-six people died in a congested lower tier at the Hillsborough football stadium in Sheffield, UK. After this disaster, one that had followed avoidable deaths at other outdated stadia (e.g. Glasgow, 1971; Heysel, 1985 and Bradford, 1987), football clubs were forced to refurbish, rebuild or relocate stadia to ensure they met new safety standards. In England, these efforts were given extra stimulus by the designation of English cities as the hosts of the European Football Championships in 1996. New stadia have emerged in sites formerly occupied by transport or utilities infrastructure, or by other forms of heavy industry. Often new venues have been funded by selling older, less safe grounds as housing or retail sites to developers. In this sense, the need to regulate events has actually provided opportunities to regenerate urban areas. This has also occurred in the sphere of cultural events, albeit to a lesser extent. Festivals that formerly took place in street settings have been encouraged to use more permanent infrastructure. The most famous example is the Sambadrome – the stadium designed by Oscar Niemeyer in Rio to host the carnival parades (they were formerly staged along the Avenida Presidente). Building these structures has produced physical effects from events which traditionally involved only a temporary transformation of urban environments.

As well as policies to regulate events, there is evidence that events can be used by authorities as a convenient opportunity to introduce new legislation. As well as new facilities, regeneration often involves new regulatory regimes.

Stricter policies are sometimes introduced for the duration of an event, and then not removed once that event has concluded.

Events as policy

Rather than simply acting as regulators of events, public bodies have also acted to instigate, fund, promote and manage events. In this sense, the provision of major events has become a form of public policy in its own right. Following the rationale that the public sector should provide amenities and services that the private sector wouldn't otherwise deliver, the public sector has instigated new events or revived events staged in the past. Since the 1970s thousands of cultural festivals have been (re)introduced. Bradley and Hall (2006) cite a study that found that 79 per cent of UK local authorities had recently established arts, cultural or sporting events. Finkel's (2009) research shows that a vast majority of UK cultural festivals originated post-1976. Whilst there is only so much that any authority could expect to achieve by staging one event, funding a regular event, or – as is becoming more common – staging multiple events over a prolonged time period, may allow more significant effects to emerge.

Events and policy

A more sophisticated approach is where public policy is formed around events to lever outcomes that are in the public interest. This is the form of public policy that has most relevance to understanding the relationship between events and urban regeneration. It has become increasingly recognised that events cannot achieve urban regeneration in their own right – even when events are regulated in certain ways to optimise benefits. Events are often used as substitutes for urban policy and this has not led to optimal outcomes. This means public bodies have had to think about how to use major events in conjunction with public policy – i.e. how to use events to assist wider policy goals. Such 'event-themed regeneration' is a relatively new concept, and how best to lever wider outcomes from events understandably depends on what those outcomes are and what event is being used. The idea of event leverage is explored further in Chapters 5 and 6.

GOVERNANCE AND STAKEHOLDERS

Before events and regeneration are discussed in more detail, it is useful to understand the different actors involved. Urban regeneration is planned and delivered by a number of stakeholders. These include governments, developers and other interested parties. Arrangements vary in different cities and countries, but municipal governments remain key actors in most major event projects. As well as identifying the roles of traditional governments, the individuals and agencies involved in urban *governance* should be acknowledged. Urban governance is a contested idea, but it is perhaps best understood as a process involving self-organising, inter-organisational networks that produce, administer and implement policy (O'Brien, 2011). It can be seen as a contrasting approach to the traditional, top-down model of governmental control (O'Brien, 2011). Broader governance needs to be discussed when dealing with major event projects, not least because such projects have helped to introduce these more flexible arrangements (see Chapter 9). In delivering urban development, municipal governments tend to work in partnership with other levels of government and with private sector partners. Thus, mega-event projects are often associated with the growth in public–private partnerships (PPPs). The rationale for these PPPs is that the public sector lacks the business acumen and financial resources to pursue ambitious projects effectively (Lever, 2001). However, the involvement of non-elected agencies in projects that involve public land and funding questions their democratic legitimacy.

Urban regeneration emerges from complex urban governance arrangements. Using major events in regeneration means adding further complexity to these arrangements as various limited-life organisations (e.g. local organising committees and event delivery agencies) and external organisations become involved. Projects may have to satisfy the requirements of sponsors, rights holders of events (e.g. FIFA, the IOC, EU, BIE) and end users in the short and long term (e.g. sports federations, local cultural agencies). Therefore, whilst major events can help regeneration projects in urban areas, they also introduce various complications. These will become apparent during the course of this book.

SUSTAINABILITY

A major concern within contemporary studies of urban regeneration is sustainable development. This is a contested term, but there is general consensus regarding the need for urbanism to be less resource intensive, whilst still allowing growing urban populations to satisfy their current and future needs. Events have been used to help regenerate dilapidated urban areas and this means some projects claim to contribute positively to both environmental and economic rehabilitation. It is within this context that many cities have come to justify event regeneration via rhetoric associated with the 'sustainable regeneration' of urban areas. The environmental and economic aspects of sustainable event regeneration are something that other literature has explored in depth. But there has been little attention devoted to the social effects and social sustainability. Therefore, one of the subsidiary objectives of this book is to assess the relationship between events and social sustainability in cities. For a more dedicated review of environmental and economic issues associated with event regeneration, readers should consult other texts (Clark, 2008; Pitts and Liao, 2009).

SOURCES

This book emerges from a series of research projects conducted by the author over an extended period. These began in the 1990s during a period of doctoral research that culminated in a Ph.D. submitted and awarded in 2002. The thesis examined sport-led regeneration initiatives implemented in Birmingham, Manchester and Sheffield. Subsequently, the author has been involved in a number of research projects related to initiatives in Barcelona (Smith, 2005b, 2007), the 2002 Commonwealth Games (Smith and Fox, 2007), the 2007 Grand Depart (Smith, 2008) and some preliminary research undertaken before the 2012 Olympic Games (Smith and Stevenson, 2009). The book draws upon the overall implications of these research exercises, as well as a large quantity of research material produced by other authors. In almost all instances, secondary material is derived from peer-reviewed journal articles rather than less robust secondary sources. This material is synthesised with the author's own research to produce the contents that appear in this book. Other texts on major events have tended to analyse individual event projects on a case-by-case basis. The aim of this book is to examine overarching ideas, issues and observations that help readers to understand the relationship between major events and urban regeneration.

THE STRUCTURE OF THE BOOK

To provide a useful introduction to subsequent material in the book, chapters on key theoretical ideas (Chapter 2) and the evolution of event regeneration policy (Chapter 3) are included. Subsequently, the structure of the book follows the conceptualisation of event regeneration outlined in Figure 1.3. Chapter 4 focuses on the development of event venues and their relationship with localised urban regeneration; it discusses the way in which the location and integration of these venues influences their success as regeneration tools. This is followed by a discussion of wider physical projects pursued in conjunction with events (Chapter 5). Cities often use the opportunity of staging events to undertake large-scale regeneration projects. These are event-themed projects because they are not essential to stage an event. Chapter 5 introduces the different ways events can be used to assist wider regeneration and the different stages of the regeneration process at which events can perform these roles. Chapter 6 also discusses event-themed regeneration, but the focus here is on socially oriented event-themed projects. This chapter outlines the social effects of event projects, but it also explains how leverage initiatives can be used to extend and optimise social outcomes. Chapter 7 discusses the way in which events are used by cities to plot a new direction for cities. This includes new ideas, images and industries. In Chapter 8 attention is devoted to tourism considerations as these are often prominent in the rationale for staging major events in post-industrial cities. Chapter 9 discusses the delivery of event regeneration. This includes the agencies responsible and the specific mechanisms that can be used to make regeneration happen. Overall conclusions are outlined in Chapter 10 and the book culminates in ten good practice principles that cities adopting event regeneration could follow. Throughout the book, case studies are used to illustrate the ideas and processes introduced. These include case studies within the main text, but also extended case studies placed at the end of Chapters 4–9. These extended cases (Cape Town, Barcelona, Manchester, Singapore, New Orleans and Gothenburg) help to illustrate points in each chapter, but they also provide self-contained examples that illustrate how post-industrial cities have used events to assist regeneration.

SUMMARY

This initial chapter has introduced the two main concepts discussed in the book: events and regeneration. The particular focus of this book – mobile, major, leisure events – has been outlined and the introduction has included a discussion of how the term regeneration will be used. The relationship between events and regeneration has been introduced and the concept of event regeneration explained and unpacked. In latter sections, the chapter explores the relationship between events and urban policy. Events have been the subject of policy interventions, but they have also been used as substitutes for urban policy. Increasingly, urban policy is integrated with events and this is something that will be discussed further during the course of the book. To provide the basis for the discussion in further chapters, the key stakeholders involved in event regeneration have been introduced. The introduction culminated in a review of the sources used for the book and the structure of subsequent chapters.

Towards a theoretical and critical understanding of event regeneration

INTRODUCTION

It is important to provide a theoretical and a historical foundation for event regeneration before specific examples are examined. In this chapter, key theoretical ideas and critical perspectives are discussed. There are a number of critical ideas that can help us to understand the way major events are linked to urban regeneration. Event regeneration can be viewed in conjunction with wider cultural movements, in particular the unfinished 'project' of modernity and dominant political philosophies. More specific theories regarding the production of – and formalisation of – time and space are useful lenses through which to explore event regeneration. Making connections to these ideas helps to understand event regeneration at a deeper level. It helps us to explore why event projects are pursued, the processes that underpin them, why they may work and why certain commentators are suspicious of them.

The chapter begins with a discussion of how event projects can be explained via reference to ideas that try to explain contemporary conditions (modernity and neo-liberalism). Critical theories that can account for the social effects of events are then discussed. In the latter sections, the fundamental concepts of time and space are explored to assist understanding of event regeneration projects. The overall aim of the chapter is to provide a theoretical platform and critical discussion to support ideas in later chapters.

MODERNITY

Using major events to redevelop cities is something very much associated with modernity. Modernity is normally considered to be a period of time (after the Enlightenment and revolutions of the eighteenth and nineteenth centuries), associated with a particular way of thinking (secularism, progress, industrialisation). The term is used colloquially to refer to the latest developments. However, modernity is not merely about newness, it is also about what is most progressive (Edgar and Sedgewick, 1999). If we adopt the conventional view of modernism – a movement promoting a departure from the past, new styles, secular values, and a positive role for science and technology (Roche, 2000) – then we can see obvious links with the urbanism that emerges from hosting major events. The pervading discourses of change, progress and economic development associated with events link them closely to the modernisation 'project'.

New event venues and landscapes often introduce new architectural styles and urban forms. Major events are also often used to celebrate and communicate technological advances. These are very modern traits. The world's mega-events are regarded as the 'timekeepers of progress' and this reaffirms their modern credentials (Roche, 2000). Most authors agree that the contemporary trend to use major events to advance urbanism dates back to the Great Exhibition of 1851. It is no coincidence that this was also the period in which modernism emerged (Edgar and Sedgewick, 1999). World Expos are particularly associated with modernity, and the relative decline of these events in the developed world may indicate a shift towards a new era of late- or post-modernity. However, it is difficult to claim that events are no longer modern phenomena, as recent events staged in Europe and North America still seem to be infused with modern credentials.

Major events are also associated strongly with the idea of the nation – a 'project' very much associated with modernism. Mega-events such as the Olympic Games and World Expos promote and legitimise the notion of nationhood, not only that of the host nation, but more generally through their conspicuous inclusion of national teams and national pavilions. This reminds us that event projects are not merely municipal endeavours: most also involve strong involvement from national governments. The buildings developed for events are often encoded with national values. This is most obvious in World Expo pavilions that celebrate individual nations, but it is also true of structures built for major sport events. Durban's stadium built for the 2010 World Cup incorporated a roof structure that was meant to imitate the South Africa flag. In a more subtle manner, the innovative roof structure (see Figure 2.1) that became the emblem of Munich's 1972 Olympic Games was deliberately designed to convey a modern and progressive nation, to counteract images of Germany's (troubled) past (Modrey, 2008).

Major events seem to be indelibly associated with modernism, but that does not mean they are always seen as agents of modernisation. Indeed, one way of conceptualising events is to view them as necessary antidotes to this movement/era. As Roche (2000) identifies, major events can act as ways for people to gain

Figure 2.1 *Munich's Olympic Park developed to stage the 1972 Games*

reassurance and control over the rapid and disorienting change associated with modernisation. The rituals, calendars and cycles associated with major events offer reassuring predictability and control over time. They also 'promise modernity the occurrence of charisma and aura in a world often appearing as excessively rationalistic' (Roche, 2000: 7). In this sense, events offer an antidote to the uniformity and associated ordinariness of modern life. This can be associated with the idea of events as opportunities to escape from modernity. One way of understanding cultural festivals is to see them as allowing people to return to a version of the medieval city: with unbridled revelry and entertainment in tents. There is often a nostalgic flavour to these events; something that allows people to 'escape' to a pre-modern existence. Conversely, World Expo events may facilitate a different type of escape, where people are transported to the future. Either way, as Greenlagh (1989) points out, major events can allow people to escape from the harshness of a modern reality.

The different roles outlined above, where events act as agents of modernity and antidotes to it, are not necessarily incompatible. Different events may play different roles: some allow people to escape modernity and others explicitly push the modern agenda forward. Major event projects still seem to be typically modernist in their ambitions and outcomes; but the way in which they are experienced may allow populations to cope, or come to terms, with rapid modernisation. Both ideas suggest modernity is still a useful lens through which to understand major event projects. And although some commentators suggest that Western nations have now entered a period of late- or post-modernity (see below), the modern 'project' is still one that is being actively pursued – particularly in parts of the developing world. Nations in Southeast Asia, South America and Africa are actively seeking major events as part of their rapid industrialisation, and this trend helps to reinforce the long established relationship between major events and modernity.

POST-MODERNITY?

Some commentators (e.g. Harvey, 1989) have suggested that the Western world has entered a period of post-modernity characterised by a revised economic system, more playful architectural styles and a blurring of the distinctions that emerged in modern society. This new era is said to have commenced in the 1970s, as the urban crisis unfolded. If we accept this interpretation, the whole era of post-industrial regeneration has occurred within a post-modern context. However, the shift to postmodernism is much contested and some noted events authors (including Roche, 2000) prefer to use the term 'late-modernity' to characterise the contemporary era. Others (e.g. Monclús, 2006) do recognise the existence of a post-modern epoch and apply it directly to understanding the urbanism associated with major events. For example, Hiller (2006) identifies a series of reasons why he thinks the Olympic Games are strongly related to the post-modern city. These range from the use of events strategies in the re-use of industrial spaces to the more destructive way events contribute to the polarisation of wealth – a noted characteristic of post-modern cities. Ultimately, Hiller (2006) sees events like the Olympic Games as a way of providing and supporting new leisure industries deemed essential to the post-modern city. In a post-modern context, the distinctions between the spheres of leisure/culture and work/commerce are said to have blurred. This has obvious connections to urban strategies that use leisure industries to generate employment and revenue and to lead urban development. Hiller (2006: 331) suggests 'Games facilities are primarily playing a role in supporting the post-modern turn towards leisure consumption.' In this sense Hiller (2006) is using the idea of post-modernism to define a mode of economic production – and an era in which boundaries established in the modern era are blurring – rather than in its other guises.

Postmodernism can also be regarded as a style, epoch or method. In terms of style, some authors make the link between major events and post-modern urban architecture. Munoz (2006) views the Olympic Villages from 1980 to 2000 as characterising the post-modern era, in contrast to the modern Olympic Villages of the 1960s. This is because architectural styles are used that playfully simulate the past – for example the Mediterranean-ness and classical references of the structures built for Barcelona's 1992 Games. The post-modern era is usually defined as one where form supersedes function in building design. Hence it is also possible to view the unnecessarily extravagant structures built as part of many event projects as exemplifying postmodernism. Examples include the Olympic stadia in Montreal and Beijing, the arches attached to new football stadia in London and Durban, and the towers built for World Expos in Zaragoza, Lisbon and Seville.

With reference to the idea of postmodernism as an epoch, some authors use the term post-modern to typify the era in which events strategies are being pursued. In some ways the whole idea that events could be central to urban development strategies is representative of postmodernism. This approach typifies an era where the symbolic value of events has superseded their use value. Wilson (1996) associates the revalorising of 'polluted, antiquated, disused and rundown' areas as something that can be associated with postmodernism. She suggests that rebuilding both the sites and their sign value has become a trope of the post-modern city. Monclús (2006, 2009) also uses the term post-modern to refer to a new era in his analysis of World Expo events. His work considers postmodernism as something that can be related to the aims of this event from the 1990s onwards. He feels that, post-1990, Expos differ because their emphasis shifted to promotion and marketing, rather than the celebration of progress. Whilst there is some value in this periodisation – promotional objectives have definitely intensified – there is a danger that we assume this is merely a contemporary phenomenon; when in fact promoting the city has been an aim of major events throughout their history (see Chapter 3).

Monclús's (2006) classification of the Barcelona Universal Forum of Cultures 2004 as a 'post-modern' event has more justification. Denied the opportunity to stage an official BIE World Expo, Barcelona decided to invent its own mega-event, and conceived one that did not feature technological objects, cultural performances or sporting excellence. Instead the draw for visitors was a series of staged debates covering the themes of cultural diversity, sustainable development and conditions for peace (Benedicto and Carrasco, 2007). The a-historical, ephemeral and unconventional qualities of the Universal Forum of Cultures certainly gave it post-modern credentials (see Chapter 5). Another recent event which seemed to demonstrate post-modern characteristics was the 'Expo 02' staged in the region of Neuchatel in Switzerland. Switzerland has an established tradition of staging national Expos outside the BIE framework: the 2002 edition followed Expos staged in Geneva (1896), Bern (1913), Zurich (1939) and Lausanne (1964). The Neuchatel Expo could be described as post-modern because of its explicit critique of nationhood and because of its ephemerality – there were multiple locations and the idea was to leave a legacy only in the minds of the visitors, with all physical traces of the event removed (Soderstrom, 2001).

BOX 2.1 EVENT REGENERATION AND 'PHANTOM' EVENTS

An example of event-led regeneration that perhaps extends Monclús's (2006) view of post-modernity from conventional place marketing to ephemeral image making was Manchester's 'Olympic' regeneration of the 1990s. For some (e.g. in the work of French philosopher Jean Baudrillard), post-modernity is defined by the triumph of representation over reality. Manchester's regeneration in the 1990s demonstrated this because it was led by an event that never happened – a phantom event. Manchester's bids for the 1996 and 2000 Games failed, but the city still managed to use the event to address prevailing image issues and to begin regenerating central and eastern areas. A velodrome and indoor arena were built anyway and Manchester became an Olympic City through mere association. Although there are usually strict limits on the extent to which official branding can be used, we have seen a series of cities using events they have never staged to promote urban development. This idea of benefiting from event associations (rather then events) is something that other cities have adopted and adapted. Like Manchester, some cities have promoted their candidacy for major events to assist urban objectives. Other cities have bid for the right to stage subsidiary events: e.g. the annual IOC meeting or Youth Olympics both staged by Singapore (see Chapter 7). These occasions are used to develop associations with the kind of mega-events that remain an impossible dream for most cities.

Post-modernism is also a term that is used to refer to the emergence of new methodological approaches. This refers mainly to the broadening of the methods deemed legitimate ways of accessing knowledge, but it can also be applied to methods used to deliver event regeneration. In a post-modern era, normative and technocratic ideas about following step-by-step plans, transferring policies from one context to another and developing sites for specific uses have become harder to justify. This applies to urban regeneration and planning for events. For example, Binks and Snape (2006: 73) suggest that using rational ideas about strategic planning when analysing the venues planned for the Manchester

2002 Commonwealth Games was 'anachronistic in what was essentially a post-modern setting'.

Whether we understand the contemporary era as modern or post-modern depends on one's own individual perspective, the context under consideration and a large dose of semantics. However, there are ways of reconciling the two positions. One of the most convincing is to acknowledge that the world's major events remain essentially modernist projects, but to recognise that there are other events that do demonstrate qualities normally associated with postmodernism. The idea that some events may be seen as post-modern even within an overall context that still has all the hallmarks of modernity is a theme explored by Stevenson *et al.* (2005). Many major events need official approval/public funding and therefore reflect the values or priorities of mainstream elites. But there are events, such as the International Gay Games (est. 1982), that seek to develop collective resistance by challenging the status quo of ruling elites. Stevenson *et al.* (2005) evaluate whether the International Gay Games 'might signify a postmodernising propensity for fragmentation, the assertion of difference and the arresting of grand narratives of progress' (Stevenson *et al.*, 2005: 468). However, these authors recognise that the event is still overshadowed by modern occasions. In their analysis of the sixth edition of this event, staged in Sydney, Australia, they conclude that the 'postmodern complexity of this hallmark event with its cosmo-politan advocacy and libertarian politics of pleasure, leaves it trailing in the wake of modernity's established global festivals of nation, commerce and the body'. The world's major events not only represent mainstream values, but they remain quintessentially modern. Nevertheless, 'alternative' events should not be under-estimated, a point underlined by the fact that participation rates for the International Gay Games now exceed those for the Olympic Games (Stevenson *et al.*, 2005).

NEO-LIBERALISM

Within critical theory, major events are not only deemed to be representative of modernity, they are seen as projects that reflect (and reinforce) dominant con-temporary political philosophies. Indeed, it is common to understand major events and associated regeneration projects as reflective of – and agents of – the prevailing neo-liberal ideology (Hall, 2006). Neo-liberalism is essentially a mode of political economy associated with removing barriers to trade, restricting gov-ernment intervention and using market forces to stimulate growth. Under a neo-liberal agenda, traditional urban policy is replaced with an approach which involves allocating a prominent role for the market, encouraging competition between service providers, seeking inward investment, empowering citizens and decentralising authority. According to McGuigan (2005), these principles were derived from the practical experiments of North American municipal governments in the 1970s. A new approach was conceived in the wake of tax revolts which discouraged public sector spending and intervention.

The contrast between the 1976 and 1984 Olympic Games provides a useful illustration of the move towards a neo-liberal agenda in this period. The 1976 Games in Montreal were staged using a large amount of public funds and left a legacy of under-used facilities and debt. The 1984 edition (staged in Los Angeles) was private sector led and turned a profit. This was representative of the political shift that had take place in the intervening years. However, the neo-liberal approach that emerged at this time has not proved to be a panacea for urban governments reeling from the effects of de-industrialisation. It is much criticised for privileging the interests of private companies, and also the elite classes.

Commoditisation

Major event strategies are not apolitical. They usually involve intense political battles between stakeholders, but they are also indicative of a broader political philosophy: the neo-liberal policy agenda. Major event strategies epitomise neo-liberal entrepreneurialism. Just as ecotourism 'neo-liberalises' nature by giving it a market value (Duffy, 2002), major events attempt to turn cultural phenomena into commercial assets. A major event is now both a product in itself, but also a way of promoting a host city as a place to visit, invest in, or live. McGuigan (2005) feels that neo-liberalism promotes the language of branding, and the extension of this practice into all spheres of life. This idea can be used to under-stand major event strategies; these are an important part of the way places and cultures are commoditised in the neo-liberal era. For example, according to Gruneau (cited in Roche, 2000: 14), the 1984 Olympic Games 'are best under-stood as a more fully developed expression of the incorporation of sporting practice into the ever-expanding marketplace of international capitalism'.

Privileging private sector interests

A further link between event regeneration and the neo-liberal agenda is the way events serve as convenient ways to promote corporate interests. In what Pine and Gilmore (1998) describe as the 'experience economy', events are products them-selves, but also vehicles used to create added value for – and interest in – more conventional commodities. Major events have become attractive to companies who want to transfer the positive associations of events to their brands. However, the significant involvement of private companies – via sponsorship – means there is a danger that they begin to direct the nature of the event itself. This is what McGuigan (2005) calls 'deep sponsorship'. Even if they have contributed funds, companies may receive disproportionately large benefits, especially when the event is being heavily subsidised by the public sector. The Millennium Festival in London is cited by McGuigan (2005) as a good example. This event was criticised for being too heavily directed by corporate interests. Glancey's (2001: 26) analysis of the event acknowledges the very visible nature of corporate involvement: 'The Millennium Experience, its entrance flanked by a branch of McDonalds, proved to be an exhibition of corporate sponsorship.' But if the event's budget is scrutinised more carefully, only £150 million of the £850 million that was spent came from corporate sponsors. The rest came from public sources; but these funds were used to pursue corporate goals. Accordingly, a common criticism of event projects is they publicly subsidise schemes that benefit corporations. This problem is exacerbated by over-optimistic projections by event organisers of income from private sector sponsors, thus creating two further problems: a budget deficit and extra pressure to conform to corporate requests to secure sponsorship.

A pressing question for this book is to what extent is privileging private interests something that pervades regeneration initiatives pursued in conjunction with events. Where event regeneration involves expensive physical developments, there is obviously a danger that they may serve the interests of the construction industry and property developers. This accusation has been levelled at various major events – including the FIFA World Cup in Japan (Horne and Manzenreiter, 2004) and the London 2012 Olympic Games (Newman, 2007). Similarly, Barcelona's 1992 Olympic Games were criticised by neighbourhood groups who pointed to the unseemly power of the 'lobby del ciment' (McNeill, 2003). Lining the pockets of property interests seems to be something that is hard to avoid – most physical regeneration projects aim to increase the value of land and property. Developers are often the main beneficiaries; but they tend to be risk averse, so projects are designed in a way that optimises their investment, not wider benefits. If events take place on/near publicly owned land, assets can be sold post-event to the benefit of public accounts. But, in an era when governments are reluctant to build anything themselves, this means balancing inducements for private sector investment (to reclaim, convert, build), with the need to maximise the value of public assets. As Prytherch and Maiques (2009: 112) demonstrate, event projects such as those pursued recently by Valencia can be interpreted as 'experiments with private development of public land'. Projects in Valencia, such as the Grand Prix circuit and America's Cup port in the city's waterfront district (see Figure 2.2), have been developed using partnerships between the public and private sectors. Hence Prytherch and Maiques (2009) assert Valencia's recent investment in staging major events is part of the new neo-liberal agenda that now characterises the city's approach to urban governance.

Figure 2.2 *The Veles e Vents building in Valencia, Spain (designed by David Chipperfield Architects). This building was developed as part of Valencia's staging of the America's Cup sailing races in 2007. It provided the base for all the teams who were competing*

In the contemporary era, major events are more commercial and more aligned to corporate interests than ever before. Even events which were once experienced as an escape from 'official life', and which have been continued or revived to represent community values, are susceptible. Davis and Marvin (2004) bemoan the corporate takeover of the Carnival of Venice which has invited private sponsorship since 1995. Some events, such as the New Orleans Mardi Gras, have tried to resist sponsorship and corporate involvement, but it is hard to prevent creeping corporatisation (Gotham, 2005b). Even those events once deemed the epitome of alternative culture such as the Glastonbury Festival of Contemporary Arts now reserve a large space for corporate guests.

Competition and globalisation

One of the key principles of neo-liberalism is competition. This is also a theme evident within event projects; not only because of the competitive element involved in many events (sport most obviously, but also arts contests, and awards of prizes at most exhibitions) but because of the competitive element that runs throughout the event's lifecycle. There is intense competition during the bidding process; when the bid is won firms compete to win tenders for event projects; and post-event, the comparative performance of the host city relative to previous hosts is highlighted constantly.

In the past forty years we have witnessed the rise of entrepreneurial urbanism: a mode of governance in which cities are forced to compete with each other for investment. Competitive pressures are one of the key forces that help to explain why cities bid for major events and why they devote large amounts of resources to staging them. Rather than collaborating or providing compatible/complementary urban strategies, cities have begun to compete with each other to secure inward investment and high calibre businesses, residents and visitors. There has always been rivalry between cities, but this has intensified in recent years. Staging major events is seen as a significant way to differentiate urban areas; with events serving as promotional tools (see Chapter 7), but also as amenities with which to the appeal to the creative classes that supposedly provide the key to urban renewal (Florida, 2002). Neo-liberalism is supposed to encourage innovation and progress through healthy competition. Thus, cities are spurred to develop event strategies that will prevent them being left behind. Cities that don't stage major events (or that don't participate in other place marketing exercises) are rendered invisible and therefore uncompetitive – even if they are managed very effectively. This can be illustrated by the status of UK cities. Places like Birmingham, Cardiff, Glasgow, Liverpool, Manchester and Sheffield have been very proactive in bidding for and staging events. But other major cities have not been willing or able to follow suit (Bristol, Southampton, Nottingham) and this makes it more difficult for them to gain the visibility required to compete in the new entrepreneurial regime.

Competition exists between cities at the regional level, at the national level and at the global level. Indeed, major events can be seen as part of the process of globalisation – a contested phenomenon which is closely aligned to neo-liberalism. Staging major events is often seen as marking the entry of cities into the global marketplace. For example several Olympic hosts (Seoul, 1988; Beijing, 2008) used the event to further their integration within the global economic systems. World events have helped to create global citizens, global products, global demand and thus global trade.

Privatisation

As well as commoditisation, corporatisation, competition and globalisation, neo-liberalism is associated with privatisation. Major events typify the way urban governments in the neo-liberal era have felt the need to work closely with the private sector. There are positive reasons to do this, including spreading any risks, maximising efficiency and utilising available expertise. But involving the private sector in events often means handing over publicly funded (or publicly owned) assets to the private sector to facilitate efficient construction or post-event utilisation. Accordingly, some major events can be seen as part of the 'project' to privatise public space and 'roll back' the traditional functions of the state – policies that are strongly associated with neo-liberalism. Due to the upgrading of various facilities to stage major events, local people have experienced reduced access to, and control of, those facilities (Owen, 2002). Even when community access is retained in privatised venues, facilities can be prohibitively expensive to use. A related negative outcome is the redistribution of funding from government programmes to allow event projects to be funded. Shifting local government priorities from reliable sources of income and the provision of social services to speculative event projects provides a good example of what Harvey (1989) terms the shift from managerialism to entrepreneurialism in urban governance. Rather than relying on traditional forms of intervention, cities are gambling that staging major events will help to encourage local economic development, leading to urban regeneration.

Challenging neo-liberalism

Most political economists agree that that the Western world is dominated by a neo-liberal ideology. Whether major events are key agents of this ideology is more controversial. An alternative to seeing major events as agents of neo-liberalism and its associated traits (commercialisation, competition, privatisation), is to view them as challenges to this dominant ideology. Accordingly, a slightly different assessment of the role of events in a neo-liberal world is provided by Black (2008: 471), who sees bids for major sport events as 'one of a relatively small number of positive, interventionist levers that remains' for the public sector in the neo-liberal era. In certain circumstances (e.g. where a government is the lead stakeholder), major events may allow democratically elected governments to yield more influence, thus contributing to a more equitable form of urban regeneration. Whilst this may appear positive, pessimists argue that if major events are now coveted by governments as ways to exert authority over their territories, this merely highlights how far the state has lost control of key functions.

Other commentators see events as useful ways of mobilising visible challenges to dominant ideologies and philosophies, as evidenced by the protests that accompanied the Beijing Olympic Games in 2008. Gotham (2005a: 235) suggests that local actors can use major events for 'positive and progressive ends' by launching a radical critique that exposes class and racial inequality. Alongside a platform for protest, public events often encourage behaviours that are not normally tolerated, perhaps paving the way for permanent changes. This positive and ideal-istic take on the transformative role of traditional carnivals and fairs is normally associated with the writing of Mikhail Bakhtin. He suggested that events could help sustain consciousness of an alternative social order even in the midst of authoritarian control and repressive orthodoxism (Morris, 2004). In Bakhtin's interpretation of the carnivalesque, events were essentially a form of escapism, but they allowed people to see an unofficial truth. The mockery of officialdom involved (e.g. parades involving a king of fools) was connected to life, rather than merely comprising a temporary inversion.

Following Bahktin's arguments about the role of events, some authors have pointed to instances where the tolerance of 'deviant behaviour' permitted during events has provided the basis for more fundamental change. An example could be the Gay Pride Parades of the late twentieth century that helped to increase the rights of gay citizens. As Quinn (2005: 932) notes, social theorists have asso-ciated festivals with opportunities to challenge the status quo and as 'possibilities for challenging social conventions, social order and authority and inverting society's norms'. Taking such a viewpoint suggests events are very much associ-ated with regeneration – albeit a regeneration of the individual's self and human spirit as much as one engineered by urban authorities.

SOCIAL THEORIES: SPECTACLES AND SAFETY VALVES

As well as political-economy perspectives it is important to think about sociological theories when trying to understand the role and effects of event regeneration. One of the aims of regeneration in the contemporary era is the 'restoration of social function where there has been dysfunction' (Couch and Fraser, 2003: 2). Many strategies are conceived to improve people's lives, and commentators have suggested how events can contribute positively and negatively to social conditions.

Critical evaluations of major events often deride them as 'spectacles'. This term was used by Debord (1994) in his book *The Society of the Spectacle* to convey the way everyday life was being reduced from active participation to passive consumerism. Considered in this light, the oft-cited 'identity making' role of events could be seen as one which is more related to consumption – with the commercial imperative and associated sponsorship encouraging people to see themselves as consumers or aligned to a certain brand. Coalter (1998) answers these criticisms by arguing that even if events are commercially orientated, they can still provide satisfying forms of social membership and identity. But major events are perhaps demonstrative of the way in which public expressions of 'collective joy' have been turned into forms of commercial leisure, consumption and entertainment (Ehrenreich, 2007). According to some, the residual effect is the de-politicisation and massification of people who become merely passive consumers of imagery. Whilst critics of neo-liberalism worry about the way major events result in the privatisation of urban space, those who deride events as 'spectacles' see them as exemplifying the privatisation of culture.

A slightly different perspective is the 'safety valve' theory, or 'Ventilsitten' (meaning steam valve in German) theory of events, in which events are staged to allow temporary and controlled outpourings of festivity, thus reducing the likelihood of demands for more comprehensive social transformations. This perspective emanates from interpretations of the role of carnivals and fairs in the pre-modern era. Many accounts of these events recognise their role in allowing people to 'let off steam'. In his book *Sketches by Boz*, Dickens (1995; first published in 1836) described the Greenwich Easter Fair in southeast London as 'a three days fever which cools the blood for six months afterwards, and at the expiration of which London is restored to its old habits of plodding industry, as suddenly and completely as if nothing had ever happened to disturb them'. The essence of this literary account is reaffirmed in academic interpretations of major events. The philosopher Terry Eagleton adopts a similar perspective in his analysis of carnival, which he considers as 'a licensed affair in every sense, a permissible rupture of hegemony, a contained popular blow-off' (Eagleton, 1981: 148). The ideas of Barthes (1973) suggest that major events might immunise the collective imagination through a small inoculation of evil. Allowing people greater freedom at specific points in the calendar increases the chances that they will conform the rest of the year. This means, rather than acting as emancipatory agents, events can be seen as part of the apparatus that helps to control society.

Whilst the safety valve theory seems less relevant to contemporary events, it could be argued that major events still allow regulated festivity of this nature. During major events it is common for rules to be waived – for example host cities of the Olympic Games or Football World Cup may relax laws governing prostitution and alcohol consumption. Many people adopt transgressive behaviour – enjoying concentrated periods of revelry and levels of drinking, singing and provocative language that would not be tolerated in other public settings. Events that encourage a temporary 'feel good factor' amongst the public can also be linked to the safety valve theory. The media narratives that may accompany the production of a feel good factor (e.g. productivity levels rising in factories after events) also indicate that the events help to perpetuate existing systems/regimes rather than providing any genuine opportunities for emancipation.

As the safety valve theory implicitly involves pacification (through temporary de-pacification), there are strong parallels with theories of 'the spectacle'.

Both theories see events as obstacles to, rather than catalysts for, more progressive social relations as they help to maintain deference to the status quo. This seems to dim the regenerative capacity of events. Whereas regeneration is supposedly about change, if we accept the principles involved in the safety valve theory, major events may be motivated by efforts to ensure existing systems and practices are retained.

To reaffirm the relationship between events and the status quo, it is useful to draw upon Bakhtin's distinction between official and unofficial events. In this book we are dealing with the former, which Bakhtin sees as tools with which to sanction the existing pattern of things, unlike unofficial versions (e.g. medieval carnivals) which he views as inherently concerned with change and looking to the future, because they allow people to escape into a utopian realm (Bakhtin, 1984). So, although contemporary major events are often presented as symbols of change beckoning in a new era, a Bakhtinian perspective would see them as efforts to maintain the status quo. The language of progress, planning for the future and regeneration which tends to pervade the rhetoric of major events may be nothing more than a 'carnival mask' – something that conveniently hides the truth.

The carnival mask

The carnival mask metaphor is a prevalent one when studying events and cities. Whereas Bakhtin (1984) is keen to emphasise the positive aspects for urban communities who wear the mask (in particular 'the joy of change and reincarnation'), in contemporary urban studies the mask is seen as a more sinister phenomenon. The carnival mask is now usually viewed as an agent of deception – a façade behind which problems can be hidden. Instead of participants wearing the mask to disguise their identities, the mask is now said to be worn by cities and their governments. Harvey (1989) is one author who uses the term 'carnival mask' with respect to ephemeral changes made to city centres in recent years. Harvey (1989: 21) feels that the superficial regeneration undertaken 'diverts and entertains, leaving the social problems which lie behind the mask unseen and uncared for'. Using Harvey's analysis, events act as tools of hegemonic power that shift attention away from everyday social needs – covering up 'real' social problems. This concurs with Greenlagh's (1989: 49) interpretation of World Expos as events 'intended to distract, indoctrinate and unify the population'. In this sense, major events could act as substitutes for regeneration – rather than agents of regeneration – providing 'smokescreens' behind which the inherent urban problems can be hidden.

As well as pacifying or distracting citizens, major events are viewed in an even more sinister fashion by those commentators who consider them key elements of 'the revanchist city'. This radical viewpoint sees events as ways of placating the masses, but also as forces with which to suppress and control those not deemed to be 'the right sort of people'. Events have long been recognised as agents of control, dating back to the infamous circuses of Rome and the city states of medieval Europe that used festivals to control their territories (Quinn, 2005), through to the modern Olympic Games. Indeed, Tufts (2004: 5) states that the Olympic Games 'are also very much implicated in the revanchist city, playing a crucial role not only in processes of accumulation, but also the social control of marginalised groups'.

The notion of events as tools of the revanchist city provides a darker version of the view that when major events are used to restructure cities, it is the most disadvantaged that usually experience the punitive costs. Olds (1998: 5) interprets major events in this manner, seeing them primarily as catalysts for long-term redevelopment planning with certain groups suffering in terms of 'displacement, negative health effects, the breaking of social networks and the loss of affordable housing'. In this sense, events may exacerbate urban social divisions, rather than heal them. The potential for negative consequences is so well recognised that those representing the rights of citizens now seek related assurances before events are even awarded to host cities (Tufts, 2004). Newman's (1999) research into Atlanta's 1996 Olympic Games provides justification for concerns about the effects of events on vulnerable residents. He found that low-income residents (most of whom were black) regarded the Games as another excuse for business leaders to reshape the city. These were the citizens most disrupted by the preparations for the Games and, rather than urban regeneration, the outcome was a 'legacy of distrust'. This account is representative of a wide body literature in which events are viewed as convenient excuses to force major changes upon urban residents, with opponents derided as conservative, myopic or even unpatriotic. The exceptional circumstances of an event become the justification for practices that would not normally be tolerated.

TEMPORAL AND SPATIAL PERSPECTIVES

As well as broad theoretical perspectives, other authors provide nuanced ways of understanding the powerful effects of major events. Many of these theories are underpinned by notions of time and space. In other words, the underlying explanation for events' role as vehicles that can help regenerate cities is because of the way in which they reconfigure temporal and spatial relations.

Events as markers of time

One key feature of events is the importance of time (see Figure 2.3). An event is defined by time – it is something that has a limited duration and which takes

Figure 2.3 *Time – a key concept in understanding events. These Olympic Rings were installed at St Pancras International Station in London to mark the 2012 Games*

place during a scheduled period. *When* events are staged is often crucially important – it helps to make events meaningful. Regular events may be staged at times in the calendar when people feel an urge to celebrate or when they need to be distracted. Others are staged to commemorate key events from the past. It was no coincidence that major events were staged in Paris in 1889 (100 years after the French Revolution), in Brisbane in 1988 (Australia's bi-centenary) and throughout Spain in 1992 (500 years since the voyages of discovery). Events are ways in which people periodise their lives, but they are also ways in which the lives of cities and nations are periodised. Some of the power of events is derived from this idea that mega-events are generational 'once in a lifetime' opportunities to make changes to host cities. An event marks a new period in a city's lifecycle – ideally, one in which the city moves away from degeneration and dilapidation. This is an idea that is explored further below.

Much of the regenerative power of events can be explained via reference to their temporal qualities. Events can help to focus attention on the future (not the past), they help to build anticipation and they provide a pivotal moment around which discourses of change can be organised. As Anderson and Holden (2008) demonstrate, it is not necessarily the event itself which provides the stimulus for positive effects but the anticipation of the event. Positive social effects are more likely during an event's 'pregnancy' than its aftermath as media coverage is most intensive pre-event and feelings of anticlimax may occur post-event. Cashman (2006), in a book tellingly entitled *The Bitter-Sweet Awakening*, suggests that Barcelona and Sydney both struggled in the years after they staged the Olympic Games despite these events being revered as the most successful of the modern era. This suggests we should see major events less as events, and more as advents (Anderson and Holden, 2008). Regeneration discourse has always been dominated by vague promises about a new future, yet to arrive. The result is hope, and it is from this feeling that many of the supposed intangible benefits of major events derive. Of course, the danger of relying on hope is the inevitability of disappointment. Alongside highlighting the importance of advent, Anderson and Holden's (2008) analysis is useful in that it emphasises the role of an event in providing a crystallising point for a range of contemporary developments, future projects and vague promises. This can allow people to feel that they have moved away from a past era, which may have been dominated by social and economic problems. In this sense events help to mark the time of a city, as well as helping to leave a lasting physical impression.

The conception of events as strategic symbols to communicate a paradigmatic shift towards a new era has close links to Jansson's (2005) mode of understanding the role of major events. Jansson's analysis is dedicated to a major housing fair in Malmö, Sweden, and he uses Goffman's (1967) concept of fatefulness to understand the often extraordinary influence of major events. Jansson suggests that these public spectacles can both produce, and act as a response to, fateful moments in a city's development. This is because, as well as providing a potent symbol of renewal, they provide a turbulent point of 'maximum visibility'. This interpretation is reinforced by Leeds's (2008: 476) justification for major events: 'there is no substitute for a rigid deadline combined with extensive public exposure of the results'. Events can communicate to residents that an important threshold has been reached, from which there is no turning back. And because events are often used in conjunction with other new developments in cities, they provide both a stimulus for, and visible demonstration of, a new direction for a city. This may make urban residents feel that the event is a fateful moment in their lives, as well as in the life of the city. As Jansson (2005) states, it can encourage social renewal, as people feel empowered to start afresh and feel part of the urban transformation. Of course, this argument could also be reversed to argue the opposite. It is this same sense of fatefulness attached to events that can be used to push through harmful changes which would otherwise be blocked. And if the event is unsuccessful the new era becomes as tainted as the past from which a city may be trying to escape.

Events as markers of space

A second important lens through which events can be understood is that of space. There is a long tradition of transforming urban spaces to stage events – even if those transformations are only temporary. To ensure that the social benefits of events are felt, organisers/participants often ensure that spaces are dressed up. An alternative approach is to use locations where people will feel free to act differently than normal. In either case, people's relationship to the space used for an event is an important part of the experience. Just as events are not staged at random moments of time, they are not staged randomly in space. Indeed, the locations which are chosen often have a significance or a particular character. A good example is the tendency for cities to stage major events on urban islands. These are spaces formed between rivers or those which are reclaimed from water courses of various kinds. World Expos in Seville, Montreal and San Francisco were all staged on such islands – and major urban music festivals in Budapest and Vienna are now staged in similar locations. This is partly because of the availability of space, but also because it allows people to feel they are entering a different world. Islands have long been associated with notions of fantasy, paradise, escapism and tourism; and these symbolic qualities are exploited by cities seeking to maximise event experiences. In this sense, whilst events can be understood as time-out time, they can also be seen as 'places out of place'; both of which add to the sense that events are special occasions.

It is important to introduce theories that attempt to conceptualise the transformation of space for events. Events have always involved these transformations, although over the past century cities have attempted to try and sustain these changes so that they are not merely temporary. Cities have tried to create spaces that retain their 'eventfulness' (Richards and Palmer, 2010) by creating areas where festivity is an enduring characteristic. Examples include large plazas in urban centres which provide the fulcrum for urban festivity, entertainment districts anchored by major sport facilities or more peripheral event zones (Smith, 2010). Cities have also developed 'festival marketplaces' to make spaces dedicated to consumption feel more like event experiences. In this sense the spirit of events has inspired urban development, as well as specific events playing important roles in place making.

Cities usually try to amalgamate event sites into the city, and turn them into a normalised piece of the urban 'jigsaw' in the post-event era. But Maddox's (2004) analysis of Seville's 1992 World Expo suggests a different outcome. Rather than an event site gradually becoming more like the rest of the city in the post-event era, Maddox raises the possibility that the city may become more like the event site. According to Maddox, the core of Seville has become more artificial and generic and the author attributes this to the effects of Expo '92. The event imposed a culture of cosmopolitan liberalism that infused the city as a whole. The concept of place making using events is an interesting one. In Seville, the residents grew to love their new event space (located on Cartuja Island), even if it seemed rather artificial. In doing so, they contributed to a process which meant that transforming one part of the city changed the city as a whole. Other forms of event-related place making are more obvious and deliberate. Parts of host cities are sometimes marked and promoted using event connections. In other examples, whole cities are promoted as event cities. For example, Edinburgh now promotes itself as a city of festivals and Melbourne claims to be the world's event city (see Chapter 7).

Events have been used to formalise time, but they have also been used to formalise space. Many post-industrial landscapes exist as vague spaces: undeveloped spaces, spaces left over from development, or spaces abandoned post-development (Solù-Morales, 1995). These are spaces that exist in between the urban and the rural (Farley and Roberts, 2011) that are 'subject to ever-changing, often improvisatory and temporary uses, and always pregnant with possibilities for peculiar practices' (Edensor et al., 2008: 286). Vague spaces exist between the formal and functional built urban environment that surrounds them. Often these are also temporary spaces: they are in transition between what was there before and what will happen soon. Vague spaces are common in post-industrial cities. One of the aims of event projects is to transform these spaces into official, functional and productive spaces. This is an attempt to formalise the space – bringing it within the confines of the programmed city. Whilst this is seen as progress by those who dismiss them as wastelands, the loss of these spaces is something that is lamented by authors such as Edensor et al. (2008). However, vague spaces are constantly being reproduced. And because of their under-utilisation in the post-event era many locations used for event regeneration projects have returned to their former status as vague spaces. For example, by the mid-1990s Maddox (2004: 303) suggests that Seville's Expo '92 site 'was reverting to wilderness'. This fate matches Edensor et al.'s (2008: 293) predictions regarding the effects of London's massive Olympic project in East London: 'The traces of the ineffable will be buried…but for how long will the entropic tendencies that transform all space and matter be kept at bay?'

BOX 2.2 VAGUE SPACES IN EAST LONDON

During London's preparations for the 2012 Olympic Games, different perspectives regarding the value of vague space were apparent. The creation of the main Olympic Park involved the removal of the Clays Lane community (425 people) and the surrounding area. During related planning meetings, the London Development Agency (LDA) was reported to have dismissed the open space adjacent to this community as 'scrubland', even though local people felt it was valuable recreational space (Porter *et al.*, 2009). Ironically, this area included a derelict sports facility. According to one observer, during an inquiry into the compulsory purchase of the land, the LDA made the case that rather than providing some form of amenity, the community was somehow 'isolated' by this vague space (Porter *et al.*, 2009). Other vague spaces within the boundaries of the planned project were also dismissed by those involved; for example the CEO of the Olympic Delivery Authority allegedly described Marshgate Lane as a 'scar' (Porter *et al.*, 2009). The representation of the space in this manner helped to justify the compulsory purchase of land. Indeed, the representation of parts of East London as derelict, dangerous and unproductive was used to justify the Olympic project as a whole. Talking vague spaces down is a general trend in cities earmarked for expansive event regeneration projects (see Chapter 5). It both helps to push them through the planning system and helps to lower the price that developers pay for land.

One useful way of understanding how events assist the production of space and place making is through the idea of 'territorialisation'. Space becomes territory through symbolic and material processes – for example the naming of a site, its organisation, as well as the construction of infrastructures. This idea has been applied to mega-events by Dansero and Puttilli (2010). These authors highlight the way in which events can be used to reconfigure space. When a city stages a major event this happens in a faster and more controlled manner than would normally be the case. They use the example of Turin's 2006 Winter Olympic Games to illustrate their argument. Dansero and Puttilli (2010) suggest the best way to understand event projects is to see them as a form of territorialisation (pre- and during event), but one that also involves a de-territorialisation (post-event) and a re-territorialisation (post-event). An Olympic landscape is territorialised for the event, and then de-territorialised at the end of the event as installations are removed. Post-event, to convert the area into a functioning part of the city, it has to be re-territorialised. All this place making enables a city to reconfigure the 'detritus' left by previous territorialisation cycles such as those which cast the area as dangerous, derelict or post-industrial. Using the theoretical lens of territorialisation, Dansero and Puttilli (2010: 337) pinpoint the critical success factor in urban event projects, the 'ability to keep and renew the territorial capital built up during the Olympics through a general re-territorialisation of the event's legacy'.

SUMMARY

This chapter has aimed to analyse some of the underpinning perspectives that we can use to understand major events and their role in regeneration. These theories provide a useful context for this book and it is important to be aware of certain critical perspectives, even if sometimes they seem overly sceptical. The ideas discussed in the chapter help to explain the role of events in regeneration and they also give us an insight into how event projects fit into wider urban change. In subsequent chapters, more specific ideas will be introduced that help to explain the mechanisms through which regeneration works. However, the broader ideas mentioned here remain relevant throughout the book. They are useful to help explain why some commentators will always be suspicious about the use of major events in urban development and regeneration (because of their associations with neo-liberalism, spectacles and political motives); and why others remain committed to this enterprise.

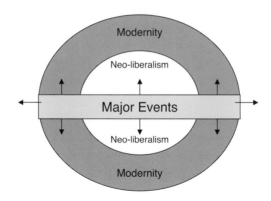

Figure 2.4 *A conceptual diagram emphasising that major events can both reinforce and challenge dominant economic philosophies and societal movements (and provide an escape route from them)*

The discussion above emphasises that there are different ways of interpreting major events. A recurring theme is that some groups see them as opportunities to challenge – or escape from – prevailing conditions, whereas others see them as a way to ensure that these conditions are maintained. This is emphasised by Figure 2.4. Major events act as critical moments in a city's lifecycle that can be appropriated by different interests; some of whom may want to introduce change, while others seek to support the status quo. There is also a possibility that events can both simultaneously support the status quo and provide a forum in which it can be challenged. The safety valve theory of events helps us to understand how this paradox could be explained. Events are viewed by some as ways of bringing communities together, inspiring them and make them feel good (i.e. social regeneration), but by others as ways to pacify people, to commoditise/ privatise culture and to distract attention from wider problems. Obviously, each event needs to be considered on its own merits, but it is useful to be aware of these critical perspectives – especially when analysing the rhetoric that surrounds major events.

The evolution of event
3 regeneration strategies

INTRODUCTION

The previous chapter of this book provided a theoretical foundation for event regeneration. This chapter provides a historical foundation. Understanding the history of the relationship between events and regeneration helps us to better understand the present. Accordingly, the discussion in this chapter outlines a chronology of event strategies to help explain current event regeneration approaches. It is impossible to trawl through the entire history of event projects, so key projects are picked out and discussed. The chapter is supported by a timeline that summarises some of the critical moments and key turning points (see Figure 3.1).

The discussion is organised chronologically. Five periods are identified and discussed: pre-1945 where the emphasis was on developing and expanding cities; the post-war period to the early 1970s, where reconstruction and modernisation were the main concerns; the 1970s/1980s where events were used to combat de-industrialisation; the marketing, economic development and private sector emphasis of the 1990s; and, finally, a twenty-first century concern with softer outcomes and legacy. Before these periods are outlined, there is a short review of how other authors have tried to periodise the use of events within urbanism.

DIFFERENT PHASES OF EVENT REGENERATION

A useful way of understanding events and regeneration is to track the development of strategies over time. Several authors have attempted to periodise major events according to their envisaged effects on urban development. This is something that has often been undertaken with reference to World Expos, as these events have a long history. Clark (2008) divides World Expo events into

Figure 3.1 A timeline chronicling the key events and key moments in the evolution of event regeneration strategies

Era of urban development	Regarded as the world's first mega-event of the modern era	1851	Great Exhibition (London)
Era of urban development	Tour Eiffel constructed. Starts a trend for creating event icons	1889	Paris Exposition
Era of urban development	Famous for the White City and the first appearance of the ferris wheel	1893	Chicago Columbian Exhibition
Era of urban development	Athens stages the first modern Olympic Games	1896	Revival of Olympic Games
Era of urban development	At start of new century, the Olympic Games are merely an appendage to more important Expo event	1900	Paris Olympic Games and World Expo
Era of urban development	The BIE takes responsibility for regulating International Exhibitions	1928	BIE established
Era of reconstruction	LA uses the Games to beautify the city, constructs an enormous stadium and builds the first purpose-built athletes accommodation	1932	Los Angeles Olympic Games
Era of reconstruction	Regarded as the first time an event is used to help redevelop the wider city (rather than just the event site)	1960	Rome Olympic Games
Era of reconstruction	Tokyo uses opportunity of Games to develop urban infrastructure rather than venues – the direct antecedent for Barcelona's Games	1964	Tokyo Olympic Games
Era of reconstruction	The first notable example of a concentrated Olympic Park hosting facilities and accommodation in an urban parkland setting	1972	Munich Olympic Games
Era of regeneration (Post-industrialisation)	The ambitious construction project for the Montreal Games is dominated by cost-overruns and project delays	1976	Montreal Olympic Games
Era of regeneration (Post-industrialisation)	The LA Games prove that mega-events can deliver a profit and rescue the Olympic movement	1984	Los Angeles Olympic Games
Era of regeneration (Partnerships)	Athens stages the first edition of the European City of Culture event	1985	ECOC launched
Era of regeneration (Partnerships)	Glasgow is nominated as European City of Culture – indicating a shift in the rationale for the event towards regeneration ambitions	1990	Glasgow European City of Culture
Era of regeneration (Partnerships)	Barcelona Olympic Games set a new benchmark for Olympic cities by using the Games to complete long-term urban regeneration ambitions	1992	Barcelona Olympic Games
Era of regeneration (Partnerships)	EU changes the name of and rules of European City of Culture event: now it is staged by member countries on a rota basis	1999	ECOC event changes
Era of globalisation (Legacy)	Several World Expos and Capital of Culture events are staged simultaneously; but at the start of a new century the Olympic Games are world's most important event	2000	Millennium events
Era of globalisation (Legacy)	More than a dozen massive projects are built to stage a bombastic Games that display the new power of the Chinese economy	2008	Beijing Olympic Games
Era of globalisation (Legacy)	The first mega-event to be staged in Africa	2010	South Africa World Cup
Era of globalisation (Legacy)	London stages the Olympic Games in East London – one of the most ambitious event regeneration projects ever attempted	2012	London Olympic Games
Era of globalisation (Legacy)	The first mega-event to be staged in South America	2014	Brazil World Cup
Era of globalisation (Legacy)	The first mega-event to be staged in the Middle East/North Africa region (MENA)	2022	Qatar World Cup

three phases: a period of 'industrialisation' (1851–1945); a period of 'cultural exchange' (1945–1991); and an era of 'national branding' (post 1992). Monclús (2007) has developed a slightly different chronology. He suggests that World Expos can be usefully categorised into 'historical expos' (1851–1929), modern expos (1930–1989) and post-modern expos (1989–present). This distinction involves discriminating between those events that were designed as ends in themselves (historical expos), events that were meant to encourage lasting urban development in the sites where they were staged (modern expos) and those where the emphasis has been on city promotion and place marketing (post-modern expos).

Monclús' (2007) categorisation is useful – and it seems possible to apply it to other events as well (albeit with slightly different timescales). For example, the European Capital of Culture event also involved an initial period (1985–1989) where the focus was on the event itself, whereas since 1990 the rationale for staging the event has shifted to one that prioritises long-term effects (e.g. on cultural provision, levels of participation and urban development). As McGuigan (2005: 235) states, after the 1990 edition in Glasgow, 'no longer was it merely about honouring what already existed: it had become about something new, about regeneration'. Although a 'post-modern' period is more difficult to identify, in the events staged post-2001 image concerns have been paramount (Richards and Wilson, 2004). However, as image development was also the main objective of Glasgow's 1990 event, this distinction is harder to justify.

The summer Olympic Games have also involved a chronology that bears similarities to Monclús's (2007) periodisation of World Expos. The editions staged in Los Angeles in 1932 and 1984 mark key shifts. Before the 1932 Games (i.e. those staged 1896–1928), the event made little physical impression on the cities that hosted it (e.g. Paris, London, Stockholm, Amsterdam). But in the period 1932–1980, the event was used as an opportunity to modernise cities such as Rome, Tokyo and Moscow. After the LA Games of 1984 we see an Olympic Games more like the ones we are familiar with today, where the focus is on commercialisation, place promotion and urban regeneration.

Several authors forward slightly different chronologies of the Olympic urbanism. Pitts and Liao (2009) differentiate between the pioneering, rudimentary projects (1896–1904); Games that involved the development of Olympic stadia (1908–1928); those which also included development of Olympic quarters (1932–1956); and those involving more fundamental urban transformations (1960–2012). Preuss's (2004) chronology focuses more on the scale, profitability and commercialism of the Games. He (2004) identifies a period of modesty 1896–1968, followed by one involving the risk, but potential rewards, of giant-ism. Since 1982 the author thinks there has been a period of commercialisation, and post-2003 an attempt to curb excesses and focus on legacy.

As Monclús (2007) recognises, any attempt to periodise events will inevitably involve inconsistencies. It is possible to find examples of major events in the early part of the twentieth century where hosts used them help to address urban problems and encourage urban development. This undermines Monclús's notion that events before the 1930s were not designed to leave permanent physical legacies. Jones (2004: 408) writes that 'Many of the built features in the [Paris] 1900 Exposition, so openly oriented around leisure and pleasure, remained in place and made a lasting contribution to Parisian infrastructure.' The event spurred the development of new bridges and stations – even the Paris Métro – and this suggests that the Expo was staged to make a lasting impression on the development of Paris. The World Expo staged in San Francisco in 1915 provides another good example. The San Francisco Exhibition was designed to reclaim part of the city and leave a permanent legacy. European examples also suggest permanent event legacies were being envisaged at this time. A year previously (1914) a Catalan politician is quoted as saying that Expos provide 'opportunities to sort out the largest number of urban problems, reforms and embellishments needed' (cited Monclús, 2007). Therefore, throughout the twentieth century there were efforts to use events in urban development.

In the review outlined here a simpler periodisation is used to chronicle the evolution of public policy and event regeneration (see Figure 3.1). Urban events exemplify wider urban processes, so this chronology corresponds more with key watersheds when urban policy in general is known to have shifted. Three key periods 1851–2000 are identified: pre 1945, 1945–1972 and post-1972 (see Figure 3.1). This latter period can be subdivided into three phases. The identification of 1945 as a turning point should be self-explanatory (the end of World War II), whilst the early 1970s are recognised by many commentators as the end of the period of modernity and the beginning of late-modernity/post-modernity. The urban crisis of the latter part of the twentieth century is often traced back to the early 1970s when political issues and an associated spike in the price of oil prompted major economic problems for industrial cities. Figure 3.1 also highlights that the major events staged by and planned for developing nations in the twenty-first century means we have perhaps entered a new era of event: one characterised by globalisation.

Pre-World War II: urban expansion

When urban objectives were attached to major events prior to World War II, the emphasis tended to be on urban development and the expansion of cities. This tradition began with the improvements associated with Paris's World Expos in the nineteenth century and the construction of parts of Kensington in London using the proceeds of the 1851 Great Exhibition. However, most World Expos in this period resulted only in superficial changes to the urban landscape of host cities. The use of events to make strategic interventions was something that only really emerged in the twentieth century.

During this early period, the smaller scale of events – and the use of temporary structures that were dismantled post-event – meant the main role events played in urban development was to demonstrate innovative urbanism. A dislocated 'legacy' emerged when these innovations were replicated elsewhere. The most famous example was the form of urbanism developed for the 1893 World Exhibition in Chicago. The Expo site was dominated by a carefully planned urban precinct with monumental buildings set in formal grounds. This event – particularly the 'Court of Honor' – provided the inspiration for the emerging City Beautiful movement: an approach to urbanism based on a visual approach to planning (Mumford, 1961). The formality and grandeur of the city were meant to civilise residents and allow them to coalesce around civic institutions. Chicago's event and its pleasing uniformity (encapsulated in its 'White City' name that was famously transposed to London) inspired new urban design in many other US cities (e.g. in Denver, Indianapolis, Washington DC and Kansas City). Indeed, the 1893 World Expo is thought to be where modern town planning in the USA originated (Parker, 2004). This was urban development, rather than regeneration, but it should be noted that Chicago's exhibition was also the first recorded use of reclaimed land to stage an event (Gold and Gold, 2005). The event was so big that it was not possible to emulate previous hosts (e.g. Paris) that had used central sites. Thus began a process of using temporary event installations to reclaim peripheral land that is then put to other uses. This tradition lives on today in other major events, particularly garden festivals.

As Pitts and Liao's (2009) periodisation highlights, sport event developments in the early part of the century (1908–1928) were usually limited to stadium projects. Event projects at this time were usually led by consortia of private sector interests. For example, the main stadium for the 1932 Olympic Games (LA) was paid for by an association of local representatives although it was then rented back to, and eventually transferred to, the city/county (Reiss, 1981). The 1928 Games in Amsterdam (see Figure 3.2) were also organised by private interests whose main motivation was to build a stadium (Westerbeek, 2009). However, the organisers still approached provincial governments for funding – making the case that the Games would attract numerous foreign tourists to the rest of the Netherlands. Pre-empting what would become a familiar scenario, the tourism effects were overestimated (see Chapter 8). In London's Games of 1908 there was no question of asking the government for money – the event was very much a private initiative. However, the public were asked to make donations and Runciman (2010) sees these contributions as an embryonic form of public 'participation' as spectating at sport events was still some way from being a mainstream activity.

In these early Olympic Games, providing a stadium large enough for the event was the main financial commitment required. For London's first Games (1908)

Figure 3.2 *The stadium built to stage the Amsterdam Olympic Games in 1928. The Amsterdam Games revived the tradition of lighting an Olympic flame and the stadium was designed with this in mind*

the stadium accounted for two thirds of the £90,000 budget (Runciman, 2010), whilst four years later Stockholm's main stadium took up 87 per cent of the money spent on staging the Games (Liao and Pitts, 2006). At the time of writing, Stockholm's stadium – largely unchanged since 1912 – was hosting the European Team Athletics Championships. In an era when the legacies of Olympic stadia are much debated, this represents an impressive achievement. Stockholm's stadium was/is fairly modest, but by the time of the 1932 Games, building a large stadium had evolved into the exercise in urban machismo it remains today. The aptly named LA Coliseum – boasting a capacity of 75,000 – was the largest Olympic arena built in the twentieth century.

Prior to World War II, building impressive modern stadia was the main preoccupation of Olympic organisers, but the long-term future of these structures was still uncertain during this period. Stadia were often built in public parks and there was less confidence than there is today about the need for such arenas after events had closed. Attendance levels at the events were often poor, with people anxious about large crowds and mixing with people of different social classes. In 1908, the Olympic site at White City was meant to be dismantled and it took a concerted campaign to persuade authorities to keep the stadium as a monument to the event (Gold and Gold, 2009; Runciman, 2010). This provides an interesting contrast to the modern legacy dilemma (see Chapter 4). The 1908 venue was kept for sentimental reasons even though the land had been designated for other uses. This is very different from the contemporary trend for urban authorities to deliberately construct permanent stadia in the hope that these structures will lead to wider development (see Chapter 5).

The modern tendency to build permanent structures to stage special events didn't really emerge until the 1920s. A series of permanent structures was developed to stage the British Empire Exhibition (1924/5), including Wembley Stadium which became England's most famous football venue (see Figure 3.3). The same site was subsequently used for the 1948 Olympic Games and for hundreds of other major events throughout the twentieth century. The development of Wembley prompted a trend for developing permanent event locations on the periphery of urban centres which had the capacity to stage subsequent major events. Other famous examples include Montjuic, Barcelona, which hosted a World Expo in 1929, the (aborted) people's Olympics of 1936 and the 1992

Figure 3.3 Wembley Stadium, London. This new arched stadium replaced the original ground that featured the famous twin towers. This site has hosted many major events including the 1948 Olympic Games

Olympic Games. Another good example is Flushing Meadows, New York. This former rubbish dump hosted World Expos in 1939/40 and 1964/5 and subsequently became the permanent setting for one of the world's most prestigious tennis tournaments (the US Open) and the home stadium of the NY Mets baseball team.

The 1920s also spawned other examples of planned permanent event venues. Amsterdam's Olympic Games (1928) involved developing a permanent sporting complex (see Figure 3.2) integrated into the city plan (Westerbeek, 2009). However, cities still tended to use existing facilities (such as military barracks, university campuses) for the support services required. By the 1930s there were ambitious schemes to promote urban development in emerging nations using events. For example, the 1932 Olympic Games were part of what Dyreson and Llewellyn (2008) term the most ambitious real-estate development project in US history – the construction of Los Angeles. The first purpose-built athletes' village was constructed for this event. The village comprised 500 prefabricated cottages arranged in a circular fashion on a 101-ha site. The organisers of the LA Games can also be credited with the process of making supplementary improvements to the cityscape in order to maximise the promotional effects. The palm trees planted as part of Games preparations were one of the more subtle legacies of the 1932 Games (Dyreson and Llewellyn, 2008).

Post-war: reconstruction/modernisation

In the post-war period, the emphasis shifted from using events to develop and promote urbanism to using events as agents for reconstruction. This involved physical regeneration, but also symbolic reparations for those cities most affected by wartime affiliations. It was no coincidence that hosts of the Olympic games in the period 1948–1972 included London, Rome, Tokyo and Munich. The exception to this was the Olympic Games of Melbourne in 1956 which aimed to generate international exposure for an emerging city (Davison, 1997).

Festivals

In the post-war period, Europe's cultural festivals were reconfigured. Before the war, cities such as Munich and Salzburg were the continent's major festival centres but the symbolic and practical problems faced by these cities allowed others to emerge in their place. The best example is Edinburgh, where the first international festival was staged in 1947. These festivals and other one-off events were motivated by the need to boost morale. The 1951 Festival of Britain was significant in that it reconfigured a large section of the South Bank in London. The Festival bequeathed a reclaimed site and new facilities including the Royal Festival Hall (see Figure 3.4). In addition to the intended morale-boosting effect,

Figure 3.4 *Belvedere Road, London, during the time of the Festival of Britain (1951). The Royal Festival Hall (foreground, right) was the main physical legacy of the event; whilst the Dome of Discovery (rear) was dismantled. The Houses of Parliament can be seen in the distance*

the Festival aimed to reconstruct an industrial area badly damaged by the war and to leave a legacy of cultural facilities. In this sense it can be considered to be an early example of the culturally oriented waterfront projects that would become a popular option for many post-industrial port cities. Interestingly, the concepts of regeneration and legacy were very much part of the rationale, with the accompanying guidebook promising that the event would:

> leave behind not just a record of what we have thought of ourselves in the year 1951 but, in a fair community founded where once there was a slum, in an avenue of trees or in some work of art, a reminder of what we have done to write this single, adventurous year into our national and local history.

> (Museum of London, 2011)

The Festival of Britain was also highly controversial as it was an expensive project delivered at a time of great hardship. It was indelibly associated with the Labour government (1945–1949), in particular Lord Herbert Morrison – whose involvement meant he became known as Lord Festival. After the election in 1951, the new Conservative government hastily dismantled the Festival. This act highlighted one of the enduring complications of event strategies – the problem of delivering long-term event legacies when the officials that commissioned the event are no longer in positions of power (see Chapter 9).

Rome and Tokyo

The Rome (1960) and Tokyo (1964) Summer Games shared many similarities. Both events were meant to be staged earlier (1944 and 1940) but were cancelled due to World War II. As a result of the war, these reconvened events were used strategically by their hosts to overcome negative perceptions about the host nations whilst introducing much needed urban infrastructure to their capitals. Officials in Tokyo and Rome conveniently avoided their inglorious recent history by emphasising connections with ancient empires. Tokyo also promoted ambitious modern imagery. The contrast between emphasising the past (Rome) and accentuating the future (Tokyo) was illustrated by the different routes chosen for the marathon race: Rome used its marathon to remind people of its illustrious classical past, whilst Tokyo devised a route that showcased its recent modernisation. Rather than using the Games to expand urbanism further, both cities refurbished existing facilities. Rome was able to use facilities and plans prepared for unrealised previous events. The Games were staged in two main sites – one which had been earmarked as the main location for the 1944 Games (the Foro Italico), and the Esposizione Universale di Roma (EUR) – a complex which had been developed for an unrealised 1942 World Expo. This created problems as the complexes had been built in the fascist era and still contained symbols and styles that were deemed by some to be distasteful (Modrey, 2008). As well as providing venues and an athletes' village, Rome's Olympic Games were also the first example of city-wide redevelopment undertaken in conjunction with an event (Liao and Pitts, 2006; Munoz, 2006). The city developed a new water system, and improved public transport, street lighting and hotel provision.

Like Rome, Tokyo used existing facilities to stage the Olympic Games and devoted more resources to developing the city rather than new venues. This strategy was a direct precursor of Barcelona's much heralded strategy for the 1992 Games which also prioritised new infrastructure at the expense of new sports facilities. In Tokyo, new expressways, major roads and underground lines were built, but event facilities were relatively modest. An existing stadium was upgraded and a former military base was used as the site for the Olympic Village. The latter was an example of event-led land reclamation of a different sort – from alien forces (the US military) rather than from nature or industry.

The 1970s

The Olympic Games of 1972 marked the end of the era where events were used to reconstruct cities symbolically and physically. Whereas the 1936 Berlin Olympics epitomised the use of monumental architecture for the purposes of regime promotion, the Munich Games were deliberately designed as the antithesis of Hitler's infamous Games. The architecture of the 1972 Games was designed to symbolise informality, democracy, humanity and quality of life. Apart from the murders in the Olympic Village, the enduring symbol of the 1972 Games was the innovative design of the roof covering the main stadium (see Figure 2.1). This was the first of many extravagant roofs that would cause Olympic budgets to be exceeded (most famously, Tallibert's design for Montreal's Olympic stadium four years later, but also Calatrava's Olympic Stadium in Athens and Hadid's design for London's Aquatic Centre in the twenty-first century – see Figure 3.5). The light and airy roof of Munich's Olympic stadium was the ultimate manifestation of the organisers' efforts to promote a new, open (West) Germany, but this philosophy was also evident in the parklands that surrounded it. The complex was

Figure 3.5 *A picture taken in 2010 of the construction of the Aquatic Centre in London's Olympic Park. The structure was designed by Zaha Hadid*

built 4 km outside Munich on undeveloped land, but instead of being designed as a self-contained, specialist 'zone', it was designed to be an integral part of the city.

The way Munich's Olympic site cleverly balanced open space and urban structures means that it can be compared to another post-war German method of using events to achieve regeneration – the *Bundesgartenschauen*. This idea – which was copied by Austria, Switzerland and France – involves taking an area of derelict land and holding a design competition to provide a suitable masterplan (Holden, 1989). The costs of developing this thorough plan are then offset by holding a garden festival for approximately six months to celebrate the formation of the new park. These events are staged every two years in Germany, with an international edition endorsed by the BIE staged every ten years (Holden, 1989). The scheme has also been expanded to include smaller, provincial editions. The key feature of these German festivals is the long lead time. There is sometimes as much as ten years' work involved in the period between conception and delivery (DoE, 1990). This allows for careful planning and allows gardens to mature through several growing seasons before events are staged. Since the first festival in 1951, *Bundesgartenschauen* have allowed many German cities to replace derelict land with attractive open space.

The urban crisis: tackling de-industrialisation

In the mid-1970s, it became clear that the developed world was facing a major urban crisis. Employment in manufacturing was declining rapidly and many cities were forced to face the dual challenge of redeveloping large redundant sites and providing employment for the people who used to work in the industries previously located there. All this had to be achieved in the context of local government budget reductions caused by political changes and the diminished tax base caused by the exodus of middle-class residents. Faced with few alternatives, many cities decided to focus on the emerging service sector. Alongside the development of retail and tourism facilities, major events were earmarked as ways of redeveloping places as sites of consumption and symbolising the shift to a post-industrial future. Events were not only staged, but 'festivity' was extended to urban management more generally (Hughes, G., 1999). Thus, as well as programmes of events, physical changes were made to promote festivity. Central areas of cities were turned into stages for events – as best evidenced by the introduction of 'festival market places' in post-industrial cities from Baltimore to Birmingham. These were pioneered by a US designer, James Rouse.

Garden festivals in the UK

In the UK, post-industrial event strategies can be traced back to the development of Gateshead's International Stadium in the 1970s and to the National Garden

Festivals (NGFs) staged by Liverpool, Stoke and Glasgow in the 1980s. Following urban riots in the early 1980s, a proposal was put before the secretary of state for the environment, Michael Heseltine. This proposal was based on the German *Bundesgartenschauen* model and the intention was to stage similar festivals in the UK. The idea was that these festivals would help to reclaim land, remove the stigma attached to post-industrial cities, attract investment and provide new services and employment opportunities for residents (DoE, 1990). In Liverpool (1984) and Glasgow (1988), NGFs were co-ordinated by Urban Development Corporations (also set up by Heseltine), agencies that took regeneration efforts out of the hands of city councils (these tended to be controlled by opposition parties). The intention was to spend public money developing the sites to stage garden festivals that would leave a legacy of land conducive for the development of commercial, residential and leisure areas. The garden festivals were intended as a way of securing image benefits, and as a way of generating revenue both from visitors and sponsors. The basic idea was that the festivals would finance themselves – but also provide a foundation for post-festival investment.

The outcomes of this interesting example of event regeneration varied between the different hosts (see Table 3.1). The 1984 Liverpool NGF helped to assist the city's image improvement, but was not so successful at securing urban regeneration. Although it made an operating loss, the event itself was deemed a success and attracted 3.5 million visitors (Holden, 1989). Contaminated land was reclaimed and part of the site was reopened after the festival as a permanent festival garden. New housing was also provided. However, in general the use of the land reclaimed was disappointing and the business park envisaged never materialised. In contrast, the 1986 Stoke NGF was less well attended (2.25 million visitors) (Holden, 1989), but two and a half years after its closure the site was bought by a developer and turned into an attractive mixed-use area (DoE, 1990). The 73-ha site had suffered from two centuries of ironworking, coalmining and claydigging and its reclamation in two years was considered to be a major achievement. Indeed, it was estimated that without the NGF it would have taken 25 years to reclaim the land (DoE, 1990).

The 1988 Glasgow NGF was the best attended of the events (4.3 million visitors) and even made a small surplus (DoE, 1990). But the scope for physical regeneration was more limited: the festival reclaimed only 49 ha of land that was less contaminated (Holden, 1989). The organisers of the Glasgow NGF enjoyed the benefits of being able to learn from the previous hosts' experiences. They even employed the designers that Liverpool had used four years previously (Holden, 1989). The Glasgow festival was only one part of a long-term programme of city promotion, which makes its effects on city image harder to determine (DoE, 1990). The physical benefits were difficult to compare to the other NGF hosts as the site was already owned by a housing developer (Holden, 1989). This meant

Table 3.1 A summary of the characteristics of the UK's National Garden Festivals

	Liverpool 1984	Stoke on Trent 1986	Glasgow 1988	Gateshead 1990	Ebbw Vale 1992
Site area	100 ha	73 ha	48 ha	82 ha	80 ha
Development period	2.5 years	5 years	4 years	5.5 years	5 years
Cost	£30 million	£30 million	£41.4 million	£33 million	£38 million
Visitor numbers	3.5 million	2.25 million	4.35 million	3 million+	2 million+
After-use	Housing + mixed leisure use and public space	Public open space + mixed commercial/ leisure use	Housing, public park, business park	Housing, public park, mixed use	Public open space, commercial, housing and recreation

Source: Based on data cited in Holden (1989)

that the site was developed soon after the closure of the festival. However, it also meant that there was less additional value generated by staging the festival, because the site would have been developed anyway.

The NGFs of the 1980s were followed by two subsequent editions in Gateshead and Ebbw Vale (South Wales) in the early 1990s. The edition staged in Gateshead was more like the German *Bundesgartenschauen* in that the site penetrated the town through a series of interconnected sites (Holden, 1989). However, it should be emphasised that the five British festivals 1984–1992 were generally very different from their German counterparts. The British NGFs were explicitly aimed at delivering urban regeneration and image/tourism benefits, whereas the German *Bundesgartenschauen* tend to be more focused on producing and protecting open space in cities (DoE, 1990). The British garden festivals were not meant to create parks – but this was not always understood by the public, causing controversy when the festival sites were redeveloped for housing (Holden, 1989). The shorter time frames in British festivals were also significant. For Liverpool's NGF, the masterplan was produced over a 10-week period (Beaumont, 1985). This meant that the detail and quality of the designs were compromised and planning to ensure effective after-use was prepared hastily. The rush to deliver the NGFs also meant that the landscaping was considered to be of poor quality. However, the British examples are still seen as successful in many ways. Derelict and contaminated land was assembled and reclaimed more quickly than it otherwise would have been without the impetus of the festival. Image improvements were witnessed and the projects were successful in attracting the private sector to lead the regeneration of these areas. The overall conclusion of the official evaluation study (which covered the first three festivals) was that 'a garden festival in isolation may not be a powerful instrument, but a festival does provide a valuable additional instrument to be included in a regeneration strategy' (DoE, 1990: 58).

The 1990s: place marketing, partnerships and economic development

The event regeneration of the 1980s was generally public sector led, with taxpayers' money used to fund and pump prime projects. Partnerships with the private sector had begun to emerge, but regulatory constraints and public reticence meant there was still a reliance on traditional forms of government. The initiative that best illustrates this approach was the World Student Games of 1991. Buoyed by the profitability of LA's 1984 Olympic Games, and – closer to home – the perceived success of the National Garden Festivals, Sheffield embarked on an event regeneration strategy that nearly bankrupted the city. In its rush to find a solution to post-industrial problems Sheffield City Council hurriedly decided to host the World Student Games in a series of new venues in the Don Valley. In 1914 this valley hosted more than fourteen companies that each employed over 1,000 people, and as late as the 1970s, 45,000 people were employed here (Lawless and Ramsden, 1990). By 1993, 90 per cent of the 45,000 steel industry jobs in Sheffield had been lost (Taylor *et al.*, 1996).

Several mistakes made by organisers in the period leading up to the 1991 World Student Games seem elementary now, but one must remember that this type of approach to regeneration was still in its infancy in the late 1980s. The leadership of the project lacked strategic experience, organisational ability and democratic legitimacy (Roche, 1994). There was a failure to cultivate a sense of public ownership of the WSG and conventional policy processes were bypassed in the rush to secure and deliver the event. Public consultation, feasibility research, monitoring and project evaluation were deficient (Bramwell, 1997; Roche, 1994). There was also a lack of strategic planning (Roche, 1994). Most of the strategies that sought to exploit the opportunity presented by the WSG were developed retrospectively – not only after the decision had been taken to stage the event, but after the event had finished. Most importantly, the project was not well integrated into long-term policy and planning. There were poor connections with the 1986 Draft Local Plan for the area, and the project was divorced from the work of an Urban Regeneration Company (SDC) which had been founded in 1987 to lead the physical regeneration of the Don Valley (Lawless and Ramsden, 1990). Ultimately, the project aimed to achieve regeneration mainly through the image benefits that officials believed would result from the event and the high-profile physical investments involved in staging it. Dabinett (1991: 15) criticises the project for attempting 'instant physical renewal', a 'quick fix' which ignored 'the less visible though more substantial process of industrial reconstruction'.

The lessons from Sheffield's WSG project were very clear, and were immediately reaffirmed by the success of Barcelona's Olympic Games a year later (see Chapter 5). As well as the strategic planning deficiencies noted, Sheffield's authorities became aware of three other key principles.

- First, not all events are the same and an event must command sufficient media attention to deliver image effects.
- Second, if events are to pay for themselves through revenues earned, it was no longer sufficient to sell tickets – the only way to make money was through media rights.
- Third, a city council could not take on event regeneration strategies without the assistance of private sector partners, or partnerships with regional, national or international governments. As Smith (1991: 10) concluded in the aftermath of the WSG, 'it is unrealistic to imagine that local authorities on their own can successfully implement cultural or sporting events on this scale'.

Ultimately, in the 1980s events were used as a way of overcoming the stigma attached to some industrial cities and as a way of attracting investment to cities that had been unable to rejuvenate themselves from within. The main idea was to reinvent cities, rather than build on existing strengths. This philosophy of urban revolution rather than gradual evolution was epitomised in the strategy used for Glasgow's European City of Culture event (1990). This is now identified in the events literature as a critical moment when the European City of Culture (now European Capital of Culture) event was transformed from one that celebrated cities with existing reputations as cultural cities (the first five Cities of Culture were Athens, Amsterdam, Berlin, Florence and Paris) to one that provided a vehicle for the reorientation and regeneration of industrial cities (e.g. Genoa, Glasgow, Liverpool, Rotterdam). As Mooney (2004) recognises, the Glasgow edition is now used as both a model and a reference point for other disadvantaged cities.

Glasgow's strategy was controversial at the time, and remains so, with Mooney (2004) suggesting that the notion of a 'Glasgow model' sustains a fallacy rather than celebrating a reality. Perhaps inevitably, concerns were expressed about the use of public money to stage a major arts festival (and build a £30 million concert hall) when housing and other key services needed investment. Alongside familiar arguments about opportunity costs, Glaswegian opposition focused on the symbolic discontinuity of an event which seemingly ignored Glaswegian traditions of industrial labour and working-class culture, in favour of new imagery dominated by arts and elite culture. Glasgow officials were staging a festival not to celebrate Glaswegian culture and life, but to promote a new vision of what Glasgow could be. The supposed 'success' of this event divides opinion, but Mooney's (2004) retrospective account is highly critical. He sees the European City of Culture policy as one that has contributed to Glasgow's worsening levels of deprivation because it diverted attention and resources from dealing with serious problems of poverty and disadvantage. In this sense, the event acted not as an agent of regeneration, but as a substitute for direct action. The strategy assumed that a wealthier city would mean a regenerated one, but the limitations of this approach are now recognised. Unfortunately, the idea that wider economic development would trickle down to disadvantaged areas not only persisted throughout the 1990s, it defined it.

Private sector involvement

In the 1990s, old fashioned managerial interventionism had been supplemented with urban entrepreneurialism and a desire to use the flexibility, expertise and efficiency associated with the private sector. Municipal authorities began to loosen their rigid structures, allowing public institutions to act more like private sector businesses, with private sector interests permitted to perform roles normally reserved for public institutions. Partnerships between the public and private sector were formed. Major events were integrated into these new arrangements in several ways.

- Events and event bids were used to help formulate new ways of working. Bids showed that the public and private sectors could work together and often new institutions formed as part of event preparations provided models for new forms of governance (see Chapter 9). The criteria for assessing event bids began to include the existence of partnerships and this encouraged their formation. In contexts such as the UK, competitive bid schemes had been developed to fund regeneration. This meant in the 1990s cities became used to competing with each other not only to stage events, but to achieve regeneration through more conventional means. This reinforces a point made in Chapter 1: event projects had begun to assume characteristics of regeneration, and regeneration projects had begun to take on the characteristics of events.
- In the 1990s the requirement for sponsors and business advocates to help fund event projects meant that city councils became more comfortable working with the private sector. Companies with vested interests in certain locations were inspired to come together to secure major events during this period. The 'growth machines' that coalesced around events were made up of private companies who might otherwise have been in competition. This made them powerful stakeholders and increased their influence within policy making. Networks were often built around clusters of stakeholders who had a vested interest in enhancing the image of a city. Henry and Paramio-Salcines (1999) cite these 'symbolic regimes' as key influences in event strategies.

In a European context, Glasgow's European City of Culture event in 1990 was perhaps the first example of this new generation of regeneration projects. As Mooney (2004) identifies, several years before the arrival of Blair and Brown's centre-left national administration in the UK (1997–2010), the local Labour council had decided that Glasgow could progress only by embracing the private sector, by forming partnerships with business representatives, by working with market forces and by attracting growth industries and companies instead of 'propping up' existing sectors and organisations (Mooney, 2004). The event was used as part of this new approach, which was essentially a place marketing strategy to encourage inward investment, new residents and tourists – rather than an urban policy that delivered change in areas that had suffered disproportionately from de-industrialisation. Another good example of how major events were used to introduce new ways of working was Lisbon's 1998 World Expo. As Nunes Silva and Syrett (2006) suggest, to deliver the major development projects associated with this event the Portuguese government thought it necessary to introduce new forms of governance. A public corporation was set up and permitted to act outside the normal restrictions placed on public bodies (Nunes Silva and Syrett, 2006). Substantial state funding was provided to underwrite private development. These new arrangements were beneficial because they bypassed bureaucratic structures, widened the financial and skills bases available and allowed greater access to EU resources. Nunes Silva and Syrett (2006: 111) conclude that the completion of Expo '98 (and later projects such as the 2004 European Football Championships) on time was 'a direct result of these special institutional arrangements'.

The event that epitomised the commercial and entrepreneurial approach to event regeneration in the 1990s was the Atlanta Olympic Games of 1996. Although event projects in the US have always been more private sector led than those in Europe, these Games were particularly notable for the influence of corporate interests. Glynn (2008) highlights how the organising committee created for the Games (ACOG) reflected the network structure already present in Atlanta – it was dominated by business interests. However, the Games also helped to reconfigure networks. The heavy reliance on sponsorship income to fund the Atlanta Olympic Games meant that officials of the companies donating money towards the event were able to enter decision-making circles that had previously been inaccessible to them. And this access to power did not necessarily end when the Olympics were over (see Chapter 9).

The increasing role for the private sector in event regeneration was not necessarily helpful. Atlanta's governance structure perhaps led to an obsession with the event itself and the image it projected, at the expense of the inner city regeneration that was seen as a priority by the mayor and other public officials. The organisation set up to spearhead the regeneration of inner city neighbourhoods (CODA) was underfunded, and when CODA asked for assistance, ACOG argued that these objectives were not part of its responsibility (Andranovich *et al.*, 2001). Whitelegg (2000) argues that ACOG's obsession with Atlanta's image at the expense of community projects was counter-productive. He suggests that had Atlanta followed Barcelona's example and focused more on community-wide projects, the improvement to the city's image would have been less spectacular but more permanent. Atlanta's regeneration may have been compromised by an obsession with place promotion at the expense of getting the 'nitty gritty' of the Games right (Whitelegg, 2000).

Glynn's (2008) work on Atlanta is important because it recognises that major events operate within the existing structure of a city, but they also give cities a 'jolt' that can mean institutional arrangements change forever. Events often provide the motivation to set up new institutions that can change the way a city is governed in the long term (see Chapter 9). In the 1990s new semi-autonomous economic development agencies or promotional agencies were created to fulfil roles normally reserved for public agencies. And major events often provided the incentive or justification to establish these agencies. Their focus was usually inward investment – either from new businesses, new residents or tourists. Accordingly, many event strategies of this era were not focused on assisting residents directly; instead the aim was to increase economic development generally.

The 2000s: a focus on people…and legacy?

With the benefit of at least 40 years of experience, event regeneration (in developed countries) post-2000 has tended to be more sensitive, more sophisticated and more targeted than twentieth-century precedents. An obsession with physical change, image enhancement and economic development has been supplemented with more attention to 'softer' outcomes. Rather than merely building venues and expecting them to lead regeneration, event projects have begun to use complementary initiatives to assist people. This reflects the wider emergence of social regeneration; regeneration that aims to improve people's lives, rather than merely upgrading places and helping businesses. Event regeneration since 2000 has been undertaken within a 'new' paradigm – that of legacy; something that has helped to refocus strategies on long-term outcomes rather than short-term impacts. Attention to legacy has helped to focus cities more on the post-event period and the need to plan for the long term before the event takes place. So rather than legacy merely being the inevitable outcome of events, it is now considered to be something that can be planned. It is also something that is increasingly considered from the outset of events, rather than merely something that occurs post-event. Confusingly, this means the concept of legacy is now associated with the pre-event period too. Initiatives pursued in the pre-event era can be used to deliver positive outcomes even before an event takes place. This idea can be traced to Toronto's bid for the 2008 Olympic Games which included the 'Legacy Now' initiative. This involved the planning, delivery and communication of benefits at each stage of the project – not just when the Games were over. This approach was adopted by Vancouver (2010) (LegaciesNow) and London (2012) (Legacy Now) in their legacy strategies for events that were actually staged.

The new legacy agenda is not merely something being advocated by host cities. Rights holders of events are interested in ensuring that their franchises are not tainted by accusations of wasteful expenditure. Interestingly, it seems that legacy is now focused on producing tangible legacies, not merely restricting negative impacts. Therefore, legacy is a justification for increasing expenditure, thus perhaps – counter-productively – increasing the likelihood of wasteful spending. For example, sports allocated temporary venues during multi-sport events now complain that there will be no legacy for their sports

(MacAloon, 2008). The idea that the new legacy focus has put more pressure on cities for permanent physical changes contradicts the wider academic literature on event regeneration where there is more recognition of intangible legacies as well as those which are tangible (Preuss, 2007). Projects such as Manchester's Commonwealth Games Legacy Programme confirm that legacy initiatives can act independently from event venues and physical facilities (Smith and Fox, 2007).

Event regeneration post-2000 also reflects changes in urban regeneration policy more generally. There has been a shift towards regeneration in specific disadvantaged neighbourhoods, rather than general assistance for whole districts, cities or regions. This is related to the realisation that increases in overall levels of economic development have not necessarily led to a better quality of life for individuals. Economic development has led to a polarisation of wealth, rather than a narrowing of the gap between rich and poor. High levels of immigration and changing lifestyles have also shifted the priorities of regeneration from merely physical regeneration and provision of new employment opportunities to more subtle aims including community cohesion, well-being and skills development. Accordingly, event regeneration has shifted to address these agendas. For example, in addition to economic benefits, the main aims of the 2006 Commonwealth Games in Melbourne were to: improve accessibility, diversity and community participation; ensure the rights of indigenous communities were respected; increase sport participation; develop a sustainable environmental framework; and maximise education benefits (Insight Economics, 2006). Similarly, in Trieste's bid for the 2008 World Expo, the city's multicultural character was heavily emphasised, with the intention of placating tensions between Slovenians, Italians and other minority groups (Colombino, 2009). And as there has been a shift to an agenda promoting inclusivity and accessibility, there has been more interest from urban governments in staging events for disadvantaged social groups including women (Potter, 2009), gay people (Stevenson *et al.*, 2005) and persons with disabilities (Gold and Gold, 2007a, 2007b).

A further change relates to who is responsible for event regeneration. Whereas event regeneration in the 1970s–1980s was all about the public sector, and in the 1990s about the increasing role of the private sector, since 2000 there has been more focus on the voluntary or third sector. The involvement of Greenpeace in the preliminary stages of the organisation of the 2000 Olympic Games was an early example of this. Other examples include the involvement of the Girl Guides in the delivery of the Legacy Programme for the 2005 UEFA Championships (Potter, 2009). In the quest to ensure that initiatives are pursued after events have finished, officials have turned to use voluntary organisations to maintain momentum. Again, this reflects a wider shift whereby the public sector has withdrawn to a 'steering' role rather than one that involves 'rowing'.

An additional development is that event regeneration is now being pursued by the world cities (London, Paris), rather than by second- (Barcelona, Atlanta) and third-tier (Gateshead, Sheffield) cities that tended to use this strategy in the post-industrial era. The cities that submitted bids for the 2012 Olympic Games read like a list of the world's greatest cities and included (shortlisted) bids from London, Madrid, Paris and New York. There are many possible explanations for this. The extra challenges associated with being 'world cities' have perhaps meant that there is a need to find new ways to solve big problems – not least the growing polarisation of wealth in these cities. The emergence of a social periphery in these cities where immigrants have inhabited housing vacated by working-class residents is another key problem (Villette and Hardill, 2007).

A final feature of the latest manifestations of event regeneration policy is the extension of planning horizons associated with these events. Host cities seem to have heeded advice to plan in advance to an extreme level. Some cities are now investigating the feasibility of staging events that are over twenty years away. Examples include Copenhagen, which has investigated the idea of staging the 2024 Olympic Games (TSE, 2010), and Amsterdam, which has developed a strategy that involves the possibility of staging the Games in 2028 (Westerbeek, 2009). Several Middle Eastern cities, including Dubai, have taken this further, by not only communicating their intention to bid for future events, but by developing the required infrastructure. This long-term strategy can involve staging interim events. The development of Durban's 2010 FIFA World Cup stadium is merely the first of a four-stage plan designed to culminate in the creation of a much larger precinct capable of staging a major multi-sport event, for example the Commonwealth or Olympic Games (Maennig and du Plessis, 2009). Mentioning cities such as Durban and Dubai also highlights one of the key features of contemporary event regeneration – the way it is now being pursued in cities all over the world, rather than merely in Europe, North America and Japan.

SUMMARY

This chapter has provided a chronology outlining the way that events have been used as part of urban development and regeneration over time. The exact timing of key turning points can be contested but there does seem to be a general pattern of evolution. The use of major events reflects urban priorities of the time: during an initial period of urbanisation they were used to achieve urban development; in the post-war period the emphasis then shifted to reconstruction; and since the urban crisis of the 1970s the focus has been on regeneration. The idea of using events to assist urban objectives is nothing new and current practice is related strongly to examples of the past. However, events are now used more extensively and more subtly in the contemporary era. They are also used to achieve a wider range of objectives. It should be noted that the chronology outlined here refers generally to Western cities, while development cycles for cities in the developing world differ. However, rather than comprising a limitation of the preceding discussion this is a further justification for analysing event projects over time. Many rapidly industrialising cities in the developing world seem to be undergoing development cycles previously seen in Western cities and this means there is added value in comparing their contemporary event projects to those from the past. This chapter has provided the historical context for the book. In the remainder of the book, historical examples are cited, but the main focus is practice from the era of urban regeneration (1970s–present). In these subsequent chapters, the different elements of event regeneration are discussed.

Event venues and urban regeneration

4

INTRODUCTION

In the first chapters of this book, the relationship between events and regeneration was discussed and a theoretical/historical foundation for the book was provided. The next five chapters are dedicated to different aspects of event regeneration as identified in Chapter 1. These include the use of events within wider strategies to regenerate cities (Chapter 5), social regeneration in conjunction with events (Chapter 6), events as ways of marking and instigating new directions for cities (Chapter 7) and their use as tools for assisting tourism development (Chapter 8). This chapter focuses on the most basic form of event regeneration – that associated with venue projects. To stage major events cities tend to develop new venues. This is principally something associated with sport events, although new theatres, museums and exhibition spaces have also been constructed in conjunction with many cultural events. World Expos are slightly different in that they have traditionally been staged in temporary buildings and structures. However, permanent facilities and buildings are now more common (Rollin, 2008).

In this chapter, the key question is whether the construction of event venues assists urban regeneration. There is a growing realisation that new venues do not automatically assist the areas in which they are located. Although regeneration is often cited in the rationale for using public funds to build and maintain these venues, it is unrealistic to expect individual buildings to deliver regeneration. However, there remains a possibility these structures could contribute to wider regeneration efforts. This chapter aims to explore how venues can be designed to ensure that they make a positive contribution to urban regeneration – physically, but also socially and economically. Well planned event venues can leave a legacy of facilities, spaces, jobs and investment that can assist regeneration. But too often venues are poorly conceived. This means they can contribute to social exclusion, costly maintenance bills and other opportunity costs. These issues are explored here.

The chapter is organised into four main sections. The first analyses the key stakeholders involved. The second analyses issues associated with venue development. These sections are followed by a third on the location of venues. The fourth section discusses principles associated with integration.

STAKEHOLDERS

Events can be useful mechanisms through which to develop new facilities for urban areas; but they also introduce various complications that will become apparent during this chapter. One of the main issues associated with event venue development is that there are usually multiple stakeholders that need to be satisfied. This creates multiple sets of requirements. Urban governments and the communities they represent are two obvious stakeholders. But building or refurbishing venues for an event is a process that also involves the rights holders of events and specialist organisations representing the activities that will take place there (e.g. sport federations). A further stakeholder group is the 'end user', the organisation that will use the facilities in the post-event period. Their requirements may be different altogether (see Table 4.1).

Due to conspicuous failures to derive value for money and long-term uses from event venue projects, there is now consensus about the need to focus on legacy. As discussed in Chapter 3, this term implies the delivery of long-term outcomes, rather than merely short to medium-term impacts. The term suggests a positive

Table 4.1 The typical legacy priorities of different stakeholder groups

Stakeholders	Legacy priorities
National/local governments	Self-sufficiency, economic development and political capital
Local communities	Improved quality of life – through enhanced opportunities for employment and recreation, better housing and public space
Rights holders	Venue use and status that reflects well on, and adds value to, their franchise
Federations/ organisations	Resources dedicated to their particular activity or interest
End users	Venue design and its suitability for post-event use

contribution, but experience suggests that legacies can also be negative (e.g. long-term debts). Despite consensus about the importance of securing positive legacies, the term is used differently by different stakeholders. Some stakeholders want to leave new facilities and opportunities for local communities, whereas others are more concerned about particular legacies for individual organisations or interests. The typical positions adopted by different stakeholder groups are outlined in Table 4.1.

BOX 4.1 THE COMPLICATIONS OF DEVELOPING VENUES IN CONJUNCTION WITH EVENTS

It is very difficult to develop event venues that satisfy different stakeholder priorities. In the literature this is illustrated well by Binks and Snape's (2006) analysis of the development of Bolton Arena in north-west England. The venue was envisaged back in the late 1980s when the local council expressed its wish for a new development that would act as both a tourist attraction and local leisure facility. To ensure funding was forthcoming, the local authority sought a partner for the project that would help to support its case for funding through the UK's National Lottery Fund. The Lawn Tennis Association (LTA) agreed to come on board because, coincidentally, it was seeking a new regional centre of excellence. However, at the same time other considerations were unexpectedly thrust on to the project. An opportunity arose when nearby Manchester was awarded the 2002 Commonwealth Games. Staging some of this event (the badminton tournament) at Bolton Arena helped to ensure the venue came to fruition – as well as providing extra visibility for the Arena.

The interesting aspect of this project is that the involvement of event stakeholders changed the configuration of the project. According to Binks and Snape's (2006: 68) research, the Manchester Commonwealth Games 'exercised an eventual influence on the design and intended function of the Bolton Arena', despite the fact that the venue would only host badminton tournaments for a few days.

The £15 million facility opened in 2001. It was paid for by a National Lottery grant (£11 million), the local council (£3 million) and the LTA (£1 million). However, this capital funding for the project was, according to Binks and Snape (2006), 'driven' by the Commonwealth Games which introduced a distorting effect. The revised design of the venue to suit the Games' needs meant that the facility was less aligned to community requirements. External interests were also unduly prioritised because of the involvement of the LTA which exerted disproportionate control of the facility, even though it had funded only a fraction of the development costs and even though it generated only £300,000 of the £2 million per year it cost to operate the facility (Binks and Snape, 2006).

Using an event (2002 Commonwealth Games) to help realise the Arena, plus the partnership with the LTA, introduced conflicting interests and a sub-optimal outcome. The danger of relying on external partners was emphasised when – due to a strategic shift – the LTA closed the centre of excellence only one year after it opened. Ultimately, these partnerships affected the impact the Arena had on the local community it was designed to serve. Binks and Snape (2006: 71) suggest that adapting the Arena in the post-event era 'has been fraught with challenges and obstacles, not least the need to alter the perceptions of the local community…that the venue is not for them'.

Ultimately, the influence of the Games was to introduce stakeholders who had no long-term interest in the venue – making it much harder for the local authority which had to retrofit a more suitable design. The local authority had opportunistically used the Games to help realise the Arena, but its designation as an event venue diminished the chances that the facility would act as a community oriented resource. Overall, the case highlights the conflicting priorities of stakeholders involved in event venue delivery and, as Binks and Snape (2006) show, it also emphasises the conflict between the temporary and long-term functions of events facilities.

VENUE DEVELOPMENT

Major event projects involve key choices about venue development. Host cities are sometimes required to invest in venues to meet the minimum requirements of event rights holders. In other instances, a host city makes the deliberate decision to invest in new facilities. One of the most widely discussed issues regarding major events is the development of superfluous new venues. Venues that are not used in the post-event era are considered to be wasteful: not just because of the cost of their construction, but also because they are often expensive to maintain. Operating under-used venues may reduce the funding available for more useful structures/provision that can make a more positive contribution to urban communities. This is known as the 'opportunity cost' of developing events venues.

White elephants and the reasons they continue to be built

Under-utilised facilities that are expensive to maintain are known as 'white elephants'. The term is derived from a Southeast Asian myth: white elephants were seen as highly symbolic specimens; they required pampering and that meant they were very costly to look after. Receiving a white elephant as a gift was a dubious honour as the recipient would have to bear the burden of the animal's upkeep. This is an apt metaphor for expensive and superfluous venue projects that continue to be a drain on resources if they are not self-sufficient. An early example was the White City Stadium built for the 1908 Olympic Games in London. This stadium was meant to be knocked down after the event, but a campaign to retain it was successful. The venue was then under-used for twenty years, meaning it can claim to be the first example of a major event 'white elephant' in the modern era (Gold and Gold, 2009).

It is increasingly acknowledged that new venues should be developed only where there is a proven need for them; otherwise existing venues, temporary venues or facilities in nearby towns should be employed. This is now widely appreciated, but host cities have continued to develop superfluous new venues. The need to impress rights holders during the bidding process; the desire to show off during the event; and/or the inflexible requirements of events rights holders are the usual explanations why mistakes continue to be made. White elephants can also result from the naive attitude that, despite the apparent lack of demand for a certain facility, a new venue will somehow generate interest and demand. These four factors (illustrated in Figure 4.1) are discussed further below.

1 *Bidding to win.* When a host city secures the rights to host an event through a competitive bidding process, this is more likely to result in white elephants. If cities are desperate to win the staging rights there is an added incentive to propose impressive venues. If proper cost–benefit analyses are not undertaken before bidding, and if the event is won, promises to develop inappropriately extravagant venues have to be kept. As Mangan (2008: 1876) points out with respect to event projects, 'aspiration does not pay attention to practicality'. The organisations that award the rights to stage events want them to be memorable and spectacular, and therefore they have little incentive to reward bidders that submit frugal bids.

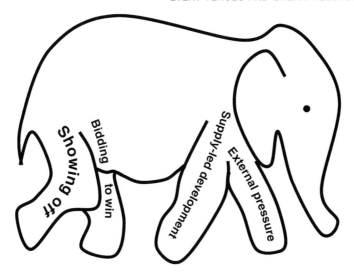

Figure 4.1 *The reasons we still get white elephants*

2 *Showing off.* Showing off – for political reasons – is also a common explanation for white elephants. With international audiences watching, there is a
temptation amongst political elites to develop venues designed to impress.
A good example was the Commonwealth Games staged in Kuala Lumpur,
Malaysia, in 1998. A new 100,000-seat stadium was built even though
the existing stadium was adequate to stage the Games (Silk, 2002). This
new stadium was surrounded by other new venues and athletes' accommodation. The extravagant spending was seen as out of line with previous
Commonwealth Games hosts. The local media blamed the 'ego and aspirations' of the prime minister for the excessive approach (Silk, 2002). Political
vanity means that the symbolic impact of venues is often prioritised at the
expense of practical post-event considerations. This is why iconic designs
are commissioned. Ambitious designs may help place marketing, but they
are more expensive to build and maintain. Innovative designs may also be
less conducive to post-event use.
3 *External pressure.* Sometimes event rights holders enforce certain requirements that encourage the development of white elephants. There are often
stipulations about the size, location and specifications of venues that mean
that facilities are inappropriate for the locations they are constructed in.
The example of the Green Point Stadium built in Cape Town to stage
the FIFA 2010 World Cup is illustrative here. This spectacular venue was
built to a scale, specification and in a location which was designed to meet

the preferences of the rights holders of the event (FIFA), rather than the needs of the local citizens (see Extended case study 1).

4 *Supply-led development (the 'if you build it, they will come' approach).* Specialist venues for events are often developed even though authorities know there is insufficient evidence that markets exist for them. The lack of existing demand for a certain activity may be part of the motivation for developing new venues. Places like Malaysia have built new facilities in the hope they will act as catalysts for sport development (Van der Westhuizen, 2004). This also applies to cultural events. Municipal authorities may want to encourage more participation in certain activities where current demand is low. When Lisbon staged the 1994 European City of Culture event it developed several high-profile cultural venues. Holton (1998) suggests a major motivation for these new venues was to inspire good behaviour and to 'train' Portuguese citizens to become cultural consumers. Adopting this 'if you build it they will come' attitude to event venues is notoriously presumptuous. There are multiple examples of event venues that have been built in the hope that a new facility will inspire interest in the activities inside. But there are very few instances of where this speculative policy has worked.

Some famous examples of white elephants

For the reasons outlined above, many venues have been planned with little or no attention to their long-term use. Costs are usually higher than anticipated and revenues generated are lower. This leaves governments with large, unwarranted debts which accumulate over time and take many years to pay off. The two summer Olympic Games staged in the 1970s made combined losses of £870 million (Walters, 2005a). The bulk of these losses were caused by the cost overruns associated with the main stadium built for the 1976 Olympic Games in Montreal. By insisting on a spectacular design, the mayor of Montreal (Drapeau) caused unnecessary cost overruns and delays. The architect (Tallibert) was overly focused on the short-term use of the stadium as an athletics venue even though it was clear that the venue would be used for baseball and football matches in the post-event era. An ambitious design was conceived involving an extravagant mast and a dome, but because of a shortage of both finance and time to realise this complicated project the venue was built without these features (Roult and Lefebvre, 2010). Since the event, the stadium has cost $40 million a year to maintain and it took thirty years for the city to retire the debts incurred (Whitson, 2004). Various design faults have meant that not enough events have been staged there since the Games to justify these costs (Roult and Lefebvre, 2010).

The main stadium built to stage Sydney's 2000 Olympic Games has also developed a problematic reputation as a white elephant. The stadium (now called the ANZ Stadium) was downscaled after the event, but it has been unable to attract enough events of sufficient scale to fill the 80,000 seats and this problem is exacerbated by intense local competition from other Sydney venues that are located more centrally (e.g. Sydney Cricket Ground, Sydney Football Stadium). The presence of the new Olympic stadium challenged the viability of existing venues and this was unhelpful, particularly as these venues were publicly owned (Searle and Bounds, 1999). Sydney's sports scene is dominated by rugby league and the main teams represent different suburbs. None of the teams attracts enough fans to warrant playing all their games at such a large stadium and when National Rugby League games are played at the ANZ Stadium the atmosphere is affected negatively by the sparsely populated stands. The Stadium is used more effectively to stage major finals and international games but the venue suffers from the lack of a regular user/anchor tenant that has the pulling power to fill the venue.

Since Sydney's Games there have been debates about why such a large stadium was built, with the IOC president claiming in 2001 that it had been built to that size 'against the advice of the IOC' (Cashman, 2006: 155). This suggests internal failings rather than unhelpful external pressure. Searle (2002: 858) questions the processes associated with the Stadium's development, concluding that 'planning considerations about whether Sydney's long-term recreational and entertainment needs required them were absent'. Searle (2002) believes that interpretation also applies to another of Sydney's venues: the Superdome (now called the Acer Arena, see Figure 4.2). Like the main stadium, this venue competes with a more centrally located indoor venue (in Darling Harbour). It is hard to avoid the conclusion that these two adjacent venues (see Figure 4.2) are entirely superfluous to Sydney's needs. Some of the smaller facilities within the Olympic Park have been more successful. The subsidiary athletics centre is now a well used venue for junior sport. Swimming is popular in Australia and this has allowed the aquatics centre to become the nation's second most visited sport venue. By 2002–3 it was attracting over 1 million visitors of varying degrees of expertise (Cashman, 2006). The critical factor that determined the success of these two facilities was that they filled a gap in the city's sporting infrastructure (Cashman, 2006). This shows the value of commissioning pre-event research to find out whether enough local demand exists to justify new venues.

Perhaps the worst contemporary example of venue legacy planning was the 2004 Olympic Games. Many of the new venues built for the Athens Games were not being used several years after the event was staged. Part of the reason for this was extended wrangling about whether the facilities should be viewed as social resources or whether their commercial value should be exploited (Mangan, 2008). A new state institution was founded in 2003 to ensure that venues were re-used or redeveloped (Gospodini, 2009). But, several years later,

Figure 4.2 *The Acer Arena (foreground) and ANZ Stadium (back right) in Sydney's Olympic Park. The area to the left is a showground that was moved from central Sydney as part of preparations for the 2000 Olympic Games*

this body was struggling to find organisations to operate the venues. The media press centre did eventually become the Ministry of Health, the badminton hall is now used as a theatre and the weightlifting centre houses a new university, but other public bodies were not interested in taking on the responsibility for operating venues. Even when uses were found, there were long delays between the end of the Games and reopening the facilities. This contrasts with Beijing, where facilities were reopened to the public very soon after the Games had finished (Kissoudi, 2010). The latest plans in Athens involve privatising the venues. Whilst this may lessen the public liability for maintenance costs, it is seen by many Greeks as a sub-optimal outcome for an event which was funded by public sector debt. The expenditure on the event raised the state budget deficit by 6 per cent of GDP (Panagiotopoulou, 2009), contributing significantly to the debt crisis Greece suffered in 2009/2010. In subsequent debates about restructuring the country's debt, privatising the country's Olympic venues was seen as one of the key priorities.

BOX 4.2 SEVILLE EXPO '92

Creating white elephants is not something that is exclusive to Olympic Games or major sport events. When World Expos have involved the construction of permanent sites and facilities, these have also been under-used. The Seville Expo of 1992 provides an interesting case. The event was deemed to be a great success, and the city's transport infrastructure was improved, but the city struggled to find a coherent use for the main site after the event. In what Maddox (2004) describes as a messy aftermath, organisers were unsure whether to demolish, maintain or sell off the main pavilions. The site needed to be remodelled rather than just recycled, but there were high expectations and local people were keen not to vulgarise the site which they had grown to love. After the event a plan was conceived to divide the site into a technology hub and a culture/amusement park. But by the mid-1990s, most of the area 'was reverting to wilderness' (Maddox, 2004: 303). The causes of this under-use are interesting. Monclús (2009) suggests that the problems were not caused by the lack of a plan, but by the co-existence of multiple schemes that hindered the execution of the original strategy.

In 1999 the plan was restructured. The former Expo site had evolved into a theme park but it had been stripped of the structures and the feel of the event that had provided its foundations (Maddox, 2004). In recent years there has been more evidence of success. By 2004, the site hosted 291 organisations and over 10,000 jobs (Monclús, 2009). This shows that event regeneration requires a long-term perspective despite the high-speed rhetoric of 'accelerated development', 'catalysts' and 'fast-tracking' that usually accompanies projects (see Chapter 5). If the legacy of Seville '92 had been judged seven years after the event, it would have been regarded as a failure. This is highlighted by the critics who maligned the project as one lacking inspiration. Even in recent accounts, the area is labelled as 'little more than an offshore ghost town' (Gold and Gold, 2005: 135). But ten years after the event, the project started to deliver the industrial diversification originally sought by organisers (Monclús, 2009).

There are several implications of the Seville Expo '92 case (see Box 4.2), but one of the most important ones is that city planners should not be afraid to radically redevelop event sites in the post-event era (to ensure use). Events sites are not usually conducive to everyday urbanism, so unless they are to be turned into theme parks or retained as event venues, they need to remodelled to allow other users and uses to colonise them. The Seville case also highlights that event projects are often long-term regeneration projects that take decades to come to fruition. Although events are often regarded as accelerators of urban development (see Chapter 5), it sometimes takes time to establish new uses for event sites. The best example of this is the Millennium Dome in Greenwich, London (Figure 4.3).

Figure 4.3 *The Millennium Dome at North Greenwich, London, during the Millennium Festival (above) and in its new guise as the O$_2$ Arena (below)*

After it staged the Millennium Festival in 2000, the facility was unused for several years. In the post-event period (2001–2007), the government spent millions of pounds to secure and maintain the large facility. Eventually, it was acquired by the American company AEG and, after being reconfigured internally, it reopened in 2007 as the O_2: a multi-purpose venue hosting concerts, sport events and theatrical shows (Figure 4.3). What was once the archetypal white elephant is now the most popular venue in the world, attracting 1.7 million visitors in 2010. This figure was 50 per cent higher than its closest revival – Madison Square Gardens in New York (Mayor of London, 2011). The O_2 case highlights that many successful event legacies are not planned and that it may take time to find suitable users for venues after an event.

Avoiding white elephants

Event organisers and rights holders are now much more aware of how to avoid white elephants. The IOC Bidding Manual incorporates suggestions for venue development including: that venues should be developed with reference to a city's long-term plan; that venues should be sustainable; that existing or temporary venues should be used if possible; and that host cities should consider flexibility from an early stage (Pitts and Liao, 2009). These and other options are discussed further below.

Using existing venues

The alternative to spending large amounts of money on new event venues is to regenerate existing venues. Olympic hosts such as Barcelona and Los Angeles have been given credit for employing this frugal approach. The Los Angeles Games in 1984 was designed as the antidote to the excesses of the Montreal Games of 1976. Organisers of the LA Games used the existing Coliseum stadium in the South Central district of the city as the main venue. The reuse of the Coliseum – originally built for the 1932 Games – meant it became the first stadium in the world to have staged two Olympic Games. Indeed, it remains the only stadium to have done so. Only four of the twenty-one facilities used to stage the LA Games in 1984 were new buildings (Munoz, 2006). This conservative approach seems at odds with the social representation of LA as a city of luxury and bombast. The explanation for this lies in the predicament the IOC found itself in during the late 1970s and early 1980s – when the Olympic Games were being undermined by a combination of political incidents, national boycotts and the fallout from the mismanagement of the 1976 Montreal Games. In this context, no city would have gambled large amounts of money staging an extravagant Olympic Games. Even for Seoul's Olympic Games, staged four years later in 1988, the organisers' approach was far less ambitious than that adopted in contemporary Games or those of the 1970s. In Seoul, only thirteen out of the 112 competition sites were newly built (Yoon, 2009). This made it very different for its closest equivalent, the 2008 Olympic Games in Beijing.

For the Barcelona Olympic Games (1992), new installations were constructed only where it could be proved that there was a need for new provision, or where new facilities would help to rebalance territorial inequity (Truno, 1995). This freed up funds for more fundamental urban transformations. Where demand for new facilities could not be proven, existing or temporary venues were used instead. Overall, the approach maximised the chances that any new venues developed would be financially self-sufficient post-Games. This is emphasised by the fact that no public financing was needed to manage the main venues (Palau St Jordi, Olympic Stadium, Velodrome, Palau Municipal Esportes) in the post-event era (Truno, 1995). However, even this example of legacy planning has not been entirely successful. Vall d'Hebron, where a series of venues was clustered (tennis, pelota, archery, velodrome) has become forlorn and dilapidated since the Games (Rowe, 2006) and people have criticised the under-utilisation of the Olympic venues on Montjuic – particularly the diving pool which provided one of the iconic images of the 1992 Games.

Securing long-term users in advance

One way of achieving efficient utilisation of new event venues is to nominate an anchor tenant for the new facilities in advance of an event. A good example is the main stadium built for the 2002 Manchester Commonwealth Games. An agreement was made between Manchester City Council and Manchester City Football Club that gave the club a 250-year lease of the £112 million stadium. The stadium was paid for by National Lottery money and public funds. To compensate, the football club agreed to hand over extra revenues the club received when attendances were over and above the capacity of the club's former stadium. Manchester City FC was also required to meet certain requirements regarding community access. The agreement ensured the stadium would be used and that there would be some benefits for local tax payers. However, transferring ownership to privately owned clubs is not without controversy. Thornley (2002) notes how public support for the Amsterdam Arena cooled when its status changed from being part of an Olympic bid to being the home of Ajax Football Club. Choosing which organisation(s) to hand it to can also be a problem. For example, legal challenges were made by other local clubs when the Olympic Park Legacy Company made West Ham United Football Club its preferred bidder for London's Olympic Stadium prior to the 2012 Olympic Games.

Recent World Expo hosts have also tried to secure tenants before the event is staged to avoid leaving a legacy of under-utilised venues. Led by BIE guidelines, hosts of 'Universal Exhibitions' have traditionally invited participating countries to construct their own pavilions – leading to a rather haphazard portfolio of buildings that are knocked down after the event. In more specialist 'International Exhibitions' that are staged in between Universal Exhibitions, the arrangements are more flexible. For example, the main pavilions for the 1998 Expo in Lisbon, Portugal and the 2008 Expo in Zaragoza, Spain, were built by the organisers. According to Rollin (2008) this is a preferable model of venue development that maximises the chances of post-event conversion. To avoid a repetition of the confused aftermath of 1992 Seville Expo, the chair of the Zaragoza Expo declared that decisions about the future uses of the buildings would be made before the event. The buildings were designed to suit these post-event uses and many were sold before the event was staged. This innovative approach did not stop many people complaining about the misuse of public funds, but it did mean that the main venues had designated post-event functions.

Using temporary structures

To avoid the desperate search for post-event tenants and uses some cities have constructed temporary venues, or – in extreme cases – demolished new structures to avoid maintaining superfluous facilities. This was the approach taken in Atlanta for the 1996 Olympic Games, which meant that the event was nicknamed 'the disposable Games'. Other hosts have adopted a similarly ruthless approach. For example, Lillehammer developed a temporary Olympic Village for the 2004 Winter Games, rather than developing permanent housing (Essex and Chalkley, 2004). Some event hosts use student accommodation, campsites or cruise ships to avoid building new facilities that wouldn't be used post-event (see Chapter 8). This trend represents a return to the early Olympic Games and World Expos where there was little expectation that facilities would be retained post-event.

Creating disposable event venues is something that can be opposed by some stakeholders. Many see this approach as a missed opportunity to leave a positive legacy. As MacAloon (2008) notes, the new 'legacy ethos' is now used to challenge bids for events that involve temporary venues. For example, some people within the equestrian community questioned the designation of Greenwich Park for the equestrian events for the 2012 Olympic Games. The construction of a temporary cross-country course, a temporary arena and temporary support facilities was seen as a missed opportunity to develop facilities that would benefit the development of the sport. This controversy highlights the essential dilemma for event organisers – whether to maximise the positive legacy of facility provision or to limit the negative, financial legacy of producing white elephants. This issue is related to the language of legacy – a term that can be interpreted as a positive 'gift' to the host city (MacRury and Poynter, 2008). However, as the white elephant myth highlights, not all gifts are welcome and many cities would now settle for a post-event period in which they are not by hampered by debts and on-going costs.

Converting venues

Major events are often criticised for leaving a legacy of under-used facilities. This highlights the value of building structures that can be converted from one use to another after an event. It may be difficult to convert large outdoor stadia to other uses, but smaller indoor venues can be designed in a way that allows them to be turned into community amenities, public institutions or business locations. In Barcelona, large flexible spaces or 'container installations' were built to host some Olympic events and there was no intention of using these areas as sport venues once the Games were over. The construction of flexible venues is a noted trend in event architecture. Ancillary facilities like media centres are particularly suited to conversion. However, it is important that venues are designed as convertible structures, rather than adopting conversion as a post hoc strategy.

A slightly different approach is to construct venues that can be downscaled after the event. Anticipating post-event under-utilisation, some host cities have deliberately designed venues to be reduced in their 'legacy mode'. Although plans changed subsequently, London's Olympic Stadium for the 2012 Games (see Figure 4.4) was originally designed as an 80,000-seat stadium that could revert to a 25,000-seat arena in the post-event era. This was considered to be a more appropriate stage for national and international athletics events – the role originally envisaged as the main function of the stadium. The design allowed the option to transfer the demountable aspects of the stadium to other host cities. Similarly, some venues (e.g. the basketball arena) were designed as temporary venues that could be reconstructed elsewhere after the event. This approach seems highly efficient, but it is not necessarily a cheap option: London's temporary basketball stadium cost £42 million (Gibson, 2011). The construction of stadia that can be relocated to other cities is also the legacy model proposed by organisers of Qatar's World Cup in 2022.

Using satellite venues

Another way of restricting the number of superfluous new venues is to build satellite venues in other towns and cities that do need them and would use them. Although the owners of event franchises often prefer to see events staged on concentrated sites, there is a realisation that geographically dispersed 'satellite' venues offer various advantages. They can generate regional/national support;

Figure 4.4 *London's Olympic Stadium during the construction phase. The original design allows the stadium to be downgraded to a smaller athletics arena. Different sections are fitted on top of one another – allowing some to be removed after the event. However, plans have since changed and the stadium will now be redeveloped to accommodate a resident football club*

they can tap into a localised passion for a particular event; and new facilities can be targeted for an area that actually needs them (Smith, 2009). Accordingly, they can help to increase the chances that new venues are utilised in the post-event era. For small towns and cities assigned certain events, partial event dislocation provides a rare opportunity to 'host' a major event.

Some events are now organised using a main venue, combined with a 'regionalised' subsidiary dimension. A good example is Lillehammer's Winter Olympic Games (1994). The organisers presented a bid to the International Olympic Committee for a compact Games, but subsequently awarded some events to regional locations such as Hamar. This town, 60 km south of Lillehammer, is known as the capital of Norwegian speed skating but its main rink needed renovation. Therefore, to maximise the legacy of the event, the speed skating was transferred to Hamar (Lesjo, 2000). Unfortunately, indecision and political manoeuvring meant that a new speed skating rink was also built in Lillehammer itself, a facility which had to be downgraded to a training venue when the final decision was made to move the event to Hamar (Lesjo, 2000). This highlights the politicisation of venue development, something that challenges the implementation of evidence based, rational planning.

Developing countries

Spending large amounts of public money on new event venues is particularly controversial in developing countries. The opportunity costs of staging events in these contexts are much higher, and there is the danger that glamorous new venues may be used to strengthen authoritarian regimes (Pillay and Bass, 2008). This seems to be applicable to Belarus, known as Europe's last dictatorship, which built several expensive venues to stage the 2014 World Ice Hockey Championships. There are other potential problems with venue projects in developing countries. If things go wrong – as they did during Delhi's 2010 Commonwealth Games – then damaging stereotypes of 'third world' disorganisation, backwardness and squalor are perpetuated. In these contexts, the appropriateness of staging major events needs to be considered carefully, and the choice of event is critical.

GEOGRAPHICAL CONSIDERATIONS

The previous section outlined why event organisers and host cities have to choose whether to build new venues or to use existing facilities, and/or whether to develop temporary venues or permanent ones. Organisers also have to decide on the location of these venues. In simplistic terms organisers have to choose between two options:

1 Using a concentrated set of venues or spreading venues around various locations.
2 Developing venues in central sites or in the urban periphery.

This dilemma leads to a series of options (see Figure 4.5). The lack of space in city centres usually means a concentred central site is unviable, although in some exceptional examples this may be appropriate (e.g. Seattle's 1962 World Expo, Berlin's bid for the 2000 Games). As well as the different options in Figure 4.5, cities can also use a combination of central sites and peripheral ones. This is very common approach in the case of Winter Olympic Games, where urban facilities (e.g. ice rinks) are located centrally, with Alpine events staged outside the city. For example, in the case of the 2006 Winter Games, the skiing events were 70–80 km from Turin.

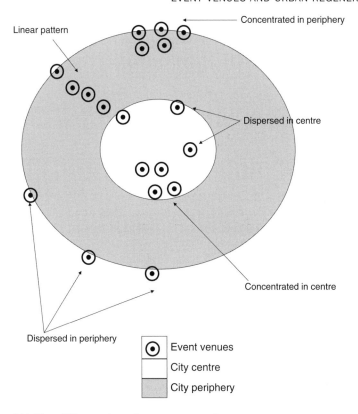

Linear pattern

Concentrated in periphery

Dispersed in centre

Concentrated in centre

Dispersed in periphery

⊙	Event venues
	City centre
	City periphery

Figure 4.5 *The different location patterns of event venues*

The geographical options available to host cities, and the implications of these choices for urban regeneration, are analysed in more detail below.

Using a concentrated set of venues versus spreading venues in various locations

When choosing where to stage events, recent hosts of the European Capital of Culture event (multiple central projects) and World Expos hosts (one major peripheral site) have tended to follow a predictable geographical pattern (van Vrijaldenhoven, 2007). But recent summer Olympic Games provide a useful illustration of the different location options available to event hosts. Whereas organisers in Munich, Montreal, Sydney and London opted to redevelop one large site, other host cities (e.g. Los Angeles, Athens, Barcelona, Rio de Janeiro) chose to locate venues in a series of sites throughout the city. Interestingly, these decisions were influenced by regeneration considerations.

Beriatos and Gospodini (2004) argue that clustering event projects in one area intensifies positive regeneration effects and allows greater opportunities to enhance city images. The Athens Olympic Games of 2004 is often cited as a case that highlights the disadvantages of dispersed sites. However, the rather disappointing outcomes of this event were not merely caused by the locations of new venues. As Beriatos and Gospodini (2004) illustrate through their comparison of Athens and Barcelona, the 1992 Games also involved dispersed interventions but city leaders integrated these within a wider plan for the city. Barcelona used its Olympic sites as part of a plan to create (ten) new areas of centrality – an idea borrowed from the municipal plan of Milan (Monclús, 2003). The new facilities were meant to unlock the potential of these areas that were well located, but where principal activities had become obsolete. Therefore, even when venues are dispersed, they can be done so in a co-ordinated fashion that contributes to urban regeneration objectives.

The decision to concentrate or spread venues depends on the availability of a site large enough to accommodate event venues. The high density of urbanism in Athens led to the piecemeal approach, as authorities found it difficult to find appropriate sites (Panagiotopoulou, 2009). The lack of available sites meant that rather than using 'brownfield' sites, some of Athens' venues were built on greenfield land. This was problematic because, as Panagiotopoulou (2009) observes, fast urban growth in Athens has led to insufficient green spaces.

There are some advantages of using multiple locations. It means that more than one urban community can benefit. In Athens, the twenty-two venues were developed in locations that privileged multiple poorer districts rather than just one. A dispersed approach also means there is less need to relocate residents/ businesses and there is less likelihood of creating what Monclús (2006: 238) calls 'investment overdose', defined as:

> the excessive concentration of resources in a limited space with the physical risk of the formation of enclaves or precincts poorly integrated to the urban structure or at the danger of an excessive standardisation, theming or banalisation of the project spaces.

Investment overdose is very common in event sites which post-event are left as vast, soulless spaces that lack social functions and social infrastructure. These often feel bereft of atmosphere because of the presence of large venues separated by enormous spaces and structural landscaping. There is a monumentality about these spaces, but one that lacks the meaning and significance of the monumentality that characterises parts of many capital cities. Several smaller interventions are easier to integrate into the urban fabric and they are less likely to cause urban polarisation or 'islands of regeneration'.

Concentrated sites

Whilst Monclús (2006) worries about investment overdose, some host cities can deliver large event sites that help to deliver an attractive new 'piece' of a city. Concentrated event venues can be used to create a zone that functions as a specialist destination in the post-event era. Creating event sites in cities has a long history that can be traced back *c.*2700 years to Olympia in Ancient Greece. Modern cities have also tended to develop clusters of venues. In the nineteenth century, sport venues were clustered in several British cities due to shared former land-use and/or owner-ship. Inglis (2004: 22) traces three clusters of sport venues in Manchester which he deems to be Victorian equivalents of 'sports and leisure zones' primarily aimed at local citizens. In the twentieth century, Moscow developed the Luzhiniki sport city that involved a main stadium for 100,000 spectators, surrounded by smaller arenas, a sporting museum and ninety sporting fields (Köhring, 2010). This was an early example of using a concentrated 'set' of sport facilities in a pastoral setting as a key part of an urban development plan. Various equivalents have emerged since this pioneering example and many of them have been built to stage major events. Munich's Olympic Park and Manchester's Sport City are perhaps the best known examples. In the twenty-first century, it is Middle Eastern and South East Asian cities that are pioneering a new generation of venue clusters aimed at attracting tourists and selling real estate. Examples exist or are currently being developed in Abu-Dhabi, Dubai (both UAE), Doha (Qatar) and Singapore. These follow more haphazard schemes used by Western cities, where sports-city branding has been used to give coherence to existing sports resources bequeathed by large events (Smith, 2010).

Developing venues in central sites or ones in the urban periphery

A related decision for event hosts is whether to locate venues (concentrated or dispersed) in city centres or in urban peripheries. Roult and Lefebvre (2010) identify three possible locations for event venue projects: city centres, edge cities and deprived neighbourhoods. These latter options are often one and the same thing. Central venues are more likely to be integrated into the city – physically, socially and economically; but they do not offer the same opportunities to assist disadvantaged areas. Edge city sites allow opportunities for urban expansion, and connections to peripheral neighbourhoods, but this location may contribute to urban sprawl. This type of urban expansion contradicts many sustainable urban design principles (Pitts and Liao, 2009).

City centre venues

Central event venues may cause problems with congestion but they assist city commerce and the pre-event atmosphere of an event. In preparing for the 1999

Rugby World Cup staged in Wales, organisers decided to redevelop a stadium in the centre of Cardiff. This decision helped to support the leisure/retail sectors in the city centre and precipitated the opening of lots of new restaurants (Davies, 2006). Central venues are more likely to encourage local spending and therefore help to support existing businesses. These venues are more likely to be used in the post-event era because of their accessibility.

The idea of using an event venue as an anchor for city centre regeneration is something that has been led by US cities. Austrian and Rosentraub (2002) highlight the trend in the USA to use sport and entertainment facilities to regenerate downtown districts. Downtown is the name given to central business districts in US cities (following the example of New York where this district is in the lower portion of Manhattan). Cities such as Indianapolis, Memphis, Cleveland, Colombus, Ohio, Seattle, Dallas, Detroit, Los Angeles, Oklahoma City, Phoenix, Pittsburgh and St Louis have all used sport venues to revive downtown sites (Turner and Rosentraub, 2002; Austrian and Rosentraub, 2002). In the 1980s, the urban cores of US cities were often viewed as unsafe places, so event venues were deployed to help reimage them as consumption oriented spaces (Silk and Amis, 2005). Newman (2002) suggests that urban authorities believed that these facilities would help to restore the historic association between business, recreation, tourism and downtown centres.

Baltimore's decision to build a baseball stadium in Camden Yards was the project that perhaps started the trend for new central venues in US cities. This venue, built in the late 1980s, provided a new landmark for the city and extended the city's entertainment district towards the waterfront. The stadium was conceived in a 'retro style' design that aimed to recreate the centrally located stadia that had been replaced by large suburban developments. Central locations were advocated by those with interests in downtown property, as businesses tended to see the value of their land holdings rise if vacant land was used for a new venue (Newsome and Comer, 2000). This was because of the improvements made, new money coming in and because they contributed to increased land scarcity. However, countering the notion that central locations encourage greater integration, event venues in some US cities have become a leisure 'bubble' divorced from the rest of the city. There is also evidence that these venues have not really slowed the process of decentralisation (of employment and housing) or contributed to regional economic development (Austrian and Rosentraub, 2002).

The advantage of staging events in central locations is that there is a beneficial, reciprocal relationship between key streets and the event. One of the best examples of this is in Gothenburg, Sweden, which has developed a cluster of central event venues along an events thoroughfare (see Chapter 9). This linear zone includes stadia, arenas, a swimming pool and a congress centre as well as an amusement park. In such examples, the events animate the city and the streets provide an extension of the venue. This enhances the experience for those attending the event and allows those without tickets to enjoy the occasion. European Capital of Culture venues are normally located in central sites. The city, rather than an individual part of the city, becomes the venue (van Vrijaldenhoven, 2007). This fits with the notion popular in the 1990s of conceiving the city as a 'stage'. It also helps with infrastructure and amenities as central areas usually boast better transport connections, and hotels and restaurants are in close proximity. The danger is that disadvantaged citizens living in peripheral parts of the city benefit little from the developments. For example, Balsas (2004) notes how Porto's Capital of Culture event privileged the central squares and streets, but neglected the urban fabric of the neighbourhoods. €180 million was devoted to cultural and structural projects, but the territorial inequity of the investments resulted in a sub-optimal outcome (Balsas, 2004).

Peripheral sites

As events have become larger, and where venues need to be concentrated together, they have tended to be located in more peripheral areas. Peripheral sites offer more space, and there is an opportunity to masterplan a whole new district (see Chapter 9). One of the keys to success is to use areas that have unrealised potential. If well located, uninhabited land needs to be remediated, events can help unlock the potential of these sites. The Olympic site at Homebush Bay (14 km from Sydney) and the Stade de France project in St Denis (1.5 km from Paris) are good examples.

BOX 4.3 THE AMSTERDAM ARENA

The Amsterdam ArenA helps us to understand how a peripheral site can benefit from a venue project. The ArenA was originally conceived as part of a bid for the 1992 Olympic Games. Despite the failure of this bid, plans for the stadium were retained and a new facility was built for the city's main football team (Ajax). The stadium was funded by a partnership that involved the City Council and Ajax Football Club, plus other private sector capital from investors and banks. The site chosen for the project (Bijlmer) was one right on the edge of the City Council's territorial boundary that desperately needed regeneration. Public authorities wanted to use the stadium to assist this area which contains the famous high-rise Bijlmermeer estate. The new stadium (incorporating an innovative retractable roof) was completed in 1996 and it was used as the main venue for the 2000 European Football Championships. Since it opened, the relative location of this district has changed radically (Helleman and Wassenberg, 2004). The venue and the surrounding retail provision have helped to address the isolation and image problems of the area (Helleman and Wassenberg, 2004). This has been assisted by numerous parallel projects, including a major urban regeneration programme – the Urban Bijlmermeer Program. The stadium has become the centre of a new entertainment district and the key role played by the venue in creating a new 'centre in the periphery' is demonstrated by the fact that the area is now referred to as Arena Boulevard or as Amsterdam ArenA.

Unfortunately, there are multiple examples of peripheral sites with a concentration of event venues that have not succeeded, and/or never been properly integrated with the rest of the city. Former Expo sites such as the EUR (Esposizione Universale di Roma) in Rome remain desolate spaces, and peripheral Olympic sites in Montreal and Sydney are visibly under-utilised. A problem with using peripheral event sites is that unless sufficient services are developed close by (shops, hotels, other amenities), the benefits of events are likely to be felt in urban centres. This was the conclusion of Connell and Page's (2005) research regarding the World Medical Health Games staged in Stirling, Scotland. City centre businesses benefited disproportionately from the event, even though it was staged in peripheral locations. The number of event venues developed on edge city sites, and the failure of these projects to instigate genuine urbanism, means some authors see these venues as key characteristics of 'edgelands' – the wilderness that exists between urban and rural areas. Indeed, in their exploration of edgelands, Farley and Roberts (2011) mention football stadia and indoor arenas as typical features of these anonymous, unpopulated zones.

INTEGRATION

Even when use long-term uses can be secured for venues in appropriate locations, that doesn't mean that the venue will assist regeneration. The key factor in determining wider success is the integration of the venue with its locality. Integration involves facilitating physical accessibility, but it is also important that venues are economically and socially integrated.

Physical integration

The physical design of event venues is crucial if they are to play a long-term role in urban regeneration. Even when venues have been developed in close proximity to a disadvantaged area, they are often not properly integrated with that community. Examples include the main site for the Lisbon World Expo staged in 1998. The disadvantaged neighbourhoods of Olivais and Chelas overlook the site but Carrière and Demaziere (2002) doubt whether the Expo helped these districts. In these instances there is a danger that an event venue becomes a 'bubble' or 'island of regeneration' separated from the district(s) it is meant to assist. This problem is often exacerbated when, as if often the case, venues are constructed in post-industrial zones that contain major roads, canals, railways and other obstacles that can deter integration. For example in Valencia, Spain, the port area has been developed as a venue for the Americas Cup and a Formula 1 Grand Prix. But despite the progress made, Prytherch and Maiques (2009: 112) suggest that 'integrating [the] new part with the centre remains a challenge'. In other cases, new obstacles are created because of poor design. Maennig and du Plessis (2009) illustrate how the moat of surface parking and wide streets isolate Durban's 2010 World Cup stadium from the downtown area (see Figure 4.6). Developing permeable event venues that have a public face is important if local integration is

Figure 4.6 *The Moses Mabhida Stadium in Durban – built for the 2010 FIFA World Cup. Built with a window that frames the city, but the stadium is not well integrated*

to be achieved. However, this is notoriously difficult, not least because event venues usually consist of closed structures of stands that are designed to face inwards, so as to isolate spectators and participants from the outside world. Unless a public face for these venues is developed, they tend to exist with their backs to urban populations.

Some critical accounts suggest that event organisers/venue developers have deliberately restricted the physical connections with disadvantaged local areas. Schimmel (2006: 267) believes that event venues are often developed as 'revitalized spaces with newly developed cultural attractions, walled off from the presumed dangerous places (and people)'. Event sites are sometimes developed as sanitised, gated communities that are purposefully designed to avoid connections with surrounding residential areas – particularly if those districts deter target audiences of visitors and investors. This reflects wider trends in urbanism. Urban regeneration is often delivered by developers working on single projects, and the combination of their profit motive and aversion to risk means developers are more likely to build inward-looking developments (Henderson, 2010). Event projects are often built like other urban developments – as individual 'pods' deliberately designed to avoid integration with other urban space (Tiesdell and MacFarlane, 2007). An alternative, more progressive, approach is needed. Safety fears and 'moral panics' can be viewed as a strong justification for building event venues near to disadvantaged communities. If venues are built in or near to these areas this can actually encourage people who would not usually consider visiting those areas to do so; and this can help to remove stigmas unfairly attached to certain urban districts.

In the contemporary era, one obstacle preventing good physical integration of event venues with local residential areas is the emphasis on security. One of the most famous security breaches at a major event occurred during the Munich Olympic Games of 1972 when eleven Israelis were murdered by intruders within the Olympic Village. At the time there was criticism of the open and accessible architectural layout of the site (Modrey, 2008). The design fitted with the organisers' aim to produce a democratic, open and amiable space, but some felt it left athletes and officials vulnerable. Event organisers are now keen to develop sites that can be easily secured and 'locked down' for major events (Murukami-Wood and Coaffee, 2007). To assist checking who and what enters event sites, spaces are developed that offer limited access. Unfortunately, this is incompatible with the design principle that event sites should be highly permeable, encouraging local people to use facilities and spaces in the post-event era. A good example is London's Excel Arena – one of the venues for the 2012 Olympic Games. This venue has been designed with its back to the East End community that surrounds it. Unless entered from one of the site's dedicated car parks or from the light transit rail system that connects the arena to Canary Wharf and the City of

London, it is very difficult to access. The segregation of the venue from its surrounding area makes it suitable for events that require high security. But it diminishes its regenerative capacity.

An example of an events venue where attempts were made to integrate the site physically with neighbouring communities is the Stade de France in Paris. This stadium was developed as the key venue for the 1998 FIFA World Cup (Dauncey, 1999). Local authorities (communes) insisted that permissions for the project would be granted only if guarantees regarding local benefits were secured (Newman and Thornley, 1996). This bargaining resulted in the removal of many physical obstacles that restricted access to the site by the disadvantaged local population. A major road (the A1 motorway) was covered and a bridge was built over the canal to link the stadium to the Franc Moisons estate – one of Paris's most troubled districts (Newman and Thornley, 1996). A public space commission was established to promote the interests of the locality – and particular emphasis was placed on efforts to make a coherent transition from the stadium precinct to the surrounding communes (Newman and Tual, 2002). However, although physical access was improved, the development has been criticised for failing to improve the lives of those who live nearby (Newman and Tual, 2002). This emphasises the need to consider social and economic integration as well as physical links.

Social integration

Even if physical access can be enhanced, there may be less tangible obstacles that prevent the proper integration of event venues with disadvantaged communities. The most obvious of these are financial constraints. In the post-event phase, there is often an emphasis on trying to recoup development costs and this may mean high entry fees/ticket prices for new facilities. Wang and Theodoraki (2007) highlight the discrepancy between levels of income in Qingdao, China, and the money required to use the new sailing facilities developed for the 2008 Olympic Games. In some cases, facilities are hired out to private users, or even sold to private operators. This makes it more difficult to ensure access for local people.

Social integration may also be deterred by symbolic exclusivity. Several authors (e.g. Lee, 2002; Binks and Snape, 2006) suggest that social access is a marketing problem, rather than one explained by financial restrictions. Because of the prevailing desire to generate image effects, new facilities are often promoted as prestigious/elite venues. This emphasis may symbolically detach these venues from the communities they are supposed to serve. As in the Bolton Arena case discussed previously, people may be given the impression that a new venue is 'not for them'. This occurs when there is divergence between the type of facility developed and the local community. For example, major sport events often leave a legacy of facilities for minority or elite sports. In the case of

Manchester's 2002 Commonwealth Games site, the people who take advantage of the new facilities tend to be enthusiastic squash, hockey and tennis players from the wider region – and not the disadvantaged people who live nearby.

Lee's (2002) research into BC Place, a stadium in Vancouver, Canada, highlights the problem of symbolic exclusion and how it can be addressed. In a community workshop, participants felt that the stadium had no connection with its surroundings. The conclusion from the workshop was that the stadium should de-emphasise its image as an elite sport venue and transform itself into a community centre. This has been addressed and now sport activities account for only 20 per cent of booked time (Lee, 2002). The reconfiguration of BC Place highlights the potential for using event venues as community resources and community hubs, rather than merely settings for external events. As Weiner (2000) states, funding for venues is more justifiable if they act as community centres and local institutions, not monuments to elite sport/culture. This is idealistic, but there is some evidence of new community oriented venues. Walters (2005b) describes how some new football stadia in the UK are designed to act as hubs for the local community by providing healthcare, training and educational services alongside opportunities for physical regeneration. Initiatives have included the provision of homework centres for schoolchildren within football stadia. This delivers multiple benefits: the venue makes schoolwork seem more exciting and it is integrated socially.

Even when facilities are accessible and affordable, the specification of venues can deter community access. There are multiple instances where local swimming pools have been closed down to fund the development of Olympic sized pools for major events. This is a good example of where social legacy considerations are not given enough priority in venue design. These factors can prevent venues from becoming the sort of resource around which local communities can coalesce.

The most enlightened venue designs are those which adopt inclusive facilities and management systems. Facilities can be reserved for community use at certain times of the week, and, even if facilities are very specialised, dedicated provision can be made for amateur enthusiasts. For example, the Sydney Olympic canoeing facility included a 'legacy loop' that facilitated public use. Similarly, anyone – regardless of their ability – is able to receive cycling tuition at the Manchester Velodrome built in advance of the Commonwealth Games in 2002. Community oriented provision can also be developed in association with elite facilities if the latter are unsuited to community use. For example, Sydney Olympic Park's Aquatic Centre has a fun pool aimed at families as well as two 50 metre swimming pools (see Figure 4.7). Sport and cultural facilities can also be configured to allow wider community activities to take place there. Open days and community events provide opportunities for local people to use these facilities; but they

Figure 4.7 *The Aquatic Centre at Sydney's Olympic Park. The Centre includes two 50 metre pools, but also a family fun pool*

also make local people feel more comfortable in these spaces. This means they are more likely to return.

Some facilities are so over-subscribed or specialised that they find it hard to justify generous public access: in these instances there is the option to donate part of the revenues earned to local outreach programmes. Weiner (2000) suggests new sport venues should set aside a percentage of revenues to fund amateur sport programmes. He feels this would help to connect new venues to local neighbourhoods.

Economic integration

It is important for venues to be physically and socially integrated, but venues have the best chance of assisting urban regeneration if they are embedded within the local economy. This means trying to build links with local enterprises, providing jobs and/or training for local people and ensuring revenues earned are invested locally. Unfortunately, the available research evidence shows disappointing levels of job creation and local linkages for event venues. This contrasts with many pre-event economic impact studies that tend to over-estimate impacts.

Event venues obviously generate employment in the construction phase and during the event, but long-term employment opportunities are harder to deliver. Even during the labour-intensive preparations for major events, workers may be drawn from a wide labour pool. Organisers tend to award contracts to multinational companies as these are the ones deemed capable of completing large, complex projects. This causes significant economic leakages. The question of who benefits is not merely a geographical one. Even when local people benefit, it is hard to ensure that opportunities go to the local people who need them the most. Organisers tend to adopt an overly cautious approach when it comes to staffing events, opting to take the best candidates rather than those most in need – even for unpaid positions.

Research into past events suggests employment levels will rise in advance of an event and then fall way as soon as the event is over; something that contributes to the hangover effect of major events. In Barcelona, unemployment rose by 21,000 persons after the 1992 Olympic Games (Brunet, 2009) and 100,000 jobs were lost in the metropolitan area 1992–1995 (Rowe, 2006). This haemorrhaging of employment was primarily caused by the recession of that period, but these figures undermine the idea that events provide a 'soft mattress' with which to offset the effects of recessions. Similar effects were witnessed in Seville, which hosted a World Expo the same year that Barcelona staged the Olympic Games. Although many jobs were created in the period leading up to the event, a year after the Expo unemployment levels had risen to 28 per cent (Maddox, 2004) and levels of economic activity had returned to those of 1987 (Maddox, 2004). Likewise, in Montreal employment doubled between 1975 and 1982 once projects for the 1976 Olympic Games were complete (Whitson, 2004).

Even where wider development has been secured on an event site, that is not necessarily an indication that employment issues have been addressed. In the area which surrounds the Stade de France in Paris, Newman and Tual (2002) estimate that 70 per cent of the people employed commute from other parts of the French capital. The improved connectivity of the site and the lack of jobs for unskilled workers have reduced the local benefits (Villette and Hardill, 2007). Villette and Hardill's (2007) research indicates that 59 per cent of people in St Denis still see employment as an issue despite the Stade de France project and the €1 billion invested here over a ten-year period (Nappi-Choulet, 2006).

The more venues are used in the post-event era, the more likely they are to support employment. Truno (1995) reported that in post-Olympic Barcelona 420 jobs were created in the new venues, plus a further forty-two in the municipal company created to oversee the installations. The O_2 is also emerging as a potentially successful example. The Dome was originally built to stage the infamous Millennium Festival but in 2007, it reopened as the O_2, with a 23,000-seat events arena at its centre. The venue now supports 2,000 operational jobs, although the accessibility of the site means that the travel to work area is very large – making employment here accessible to millions of Londoners. Nevertheless, the aim is that 40 per cent of operational jobs will go to local residents and currently 43 per cent of employees are residents of the local borough (AEG, 2007). The local borough council also has a job brokerage agency that aims to direct these jobs to those who need them the most (see Box 4.4). These agencies are important if host cities are to ensure that economic benefits of major events are felt in areas that require assistance.

BOX 4.4 THE GREENWICH LOCAL LABOUR AND BUSINESS INITIATIVE

One example of good practice regarding the economic integration of events venues is the Greenwich Local Labour and Business (GLLaB) initiative (see Figure 4.8). This organisation was established in 1996 by Greenwich Council in advance of the Millennium Festival staged at the Millennium Dome. Planning permission for the Dome included the stipulation that developers engage with GLLaB and deliver local employment benefits. The organisation was retained after the event and it continues to work with local people to help them find employment and training opportunities. The organisation recently placed its 10,000th resident into work. GLLaB has recently developed a Major Events Programme that it runs in conjunction with a local volunteering organisation and AEG, the operator of the O_2 venue. The aim of the programme is to give support and training to local people and to provide a pool of volunteers to work at not-for-profit events such as an annual half marathon and major sport events (e.g. the 2009 World Gymnastics Championships). Volunteers receive four days training and receive certification if they complete the training provision successfully. The idea is that this will increase skills and confidence amongst unemployed people, but it also helps people to access paid work at the venue. Indeed, the GLLaB set a target that 20 per cent of graduates of the programme would gain employment at the O_2. The nomination of Greenwich as a key venue for the 2012 Olympic Games has provided a further opportunity for the organisation to assist hundreds of local people through volunteering initiatives. GLLaB has co-ordinated the local version of the 'Personal Best' pre-volunteering scheme for the 2012 Games. Graduates of the scheme receive a nationally accredited qualification and a chance to gain new skills and experience, plus an enhanced opportunity to become a 'Games Maker' – an official London 2012 Volunteer.

Using events to help local businesses and build better relationships between them can be assisted by establishing business clubs or associations in conjunction with events. These clubs help to capitalise upon the business and networking opportunities that may arise. Sjøholt (1999) argues that some of the most important outcomes of the 2000 European Capital of Culture event in Bergen, Norway, were the international contacts and networks that were cemented. Smith and Fox (2007) identify the benefits provided by the business club that was formed as part of the 'Prosperity' project run in conjunction with the Manchester Commonwealth Games in 2002. The club gave trading advice to

Figure 4.8 *The rather undistinguished headquarters of the award-winning GLLaB organisation in Greenwich, London*

more than 500 businesses and set up over 250 one-to-one businesses meetings on behalf of its members. It also helped members to collectively tender for, and win, around £45 million of sub-contracting work (Smith and Fox, 2007). This shows that business clubs can contribute to other objectives such as the use of local suppliers discussed above. O'Brien (2006) contends that Manchester's business club was inspired by the approach adopted by organisers of the Sydney Olympic Games (2000). Sydney officials had capitalised formally on the number of business people they knew would be 'floating around' the event by creating Business Club Australia (BCA). O'Brien (2006) claims that BCA consultants were involved in Manchester's subsequent project and in similar projects adopted by Salt Lake City in the USA, host of the 2002 Winter Olympics.

SUMMARY

This chapter has highlighted the challenges faced by host cities who want to use new venues as tools for urban regeneration. The discussion stresses that host cities need to think imaginatively when planning venues if they want to achieve regenerative effects. Too often cities have not established the levels of demand for venues, or thought enough about their location and integration with local communities. Where demand cannot be proven there is a strong case for using existing or temporary venues, or building flexible venues that can be easily converted/relocated after an event. This may restrict the positive legacy of events, but it ensures that budgets for other community services are protected from negative financial legacies. Location decisions need to be carefully related to the existing morphology of, and plans for, a city. Wherever venues are located, the best regeneration outcomes tend to occur if they are integrated with local communities – this means they can act as centres for employment, entertainment and community use rather than specialist facilities for external audiences. As well as considering appropriately flexible design, the ownership and management arrangements seem to be important. These arrangements need to balance key priorities that may not necessarily be compatible: for example, community access and financial self-sufficiency. Lessons from Montreal, Athens and other high-profile failures highlight that the post-event use of venues needs to be considered as early as possible in the lifecycle of an event and the design of venues should be driven by long-term uses, rather than the requirements of a one-off event. This chapter has considered the most basic form of event regeneration: venue projects. In the next two chapters, the idea of event-themed regeneration is discussed. This refers to regeneration projects that are undertaken in association with events. In these instances, events are used as part of wider efforts to achieve wider urban objectives, rather than as something that leads regeneration efforts.

EXTENDED CASE STUDY 1: VENUE DEVELOPMENT FOR THE SOUTH AFRICA WORLD CUP 2010

In 2010, South Africa hosted the FIFA World Cup football tournament. Despite fears over security problems, labour strikes and transport provision, the event itself was staged successfully. This has helped to dispel the clichéd view that developing countries are incapable of organising events on this scale. The rationale for staging the World Cup always included helping disadvantaged people in South Africa. Football is a sport that is associated with urban black communities. This meant there was a good fit between the event and disadvantaged South Africans who required assistance. The commitment to build stadia in disadvantaged areas – most famously the main SoccerCity stadium in Soweto – also helped to encourage support from, and benefits for, some of the poorer citizens.

The South African government's investment in staging the 2010 World Cup was motivated primarily by the desire for economic growth – in particular the need for infrastructure development, external image enhancement and new employment. As Chapters 5 and 7 of this book illustrate, these objectives have close links with urban regeneration. Prior to the event, the South African government consistently expressed the view that World Cup venues would help to kickstart urban development (Swart and Bob, 2009). The urban objectives of the event were particularly interesting as there was an opportunity to address the negative legacy of the apartheid era. Back in 2008, Pillay and Bass suggested that the World Cup could help to rectify some of the structural problems caused by the spatial planning policies of the apartheid years. This ambitious objective was always likely to be difficult to achieve, but the 2010 project's evolution and impact provides rich material for understanding the challenges associated with using events to achieve urban regeneration. The project highlighted different approaches to event regeneration: some thought the priority should be broad based economic growth, whilst others favoured specific assistance for poor and disadvantaged people.

A large proportion of government investment in staging the 2010 World Cup was spent on constructing new stadia and refurbishing existing venues. There were other physical interventions – e.g. the Gautrain public transport project in Johannesburg – but stadium projects dominated. At the time of the bid R818 million (£75 million) was allocated to stadium development. Later estimates suggested the cost of the stadia would rise to R2.5 billion (£225 million) (Cornelissen, 2007). The final bill eventually amounted to R8.4 billion (£757 million) – a figure that represented over 50 per cent of the total spending on the 2010 World Cup (Maennig and du Pleissis, 2009). Expensive projects in a developing country are always likely to cause controversy. Therefore, it is interesting to note how organisers tried to optimise the benefits for disadvantaged people.

As with most mega-events, these decisions were influenced by external stakeholders – in this case the rights holder FIFA. Indeed, there is evidence to suggest that FIFA's interventions made it harder for South African cities to use the event to assist disadvantaged people. Cornelissen (2007: 250) suggests that 'heavy handed interventions' by FIFA 'redirected many of the initial objectives identified in the bid'. This was despite FIFA's enthusiasm to promote the event as one that would accelerate levels of economic and social development in South Africa.

The multiple matches of the 2010 World Cup were staged by several South African cities. Originally, thirteen cities had been earmarked as hosts, but over time this was reduced to ten. In 2006, four years prior to the event, nine cities were confirmed as hosts: Johannesburg, Pretoria, Cape Town, Port Elizabeth, Durban, Bloemfontein, Polokwane, Nelspruit and Rustenburg. The first six cities in this list were obvious candidates, but outside South Africa little was known about the northern cities of Polokwane, Nelspruit and Rustenburg prior to the tournament.

Cape Town

Decisions about where to stage the matches were heavily influenced by FIFA (Cornelissen, 2007). There was a series of interesting disputes within and between cities regarding where host grounds should be situated, whether existing stadia should be used and which grounds should be designated as training or support venues. The most interesting of these disputes occurred in Cape Town, Western Cape. During the short period of time when alternatives could be considered, three potential options were proposed in this city: building a new stadium at Green Point in the centre, refurbishing the existing central stadium (Newlands) or upgrading a local stadium in nearby Athlone. As this was an event that was meant to assist and engage Cape Town's black communities, it made logical sense that Athlone was identified as a potential site. This suburb 10 km east of the city was considered to be the home of football in the Western Cape and was an area where residents desperately needed new social and economic opportunities.

In the initial bid submitted to FIFA, Athlone was identified as a practice stadium, with the existing Newlands stadium designated as the main venue. But after political intervention in 2005, Athlone replaced Newlands as the main site. Subsequently (in 2006) there was an announcement that – contrary to all the previous indications – a new stadium would be built at Green Point in the city centre (see Figure 4.9). The official rationale for this u-turn was that a new stadium would allow one of the prestigious semi-finals to be staged in Cape Town. But Swart and Bob (2009) allege that the decision was made because FIFA delegates had objected to the low-cost housing around Athlone Stadium as it

Figure 4.9 *The view of Cape Town Stadium from Table Mountain*

would not impress those watching on TV. According to Cornelissen (2007), FIFA also forced the city to abandon the idea of refurbishing Newlands and insisted on the new stadium at Green Point – a spectacular location that was very media friendly because of its coastal location and proximity to Table Mountain (see Figure 4.9). The imageability of the site was emphasised by the decision of the BBC to base its main presenters in a studio that overlooked the stadium (even though the final would be in Johannesburg). However, as the site for an urban regeneration project this location had several disadvantages. A new stadium at Green Point didn't promote engagement with disadvantaged communities, it represented an inefficient use of existing resources, and it resulted in the loss of open space.

The stadium was built on a site that formerly housed a golf course and a public common. Even once the decision to use Green Point was made, there were two possible alternative locations for the stadium. The decision was made to build on the golf course instead of a site that already had an athletics stadium because there would be less visual impact and inconvenience for existing residents (Environmental Partnership, 2006). The rationale also included the argument that removing the golf course and replacing it with a stadium and accessible open space would actually increase the number of people who could access the site (Environmental Partnership, 2006). The stadium was built using an undulating

Figure 4.10 *Fans leaving Cape Town Stadium during the 2010 World Cup in South Africa*

membrane design so that the structure integrated with, rather than imposed itself on, its surroundings (Maennig and du Plessis, 2009). The shape of the stadium was meant to represent the hats worn by women of the local Venda community (see Figure 4.10). However, the spectacular stadium design and its large size (68,000 seats) meant that costs escalated. The stadium was estimated to cost R2.85 billion (£257 million), with R400 million (£36 million) contributed by the city (Swart and Bob, 2009). However, the final bill was estimated to be R4 billion (£361 million). The large size of the stadium and its bold design also makes it harder to adapt to regular use in the post-event period. Indeed, Maennig and du Plessis (2009) describe the design used as 'innovative' and 'unique' but essentially 'impractical' and 'non-functional'.

In Durban, an iconic venue was also built. The municipal government decided to build this type of venue to pursue established tourism and image ambitions. As Roberts (2010: 1494) states, here 'the decision to construct a new stadium was not based on the requirements of the tournament, nor requests from FIFA as Asba Rugby Stadium was already deemed adequate to host World Cup games'. In Cape Town, the decision to build a World Cup venue at Green Point was taken despite the fact that the newly elected local administration was not in favour of this option. This obviously indicates a problem with major event strategies: even when events are staged to help disadvantaged people, the demands of event organisers, media and other external agencies are prioritised. Local organisers often struggle to maintain control, especially in an event such as the FIFA World Cup which involves an international organising committee, a national co-ordinating agency, as well as multiple local committees. The case illustrates the differing priorities of stakeholders when it comes to planning venues for major events. In the case of the 2010 World Cup, Cornelissen (2007: 255) suggests that the interactions between Cape Town's leaders and FIFA officials were characterised by 'processes of negotiation, bickering and to some extent bullying'. This rather damning conclusion helps to illustrate many of the ideas contained in this chapter regarding the difficulties of satisfying multiple stakeholders – and in particular the worrying power exerted by external interests that have the lowest stake in the long-term impacts of the event.

Events and the parallel physical regeneration of cities

5

INTRODUCTION

The previous chapter illustrated how event venues are allocated a role in the development of specific sites or surrounding districts. But major events have also been associated with more fundamental urban transformations where large areas of cities have been redeveloped. Changes to the wider physical urban fabric are the most visible effects of event projects and many cities now bear the physical imprint of events they have staged. This chapter explores the relationship between major events and wider physical regeneration. It is now generally recognised that physical changes must be linked to the wider social, economic and environmental development of an area. But to avoid duplicating ideas in other chapters, the discussion here is focused on physical changes. The chapter focuses on sport events and World Expos because these are the events normally associated with major urban development programmes.

Major events have helped to deliver a range of wider urban transformations: new housing, commercial, transport and infrastructure projects, plus improvements to the public realm. When these projects are spatially concentrated, major event projects exhibit similarities to urban mega-projects that have been discussed by a number of authors. These are defined by Orueta and Fainstein (2008) as large schemes with huge edifices, strong symbolic significance and complex content. This definition – usually reserved for large-scale transport or waterfront projects – seems equally applicable to major events. Therefore, some event developments are just like other urban mega-projects and they are vulnerable to the same criticisms (e.g. cost overruns, gentrification, sterilisation, standardisation). However, urban regeneration inspired by major events has some distinctive qualities and these are outlined here.

The chapter has two key aims: first, to explore the different ways that major events can assist wider urban regeneration. Second, to identify the stages of the regeneration process when events can play a role. Wider urban regeneration associated with events can be controversial; so this chapter also aims to identify the problems that can occur by using an event within projects. A recurring theme in the chapter is that major events are best used as integrated aspects of existing, wider urban regeneration plans, rather than individual projects in their own right. However, as the discussion below emphasises, this principle is not always followed.

This chapter is divided into two main sections. The first addresses the different role that events play in wider regeneration. The second section is more critical, and in this part of the chapter the inefficiencies and problems associated with event projects are considered.

THE DIFFERENT ROLES OF MAJOR EVENTS WITHIN WIDER URBAN REGENERATION

Major events are used within urban regeneration projects in different ways and at different stages of the process. Some event projects are intrinsically associated with the initial stages of a wider regeneration project, for example:

- Providing flagship projects to stimulate future development
- Overcoming established structural imbalances.

Other event projects are more associated with the intermediate stages of projects:

- Accelerating existing plans
- Extending existing plans
- Providing narratives for wider developments.

Finally, some event projects are undertaken at the end of wider regeneration projects:

- Showcasing completed projects.

These different roles of major events are explored further below.

Major events as flagships to stimulate future development

A flagship is the most prestigious of a set of related phenomena. In this sense, a high-profile event project can act as a flagship for a major event or an institution, but also more generally as a flagship for the area in which it is located. In the context of urban development, the term flagship is also used for projects that act as a 'marshalling point for further investment' (Smyth, 1994: 5). This implies that flagship projects are the cause of further developments. Indeed, Bianchini *et al.* (1992) state that projects should be considered to be flagships only if they succeed in attracting a flotilla of other developments in their wake. In brownfield or peripheral sites, event venues are often used as flagship projects to encourage subsequent investment from other sources. Investors are hesitant to commit to an area which has a poor reputation, poor infrastructure and few amenities. So an event project can provide the foundations from which an area can be redeveloped by providing a sufficient incentive to invest in the area. Event projects are often underwritten by national governments – so investors know that public bodies are committed to delivering them. This increases confidence. The official (hard) or unofficial (soft) branding of these areas as event sites may also be conducive to investors. Therefore, major events can play a role in urban regeneration by providing 'flagship developments' to lead the development of an area that would otherwise remain undeveloped.

A good example is the Stade de France, built as the centrepiece of the 1998 FIFA World Cup. This stadium has acted as a flagship for the regeneration of St Denis, an area 1.5 km north of the centre of Paris (Thornley, 2002). St Denis was affected negatively by de-industrialisation and by obstructive transport infrastructure. The site for the new stadium was formerly a gasworks which had been derelict since 1980 (Newman and Tual, 2002). Prior to the Stade de France project local authorities had striven to stimulate development there – but with little success (Newman and Thornley, 1996). According to Newman and Thornley (1996), the decision to use St Denis as the centrepiece of the 1998 World Cup radically changed the area's fortunes because it brought strong planning, state funding and gave the private sector sufficient confidence to invest.

The Stade de France project was delivered using an established formula, with the state providing a basic masterplan (see Chapter 9) and delivering key infrastructure. This provided the platform for subsequent private sector investment (Nappi-Choulet, 2006). The national government delivered a series of infrastructural improvements including covering the motorway, new parks, a new railway station and improvements to other local stations (Newman and Tual, 2002). A public–private partnership developed (and managed) a mixed-use development next to the stadium (Newman and Thornley, 1996). This included canalside housing, shopping and leisure facilities and new office development. Further development was achieved by attracting short-term 'pioneer' investors (Nappi-Choulet, 2006). So, although the Stade de France helped to attract companies to invest in the area, these investors only aimed to own assets for a short period of time (2–5 years). Nappi-Choulet (2006) thinks the case shows that long-term regeneration can be achieved by attracting short-term investors. In the years since the construction of the Stade de France, the area has become a new business district which has attracted a lot of investment, including a large number of foreign investors and an estimated €1 billion in public funds (Nappi-Choulet, 2006).

In line with the definitions of flagships above, development has now spread from the immediate vicinity of the stadium. The area directly to the south (i.e. towards the centre of Paris) has attracted a cluster of creative industries including fashion, media and internet companies (Newman and Tual, 2002). According to Nappi-Choulet (2006: 1512), St Denis 'has successfully turned itself into a new business district for the greater Paris region'. The role of the stadium remains crucial. Newman and Tual (2002: 833) suggest 'employers who want to impress prospective employees bring them to the stadium'. This is no ordinary stadium project; the links to the event that spawned its development give it extra symbolic power. This power is exaggerated because of the victory of the French team in the World Cup Final that was staged here. However, despite much vaunted rhetoric about the ethnic diversity of the French team inspiring the local immigrant population, the redevelopment of the area has not necessarily benefited those most in need. Pockets of deprivation remain and the lives of residents living in nearby estates have not improved (Newman and Tual, 2002). Newman and Tual (2002) highlight the risk that a dual society may have been created – with ongoing interventions required to avoid the new commercial district being segregated from the existing residential community. This demonstrates that even when urban regeneration is successful, nearby disadvantaged communities do not necessarily benefit. The problems here were social issues that needed more than physical/technical solutions.

Major events as ways to address structural problems

Alongside instigating urban regeneration, major events are often used when there is a need to address a major structural problem. As Westerbeek (2009: 785) suggests, one of the reasons cities want to stage the Olympic Games is to try to 'solve complex urban planning issues' and to transcend key barriers. A city may have a problem that has been long recognised, but one that has been too difficult to address using conventional approaches. An example is the imbalance between West and East London. The east of London is an area that was disadvantaged disproportionately by de-industrialisation and the destruction of World War II. Eastern parts of UK cities are often poorer than their western counterparts because of the prevailing winds that direct pollution to eastern suburbs. The lack of territorial equity between east and west is something that London's public authorities have been struggling to tackle for many years. A major event (the 2012 Olympic Games) was seen as one of the few vehicles that could make a difference in the medium term. The 2012 Games are being used to implement an ambitious Strategic Regeneration Framework that aims to close the disparities between East and West London over a twenty-year period. Following the same logic, when Berlin was faced with the difficult task of reuniting its disparate halves after the fall of the Berlin Wall in the early 1990s, an Olympic bid was submitted (Alberts, 2009). Fundamental urban problems in South Africa were also addressed by staging a major event. The 2010 FIFA World Cup was identified as a way to 'make significant inroads in changing the anomalous form and structure of South African cities, brought on by a decade of apartheid spatial planning' (Pillay and Bass, 2008: 343).

There seem to be three specific contexts in which major events are used to address fundamental structural issues. The first is in a post-conflict scenario (e.g. Rome 1960, Tokyo 1964) where a city has been held back or partially destroyed and requires fundamental modernisation. The second is where urban development has become unbalanced by de-industrialisation, disadvantaging some parts of the city (Barcelona 1992 Olympic Games; London 2012 Olympic Games). The third is where a city is seeking to expand and/or integrate its periphery. In all these instances, a major event is not merely viewed as a way to develop certain sites, but it is seen as a 'once in a lifetime' opportunity to restructure whole cities. Citing these structural problems within bids for major events may assist a candidate city's chances of success. One of the reasons Barcelona became a model of Olympic urbanism was because the city was given the opportunity by an organisation (the IOC) that was sympathetic to its plight. Similarly, London's plans to regenerate East London gave it a competitive edge over Paris in the bidding process. In Paris the proposed event projects would have had a less dramatic effect on the city's structure. Therefore, the reason urban restructuring has emerged as a key aspect of event regeneration is not simply because of the ambitions of urban authorities, but because of the motivations of event franchise holders. FIFA, the IOC and the BIE may be interested in helping cities to overcome long-term problems, but they are more interested in being associated with successful urban transformation. This helps to explain why the term catalyst may not be the most appropriate one here. The word catalyst refers to something that instigates or accelerates a process without itself being affected. But events are affected by the way that each host city stages an event – and when they are cited as being responsible for fundamental change in city's fortunes, this can add to the value of the 'franchise'.

Major events also have a track record of helping cities to overcome literal obstacles that restrict urban development. Often sites remain degenerated because they are cut off and host cities have sometimes used events to integrate these areas more effectively. For example, Hangzhou, China, used the World Leisure Expo to encourage development to jump from an area near Xihu Lake to the outer area at Qiantang River. Zhang and Wu (2008) call this 'leapfrog development', with the event credited with allowing the city to extend its boundaries south of the river. This type of development is often part of major event strategies because events have a tendency to be staged in waterfront zones. These locations – reclaimed from military or industrial uses or from nature – provide enough space to develop the facilities required for a major event such as a World Expo or Olympic Games. They allow these peripheral sites to be integrated into the city, and for urban development to be continued on the other side of riverside locations. A good example is Nation's Park – the former industrial site that was redeveloped as a new urban centre for the Lisbon 1998 World Expo. As Carrière and Demaziere (2002) explain, this project was an opportunity to integrate the eastern part of the city's riverside more effectively into the metropolitan area.

There is a particular trend for World Expos to be staged not only in waterfront locations, but on peninsulas and urban islands. Famous examples include the 1992 Seville Expo staged on the Cartuja 'island' in the middle of the Guadalquivir River and the Montreal 1967 Expo staged on two artificial islands in the St Lawrence River. There are three plausible explanations for the common use of islands. First, events provide opportunities to reclaim these islands from waterways thus providing sufficient space to stage events. Second, islands allow events to communicate that attendees (even long-term residents) are entering a world distinct from the rest of the city. This is important to encourage the sense of festivity deemed to be an essential part of successful events. Third, an event can be used to improve access, provide new attractions and infrastructure that means these peripheral spaces can be integrated within the rest of a city. However, this has proved to be difficult to achieve. Despite the construction of several new bridges, the site of Seville's Expo 1992 was, until recently, under-used. A theme park and technology cluster are now located there, but the area remains poorly integrated. This may be explained by somewhat conflicting objectives of major event strategies. Event sites are designed as distinctive spaces, lessening the likelihood that they will be blended successfully into the rest of a city. This is another way in which the short- and long-term objectives of a major event fail to correspond.

Major events as ways to accelerate existing urban regeneration plans

Justifications for staging major events may include the notion that urban development projects normally envisaged for the long term can be achieved in a shorter time frame. This 'acceleration' is a fundamental part of the way events are used to achieve physical regeneration. Usually, major urban regeneration projects are scheduled over 25–30 year periods. To stage the Olympic Games, these projects are scheduled to be completed in a fraction of this time. For example, the redevelopment of Homebush Bay was scheduled to take thirty years, but Sydney's successful bid for the 2000 Games meant it was to be delivered in fifteen years (Wilson, 1996). Using events to accelerate urban development is not restricted to the Olympics, nor is it an exclusively contemporary phenomenon. For example, Mayor Belloch believed that staging a World Expo in 2008 meant Zaragoza 'achieved in 3 years what would have normally taken twenty' (Rollin, 2008) and, as previously stated, the National Garden Festival in Stoke (1986) involved the reclamation of land in two years: without the event this would have been scheduled over twenty-five years (DoE, 1990). Such accelerated development may be particularly useful in areas where redevelopment has stalled, or where remediation is particularly difficult.

Accelerated development is enabled by a series of subsidiary factors. The most important of these is the imposition of strict deadlines for project completion. To a lesser extent it is also facilitated by the greater likelihood of 'buy-in' from key stakeholders. These, and other factors, are addressed below.

The imposition of strict deadlines

The key characteristic of event projects that differentiates them from other modes of urban regeneration is their inherent time-based element (see Figure 5.1). Events, by definition, occur at particular points in time, and using them within urban regeneration introduces a heightened temporal dimension. Completion deadlines are introduced, even for projects that are not essential to the event. Many urban development projects are never completed, only partially completed, or fully completed but only over a frustratingly long time scale. Incorporating a fixed associated deadline can help to avoid this. Hosting a major event may also give incentives to the private sector to accelerate housing, infrastructure and commercial projects so that it too can benefit from event associations. As Ren (2009: 1025) states with reference to the Beijing Olympic Games, 'both private and public developers raced to complete construction before the 2007 deadline'.

However, there are disadvantages with the introduction of deadlines for project completion. Often, there are good reasons why urban regeneration projects take so long and these apply to both the planning stage and the delivery phase. McManus (2004: 164) claims that plans for Olympic projects in Sydney were prepared 'with frantic haste' resulting in inappropriate developments. During Sydney's Olympic preparations, a new State Environmental Planning Policy (#38) was created which exempted Olympic proposals from proper assessment (Kearins and Pavlovich, 2002). Tight time scales allow fewer opportunities for consultation with the local population and other planning procedures may also be compromised. Carrière and Demaziere (2002: 78) suggest this occurred during preparations for the 1998 World Expo in Lisbon: 'the urban development

Figure 5.1 *Time pressures. The clock in Trafalgar Square, London, counting down the time until the start of the 2012 Olympic Games*

operation was faced with tight time constraints relating to the opening of the exhibition, leaving few opportunities for consultation'. With reference to preparations for the London 2012 Games, Porter *et al.* (2009: 406) suggest that the Olympic Delivery Authority had 'barely completed the process of uploading the [planning] documents onto their website before the time to object had run out'. So the pressure for timely delivery is a convenient way for event organisers to circumvent normal processes. Worryingly, this may suit projects that involve the displacement of people or other controversial aspects (Broudehoux, 2007).

Having a universal development deadline is not necessarily a good thing. In the delivery phase of event projects there may be technical complications and rushing to finish work may lead to a reduction in quality. Delivery organisations often have to make extra payments to contractors to ensure timely completion and this pushes budgets higher. Mistakes may also be made in the rush to complete projects. These may be regretted later. In Beijing, prior to the 2008 Olympic Games a 'building frenzy' removed valuable heritage assets (Ren, 2009).

There are other problems with universal deadlines for major regeneration projects. When a series of large-scale projects is completed at the same time this can add to a noted 'hangover' effect. The hotel sector provides a good example. When several new hotels are all completed just before an event a host city will experience a sudden increase in the number of rooms available. This inevitably leads to problems with over-capacity and a downward pressure on prices in the immediate post-event era (see Chapter 8). A similar problem exists with respect to employment in sectors such as construction. When projects all come to fruition at the same point in time, alternative employment is needed for a large number of workers. In both cases, the problem of over-capacity in the post-event era is exacerbated by the corresponding decline in demand for hotel and construction services. This means host cities have to follow events with other large-scale projects to utilise capacity created during the build-up to the event. Housing provision associated with events is susceptible to the same problem – releasing large amounts of units simultaneously for private sale may make it harder to achieve the returns needed to fund investments.

It is also possible to question the notion that events deliver accelerated regeneration at all. Although major event projects are said to be useful catalysts for urban regeneration projects, it should be acknowledged that these projects often remain unfinished long after the event. In Sydney, work is still being undertaken to redevelop the main site of the 2000 Olympic Games and the latest masterplan provides a vision for 2030 (see Chapter 9). Similarly, the 'legacy phase' work for London's 2012 Olympic Park is programmed to 2030. The need for redevelopment in the post-event era to turn sites into functioning areas means that the danger of slow, or stalled, urban (re)development still persists. Major events may ensure ambitious urban regeneration projects are started, but they do not guarantee completion. Although events are seen as accelerators of urban regeneration, in several of the cases discussed so far (Seville, Paris, Sydney) evidence suggests that cities may have to wait decades before effects are fully realised. In other cases, such as New York's Flushing Meadows, a second major event was required to ensure that the regeneration plans for a site were fully realised (World Expo 1939/40 and World Expo 1964/5). The regeneration of former industrial sites in Vancouver has also been assisted by staging multiple events. The (northern) shores of Vancouver's False Creek were redeveloped to stage Expo '86; the 2010 Winter Olympic Games were used to extend the regeneration project to the southeastern side of the Creek (see Figure 5.2).

As well as the fear of embarrassment caused by missing deadlines, there are other incentives for cities to complete prestigious urban regeneration schemes in time for an event. Governments want these projects to be complete when a city is subjected to intense media exposure during an event. However, if this incentive is prioritised too much there remains the danger of superficial redevelopment where resources are concentrated on the most visible projects. As Greene (2003) reminds us, events inspire host cities to improve their appearance in a very

Figure 5.2 *An aerial view of False Creek, Vancouver, the site of the Olympic Village and other key venues for the 2010 Winter Olympic Games. The shores on the more bulit-up side of the Creek were developed for the 1986 World Expo*

condensed time frame. This means there is a temptation to address the visibility of underdevelopment, rather than the underlying problems. For example, Newton (2009) shows that the N2 Gateway project in Cape Town was prioritised by South African authorities during preparations for the 2010 FIFA World Cup because of its high visibility on the transport corridor linking the main venue and the airport. Because of the pressure to relocate residents quickly and cheaply, large sites on the urban periphery were used to rehouse citizens. This means the project may contribute to, rather than help to reduce, the spatial inequities forged during the apartheid era.

More buy-in from key stakeholders

The other reason urban development can happen more quickly when it is associated with an event is because the event may generate a greater sense of purpose amongst a wider group of stakeholders. Influential stakeholders are more likely to engage with the project and stakeholders may commit more time and resources.

This makes them easier – and therefore quicker – to implement. For example, progress in East Manchester was accelerated by the consensus achieved during bids for the 1996 and 2000 Olympics and preparations for the 2002 Commonwealth Games. These events helped to forge an effective partnership between different levels of government (national government, a national regeneration company, the regional development agency, plus Manchester City Council) but also between the City Council and the private sector (Evans, 2007). This allowed venues for the Commonwealth Games to be completed in a timely fashion, but it also helped to deliver regeneration effects in other parts of East Manchester. Therefore, whilst the number of stakeholders involved in event development can be seen as inefficient, if the event has encouraged influential stakeholders to co-operate then the opposite effect can be observed. Most importantly, this joint working can persist after the event, allowing other long-term regeneration objectives to be addressed.

Events as vehicles to extend existing plans

As well as accelerating plans, major events can be used to extend existing urban regeneration plans. This fits with noted good practice that advises that events be incorporated within established projects and long-term ambitions. There are several instances where events have been incorporated into an existing project, allowing regeneration to be extended over a larger geographical area. Marseille's long-term regeneration ambition to revitalise an area near its water-front is a good example. Marseille is a city that has long been associated with ethnic ghettoes, port de-industrialisation and middle-class flight (McNeill, 2003). A project was instigated in 1995 to regenerate a 313 ha site near the port, which included brownfield land, derelict housing and public buildings (Andres, 2011). In conjunction with winning the right to stage the 2013 European Capital of Culture event, the project has now been extended to a 483 ha site. The ongoing project helped the city to win the bid, but the bid has also helped to extend the project – not only in terms of the size of the area, but the ambitions of the plans (Andres, 2011). Staging the event has helped to secure national funding for a new museum: the Museum of Civilisations from Europe and the Mediterranean. Andres (2011) suggests that the event provided an 'electro-shock' to secure the realisation of extra facilities.

A coherent narrative for wider projects

Major events can provide a useful narrative for wider regeneration projects. A narrative is a story formed to communicate ideas more effectively. New roads, bridges, sewerage systems and housing projects may have little direct relevance to a major event, but including them within an event 'package' helps to justify staging the event, whilst simultaneously allowing mundane projects to be associated with an event's excitement/publicity. The association of these projects with an event helps to tell the story of regeneration. This is becoming an increasingly familiar tale!

Providing a unifying events theme for a diverse set of projects also allows them to be communicated easily to internal and external stakeholders. This helps to publicise them. Developing this overarching theme may be particularly important for areas that have been stigmatised as rundown. Simply adding event venues to an area may not convince people that this area has changed, but if there are well known wider changes occurring simultaneously, this may provide the critical mass that is required to change people's mindset.

The major disadvantage with this approach is that it gives critics an opportunity to raise questions about how much it costs to stage major events. If host cities incorporate a series of wider physical projects into their suite of event projects, then the budget may appear artificially high. Therefore, host cities tend to include wider projects when they are citing the rationale for staging events, but try to separate them off when discussing the budgetary considerations (Smith and Strand, 2011).

BOX 5.1 OLYMPIC HOUSING

Events can be used to help deliver and promote new housing units. This is particularly true for the Olympic Games, an event that now requires host cities to provide housing for athletes. The idea of a dedicated Olympic Village is a phenomenon that dates back to the prefabricated units built for the Los Angeles Games in 1932. The Helsinki Games (1952) were the first time permanent housing was prioritised as a key outcome of the Games.

Apart from Athens's Olympic Village – which houses over 2,000 families on low incomes (Panagiotopoulou, 2009) – most other permanent Olympic Villages have been inhabited by affluent groups in the post-event era. Accordingly, the lack of social diversity is a serious challenge to the regenerative power of this new housing provision. Barcelona's Olympic Village provides an interesting case. Here, renowned architects built good-quality 5-storey apartments on a 47 ha site between the city's main park and the beachfront. Originally, the plan was to offer them as subsidised social housing, but the escalating costs of staging the Games meant that their private sale proved too tempting for municipal authorities.

This introduces a key problem with event-inspired communities: the social objectives of event planning are often compromised because of the need to maximise revenue to pay for venues. When cost savings have to be made, social housing ambitions are usually one of the first elements of event projects to be cut. During preparations for the 2010 Vancouver Winter Games, residents were promised a legacy of affordable housing. The city has a large problem with homelessness. The Downtown Eastside area (see Figure 5.3) is one of the poorest parts of the city, and one where housing for homeless and disadvantaged citizens is urgently required. This area has a population of around 14,000 and is located near BC Place – one of the main arenas used for the Olympics. In the run-up to the Games, the City of Vancouver produced an 'Inner City Inclusive Commitment Statement' (ICI) that promised affordable housing, no displacement of existing residents and consultation regarding a feared security crackdown. According to Porter *et al.* (2009: 411) 'the 'ICI promises have been almost completely ignored'. Just before the Games it became clear that no new Olympic related social housing units would open before the Games and that the Olympic Village was 'now unlikely ever to be occupied by any currently homeless individuals due to cost overruns' (Porter *et al.*, 2009: 411). Of the multiple units that were constructed near False Creek in advance of the Games, only 250 have been designated as affordable housing (VANOC, 2010b). VANOC contributed $30 million to the City of Vancouver to pay for this provision (VANOC, 2010b).

Branding new units as Olympic housing is something that relies on soft branding, rather than hard branding, because of the restrictions imposed by the IOC. In Barcelona, the housing project that included the Olympic village was named Nova Icaria, after an ideal 'workers community of the future' conceived in the nineteenth century (Hughes, R. 1999). But 87.5 per cent of its residents instead call the area Vila Olimpica (Valera and Guardia, 2002). This is perhaps symbolic; not only of the rejection of the area's original social ambitions, but also of the importance attached to the event which inspired its reconstruction. Consensus on an area's name is also an indicator of the social homogeneity of a newly formed neighbourhood. Valera and Guardia (2002) concluded that Barcelona's Olympic Village has gained a distinctive image amongst its residents. This highlights a key advantage of event communities. For new housing projects it may make it easier to forge a temporal/historical identity.

Figure 5.3 *A crane and the mist hang over Vancouver's Downtown East-side district*

Barcelona's Vila Olimpica was planned to encourage socialising: it was organised in blocks, with inner courtyards and gardens for public use. But the onerous work commitments of the affluent residents that have moved there have contributed to somewhat distant relations between neighbours (Valera and Guardia, 2002). Although the community may not be cohesive or diverse, the opportunities, facilities and services provided for residents contribute to Hemphill *et al.*'s (2004: 770) conclusion that Vila Olimpica 'displays a high degree of adherence to sustainability principles'. Their assessment used a series of weighted indicators to measure 'sustainable urban regeneration performance'. Of six developments analysed (in Belfast, Dublin and Barcelona) Vila Olimpica scored highest, with the authors surmising that it was a notable example of good practice. One key factor that differentiated it from projects deemed less successful was the significant presence of education and medical facilities.

Bids to stage the Olympic Games, as well as events that were actually staged, have also been used to instigate new housing developments. A good example is South Hammerby in Stockholm – designated as the 'Olympic Village' in Stockholm's unsuccessful bid for the 2004 Olympics (Khakee, 2007). The development went ahead anyway, emphasising how important events can be in securing the required plans, funding and partnerships required to deliver innovative urban development schemes. Although this area has impressive ecological credentials, its social sustainability is hampered by the lack of certain services (e.g. childcare) and the exorbitant price of accommodation. A privileged and socially homogeneous community is the inevitable outcome. Such homogeneity seems to be a key limitation of event-led development. In other examples, promises to build new housing as part of event projects regardless of the outcome of event bids have not always been fulfilled. Despite promises to build the 2,300 homes in Berlin as part of preparations for the 2000 Olympic Games, the project was abandoned when the city was not awarded the Games (Alberts, 2009). However, the proposed media centre site was developed as a residential area.

One of Stockholm's rivals for the 2004 Olympic Games was Cape Town, South Africa. Although Cape Town's bid included a commendable social orientation, the city soon realised that delivering a sustainable housing legacy would be very difficult. High IOC standards meant that construction costs would have made the new housing more costly than needy residents could afford (Hiller, 2000). Such demanding stipulations emphasise a key problem with housing projects associated with events – the need to satisfy an external stakeholder. This, plus the related motivation to develop Olympic Villages as prototypes of new forms of urban design (see Chapter 7), and the use of high-profile architects, often produces 'high spec' and thus high-priced residences. This limitation is supplemented by other reasons why event planning often fails to deliver a sustainable mix of different housing. For example, the requirement in many event budgets for the sale of redeveloped land to help pay for expensive events means there is a disincentive to use such initiatives to provide low-income housing or even mixed occupancy developments.

Events as platforms for showcasing urban development

Major events do not merely act as ways to instigate, accelerate or extend urban development; they provide vehicles to communicate wider achievements.

A major event is sometimes the platform for the dissemination of messages about a city's regeneration. These messages are meant to influence a range of internal and external audiences including city residents (voters), tourists, potential residents, external investors and other influential decision makers. A city may choose to stage an event at a time immediately after it has been renovated and where positive images can be projected. In these instances, events are not instigators or accelerators of development, but simply projects that provide opportunities to showcase recent works already undertaken in a city. As Ren's (2009) analysis of Beijing highlights, sometimes the primary role of events is to provide a worldwide ceremonial launch for projects. However, Faulkner *et al.* (2001) suggest that the showcase effects of major events are often 'marginal' because these events take place in large cities that are generally well known. The implication of Faulkner *et al.*'s (2001) observation is that showcasing may work better for smaller, less well known cities.

A good example of regeneration 'showcasing' was Lisbon's European Capital of Culture event in 1994. Holton (1998: 78) described this event as one where 'Lisbon took off her braces and glasses, proudly displayed her "traje de gala" (ceremonial gown) and with an eastern rotation of her clean face invited the rest of Europe to witness her spectacular urban makeover'. Holton (1998) described how Lisbon used the event to 'showcase' several new constructions including the Centro Cultural de Belem and Culturegest – enormous modernist cultural venues financed by the state.

Melbourne's Commonwealth Games of 2006 is another good example of how events are used to showcase recent changes. One of the objectives of staging the Games was to emphasise the newly regenerated Southbank riverside zone (see Figure 5.4). This area – blighted by its former use for transport infrastructure and waste disposal – was redeveloped by successive state governments and the Liberal-National Kennett administration had completed the transformation in the 1990s (Sandercock and Dovey, 2002). The area now includes the corporate headquarters of Exxon, a new exhibition centre, a trade and convention centre and a casino, as well as the pre-existing arts centre. A key objective of the Victoria Government and City Council was that: 'The Yarra River corridor will be opened up to become the heart of city life' (cited in Sandercock and Dovey, 2002: 158). So, when Melbourne was awarded the 2006 Commonwealth Games, rather than redeveloping another part of the city, the main aim was to emphasise the river zone's recent redevelopment. This was confirmed in the 2010 Melbourne City Plan (developed in 2002) that stated: 'The river will be a key focal point during the 2006 Commonwealth Games' (Melbourne City Council, 2002: 14).

Rather than merely hoping media editors would emphasise the riverfront, the state and city authorities implemented a number of dedicated initiatives. Melbourne City Council provided a AUS$3 million (£1.2 million at 2006 rates)

Figure 5.4 *Melbourne's regenerated riverscape that provided the centre-piece of the 2006 Commonwealth Games. The city's impressive events infrastructure can be seen in the distance*

grant to deliver a 'River Show' (of lights and sounds) that took place during each night of the Games. The Council claimed that 'The River Show showcased Melbourne to a world-wide television audience and attracted a crowd of around 100,000 spectators on the opening night' (City of Melbourne, undated: no pages). To improve access to the new river zone, the Victoria Government also converted an old railway bridge into a footbridge over the Yarra River. This crossing opened three days before the start of the Games. It was flanked by glass panels depicting the diverse range of communities that inhabit contemporary Australia – a key theme of the event. The City Council also installed seventy-two fish sculptures over the regenerated stretch of the river – each representing one of the competing nations. These riverside initiatives and their connections to the event meant that Melbourne's waterfront regeneration became associated with the 2006 Commonwealth Games even though the most significant projects had been completed several years previously.

THE INEFFICIENCY OF URBAN DEVELOPMENT ASSOCIATED WITH MAJOR EVENTS: THE TAIL WAGGING THE DOG?

As well as discussing different ways that mega-events can play a role in parallel physical regeneration, it is also important to highlight the associated problems.

One of the main worries about urban regeneration that involves an event is that a temporary phenomenon involving external stakeholders starts to dictate important decisions regarding urban regeneration. In other words, a short-term event can unduly influence long-term plans when, ideally, the reverse should be true. Whilst some host cities have cleverly used events to assist or extend long-term projects, others have been overwhelmed by the needs of the event itself. The multiple examples of under-used venues and vacant development projects prove this (see Chapter 4). But there are also more subtle examples where the *design*, *location* and *scale* of wider urban regeneration projects have been unduly influenced by event considerations. Major events may also encourage developments that are simply *unnecessary*. These four problems are analysed below.

Some projects are meant to assist urban development, but their temporary role as event facilities can affect their design and their suitability for end users in the post-event period. Binks and Snape (2006) provide an insightful account of how the design of a long awaited community facility in Bolton became hijacked when it was designated as the badminton venue for the Manchester Commonwealth Games (see Chapter 4). This is also true of many new housing projects earmarked as athletes' accommodation during mega-sport events. In several instances (e.g. Vancouver 2010, Melbourne 2006) event stakeholders, such as local organising committees (LOCs) or rights holders, have insisted on specifications that make it harder for housing units to be adapted for conventional use after the event. Cases such as these highlight the conflicting priorities of event stakeholders, developers and those representing urban areas more generally. Organisations responsible for delivering events often complain that they are not sure who their client is. Is it the local organising committee, the rights holder, the end user or the government/ taxpayer? As Binks and Snape (2006) identify, partnerships assembled to develop venues and supporting infrastructure often have no responsibility for those facilities in the post-event era. This can result in the long-term interests of end users being compromised.

The location and scale of urban regeneration initiatives can be unduly influenced by major event projects. For example, transport projects are sometimes redirected to include event related locations, even though existing communities may remain under-served. Examples include Sheffield's supertram system where the route is dominated by the four main venues for the 1991 World Student Games (the Don Valley Stadium, Sheffield Arena, Ponds Forge and Hillsborough Leisure Centre). The transport legacy of Sydney's Olympic Games was also undermined by the focus on the event, rather than wider considerations. The principal transport initiative developed as part of the Sydney 2000 Games was the rail loop at Homebush Bay that linked the Olympic Park to the existing rail network (Cashman, 2006). Services on this facility are now irregular and the chronic public transportation problems endured by Sydney's residents remain unresolved

(Cashman, 2006). Similarly, Prytherch and Maiques (2009: 114) note that recent public investments in Valencia's transport system 'have focused on linking the airport to the city centre and America's Cup port, and thus are geared primarily to visitors while poor and peripheral neighbourhoods lag behind'. Again, this suggests an event (in this case the America's Cup sailing race) has relocated regeneration away from areas where it is needed most.

Major events may also encourage a scale of development that is out of proportion with the development required for an area in the long term. Sydney provides a useful illustration. Before the 2000 Olympic Games, Wilson (1996: 611) questioned whether the 60 m wide streets and the large-scale buildings in the Olympic Park would provide useable human space (see Figure 5.5). This view was vindicated after the event and developers are now retrospectively overlaying the monumental urban structure with smaller buildings (Lochhead, 2005). Event sites seem to be the new version of monumental government precincts – where the overall feeling of the user is one of awe. The problem of inappropriate scale can also affect the legacy of smaller events. The National Garden Festival staged in Gateshead, England, in 1990 allowed a site to be regenerated for housing and parkland, but a recent report highlighted the problematic influence

Figure 5.5 *The wide Olympic Boulevard in Sydney's Olympic Park. Several hotels have been developed on the site and two of them (Ibis, Pullman) can be seen on the left of this picture*

of the event: Eslington Park was one of the main legacies of the festival, but because landscaping was designed to accommodate large numbers of people, the park has large sculpted earthmounds and inappropriate planting. This means 'the effect on the visitor's sense of personal security can be quite disconcerting' (GVA Grimley, 2006: 37).

A final way that events can unduly influence the direction of urban development is to assist the delivery of projects that in normal circumstances would be rejected. In this sense major events may encourage unnecessary urban development. This is partly explained by the short time frames and deadlines that hinder planning procedures (discussed above), but unnecessary development also occurs because of the pervading discourse and hype that surrounds major sport events. As McManus (2004: 164) argues with reference to the Olympics, it is 'possible to appeal to the discourse of the Olympic City in order to gain support for a project that...otherwise may have been unnecessary'. The example he gives is a super-yacht marina in Rozelle Bay, Sydney, built in advance of the 2000 Olympic Games – a particularly interesting example because it was partly justified on the basis that it would be temporary, but by 2003 it still had not been removed (McManus, 2004). This is another important characteristic of major event strategies – the retention of developments envisaged as necessary only for the duration of the event. These developments may not be a problem in themselves, but they may encourage related development not envisaged by municipal planning agencies. Unnecessary development is of particular concern when it takes place on sensitive or previously undeveloped sites. For example, many of the venues for the 2004 Olympic Games were developed on greenfield sites even though Athens urgently requires more, not less, open space. This makes the under-use of these venues even more galling for the people of Athens. The decision to develop a stadium in Cape Town on the city's Green Point Common for the 2010 FIFA World Cup is a further example. The decision caused a double whammy effect: fewer benefits for a disadvantaged peripheral district and the commercial development of open space near the city centre (see Chapter 4). Interestingly, Swart and Bob (2009) suggest that the tight time frames associated with the event contributed to the decision to build the stadium at Green Point. As time passed this location became the only option that could be developed on schedule. This reaffirms the discussion above about the problems caused by the inherent time pressures attached to major event projects.

The dark side of events

The discussion above has highlighted how major events can be used within wider urban regeneration projects and some of the inefficient ways that events can influence these projects. It is worth emphasising that the development effects of major events have been criticised by urban planners, but also by human rights organisations and citizen groups. Perhaps the most damaging characteristic of event projects is the noted dislocation of housing and businesses. A UN report in 1996 suggested that, of the thirty-four recent examples of mass evictions, five were related to major events (Greene, 2003). Fifteen years later, the UN Special Rapporteur on Housing expressed concerns that Brazil's preparations for the 2014 World Cup and 2016 Olympic Games were having harmful effects on poor citizens (United Nations, 2011). Allegations concerning displacement and evictions were received by the UN from a number of cities, including São Paulo, Rio de Janeiro, Belo Horizonte, Curitiba, Porto Alegre, Recife, Natal and Fortaleza (United Nations, 2011). The main problems noted were insufficient time for stakeholders to propose and discuss alternatives, inadequate plans for relocation and the very limited compensation offered to the affected communities. The paltry compensation levels were considered to be particularly galling by the UN's special rapporteur given the increased value of real estate in cities where event projects are underway (United Nations, 2011).

The Olympic Games and FIFA World Cup have a record of residential displacement. It is estimated that 2 million people have been displaced by the Olympic Games in twenty years (Glynn, 2008). As part of the preparations for Seoul's Olympic Games (1988), 48,000 properties housing 720,000 people were destroyed (Greene, 2003). Only 10 per cent of these people were rehoused on site. Prior to the 2010 World Cup, Newton (2009) notes how the N2 Gateway project in Cape Town resulted in the eviction of 20,000 poor people. The high visibility of this area on the corridor linking the airport with the city meant that slum clearances were fast-tracked without proper consideration of the effects on those dislocated.

This practice continues in the contemporary era, with Beijing a notable example. The Olympics were used as an excuse to 'beautify' several areas, including Qianmen, a historic area that had previously been spared redevelopment. The Games deflected attention from the controversial changes to Beijing's urban fabric – the new Qianmen was 'opened' the day before the Games commenced (Ren, 2009). Thus, major events not only provide a showcase to illustrate new changes to outsiders (Qianmen was on the marathon route), but a way of diluting internal opposition. It is mistaken to think this is a problem restricted to authoritarian regimes. In a damning editorial, Porter *et al.* (2009: 397) describe how in Vancouver 'the existing population and neighbourhood … are invisible to the bureaucratic abstraction of delivering major venues and new infrastructure' for the 2010 Winter Olympics. During the land acquisition and delivery work for London's 2012 Olympic Games, a community of 425 people at Clays Lane was evicted and dispersed. The compulsory purchase of property was allegedly assisted by the London Development Agency's depiction of the area as decayed and isolated. This view was contradicted by those who saw it as the home of a functioning community easily accessible by bus and tube (Porter *et al.*, 2009). Somewhat ironically for a project justified by the delivery of a sport event, new amenities in this area will be built on an area that used to include a sport stadium and a cycle circuit. This highlights a key problem with regeneration associated with major events – it tends to replace what was there before, rather than building on existing resources (Raco, 2004). Even when residents and businesses are not forcibly removed from sites, they may be pressured to leave – either by rent increases or by fears of future changes. Placed alongside concerns about the design, location, scale and necessity of certain projects, the displacement of resident populations reminds us that physical regeneration in association with events is not always a positive phenomenon.

SUMMARY

This chapter has explored the relationship between major events and wider urban regeneration. Distinctive qualities that major events can bring to wider regeneration processes have been noted. Events can help to instigate, accelerate and showcase urban regeneration. These roles for events occur at different stages of the regeneration process (see Figure 5.6). Several major disadvantages of event developments have also been observed. As well as serious ethical concerns regarding the displacement of existing communities and businesses, events can result in urban development that is inefficient – because it is in the wrong

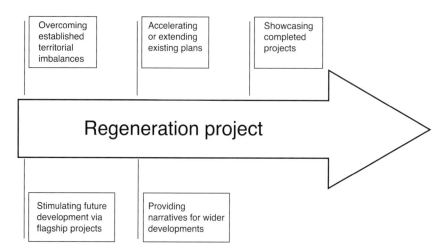

Figure 5.6 *The different ways that events can be used within regeneration strategies and the stages of the process at which they are deployed*

place, at the wrong scale, or simply unnecessary. Major events can also unduly affect the design of urban development projects because of confusion regarding whose interests should be prioritised. Whereas conventional urban regeneration usually involves a clearly defined client, this is not the case for many event projects.

The examples cited here suggest that urban regeneration needs to be guided by local needs and conventional planning procedures, rather than being indirectly led by event priorities. Ultimately, major events should only be used in urban regeneration when there is a strong case that they are the best way of achieving the outcomes desired. It is difficult to justify urban regeneration projects that are led by transient events, but that is not to say events cannot be useful tools within regeneration projects. The potential of well located, brownfield sites can be unlocked by events and event associations can provide useful 'place making' tools that add value to land in areas where market forces have failed to deliver renewal. Ultimately, the best outcomes seem to emerge when events are integrated within long-term urban regeneration plans. The worst outcomes occur when events distract urban authorities from their existing plans: this is where the opportunity costs of staging mega-events become dangerously high. Unfortunately, the unpredictable bidding process and inevitable opportunism associated with staging events means that rational planning is very difficult. This – alongside the political capital at stake – means that, despite the burgeoning amount of best practice available to guide key stakeholders, we are unlikely to see an end to inappropriate urban regeneration inspired by major events.

EXTENDED CASE STUDY 2: BARCELONA, A TALE OF THREE AND A HALF MEGA-EVENTS

The most famous example of a city that has undergone a fundamental physical restructuring in association with major events is Barcelona. The Catalan capital's regeneration associated with the 1992 Olympic Games is a well known case, but it is also one that is sometimes over-simplified and misrepresented.

The case is often misunderstood for three main reasons:

1 The direct influence of the 1992 Olympic Games is sometimes over-estimated.
2 The contextual uniqueness of the case is often overlooked.
3 The role of other events in the city's development tends to be neglected.

This case study aims to explain the factors that underpinned Barcelona's regeneration and to show how the 1992 Olympic Games were merely one project of a series of events that have shaped the city.

An introduction to the regeneration projects associated with the 1992 Olympic Games

The most important point about Barcelona's Olympic redevelopment was that it was linked to wider city plans and long-term objectives for the city. The city's Olympic regeneration was assisted greatly by the actions of previous city leaders who had bought large quantities of land when prices were low during the period of transition (1975–1979). Some of the key initiatives (e.g. the Port Olímpic development) consciously implemented plans that had been developed sixty years previously (Woodward, 1992). Others (e.g. the city centre waterfront development – see Figure 5.7) had been envisaged since the 1960s. An ambitious General Metropolitan Plan was in place ten years before the Olympic Games were secured. This plan was a useful compromise between development objectives and the interests of local people and it prioritised the production of new public spaces and local amenities (Monclús, 2007). The urban public space projects that were part of this plan were largely completed 1981–1987 (Rowe, 2006). These focused on residential neighbourhoods, rather than the central areas; and on small interventions, rather than prestige projects. Projects were designed from the

Figure 5.7 *Barcelona's reconfigured waterfront. This coastline was developed for two different events (the 1992 Olympic Games and the 2004 Universal Forum of Cultures)*

bottom-up (at the neighbourhood level), rather than imposing a rigid top-down masterplan. These initial efforts explain Calavita and Ferrer's (2000: 805) assertion that Barcelona's regeneration was 'remarkable' because the emphasis placed on the Olympic Games and associated marketing 'has not hampered, as is generally the case, the pursuit of an ambitious social agenda'. This was reaffirmed by Garcia and Claver (2003: 116) who suggested that in Barcelona 'projects achieved urban restructuring with a degree of redistributive justice'.

The Barcelona Olympic Games were perhaps a good example of themed event regeneration – where a diverse range of projects is united under a unifying narrative. Only a small proportion (Brunet (2009) suggests 9.1 per cent) of the total investment was spent on staging the event directly. As highlighted in Chapter 4, existing venues were used wherever possible. This contrasted with previous projects like the 1976 Montreal Olympic Games, where 90 per cent of the budget was allocated to Olympic facilities. In Barcelona, the focus was on providing public space, updating infrastructure and adapting the morphology of the city. According to Monclús (2007), these objectives were achieved through the enterprise of the political class and the spirit of citizen co-operation. The involvement of knowledgeable planners and other urban experts was also significant.

The Games did influence Barcelona's development – changing its speed, direction and scale. As Monclús (2007) identifies, one of the key role of the Games was to increase the levels of ambition, with small projects superseded by more extensive projects. The Olympics hastened and secured the delivery of several projects, but many of the changes would probably have been delivered without the event. The four main Olympic venue sites were perhaps the exception, but even in these locations there were efforts to link initiatives into the wider plans for the city. Olympic projects were dispersed to strategic points on the edge of the city centre as part of a plan to create new areas of centrality. The Games projects involved remodelling several key locations, rather than delivering regeneration in one concentrated zone (see Chapter 4). But the four main sites were given some coherence by the improvements made to the road infrastructure that linked them and by their integration into city plans. Although the projects on Montjuic (the Olympic Stadium, Palau St Jordi, swimming and diving pools) are most well known, the Olympic Village and the improvements to Vall d'Hebron were the main urban regeneration projects. These are discussed further below.

The Olympic Village

Several locations for the Olympic Village were considered, but a site between the centre and the sea (Parc de Mar) was selected to maximise the urban regeneration legacy of the Games (see Figure 5.7). Redeveloping this strategic location allowed the opportunity to make the morphology of the city more coherent. A special Town Plan was formulated in 1986 to reclaim 100 ha of industrial land and turn it into a new urban district. As well as providing 2,400 new housing units, the project delivered other benefits. Railway lines were re-routed, a major road was covered, the promenade extended, a new marina created, beaches rejuvenated and new hotels and office space constructed.

Vall d'Hebron

The sports complex developed at Vall d'Hebron is the least well known of Barcelona's four main Olympic sites. This site 'in the first periphery' (i.e. just outside the city centre) was already semi-developed and the opportunity was taken to organise this 'chaotic urban space' (Truno, 1995). The idea was to create a platform for the subsequent utilisation of the space. The velodrome already existed, but tennis, pelota and archery facilities were all added. Fifteen-storey housing estates were constructed next to the sports facilities (Rowe, 2006). However, the area has not been as successful as the Olympic Village development. According to Rowe (2006), in the years following the Games the area became forlorn and dilapidated.

A 'Barcelona model'?

The success of Barcelona's Olympic initiatives means they are sometimes discussed as a 'model' that other cities could seek to emulate. There are a number of problems with the notion of a Barcelona model of event regeneration. These are summarised below.

1 *There were some negative aspects of Barcelona's initiatives that other cities would not want to emulate.* Despite the widespread recognition of success, a number critiques have emerged in recent years that question aspects of Barcelona's Olympic regeneration. One recurring criticism is the neglect of social considerations. Some link this to an overemphasis on place marketing and economic considerations in the latter stages of Olympic preparations. Calavita and Ferrer (2000) doubt whether a more participatory process was possible without jeopardising the timely completion of all the facilities. The Olympic Village is used as an illustrative example of some of the social failings of the project. Here, initial plans to provide social housing were abandoned when the (high) value of the new housing stock on the private market became clear. More general issues with housing legacies have also been raised. The Olympic projects were partially responsible for rises in house prices that have displaced people and public sector housing to the metropolitan periphery. The new zones of centrality created were built in

deindustrialising areas, but they were not aimed at working-class residents (Balibrea, 2001). This contributed to the dislocation of original neighbour-hoods. Other criticisms include Marshall's comment (1996) that employment objectives were unclear and weakly developed and Monclús's (2007) conten-tion that there was too much emphasis on private transport, at the expense of public provision.

2 *The ideas for major projects were borrowed from elsewhere and the strategy involved a complex mix of individual initiatives rather than one coherent model of development.* Whilst the city is now a favoured model which other cities seek to emulate, Barcelona's initiatives were themselves influenced by initiatives pursued elsewhere:

- The waterfront project was strongly influenced by the designs for US cities by James Rouse – in particular Baltimore's Harborplace (Monclús, 2003). Major events had already been used to recover dilapidated and obstructed waterfronts before Barcelona pursued this approach (e.g. in New Orleans: see Chapter 8).
- The idea for new areas of centrality was borrowed from Milanese urban planning (Monclús, 2003).
- The strategic planning processes that were developed in association with the Games were influenced by North American Plans, particularly San Francisco's 1984 Plan (Monclús, 2007).
- Some of the principles of urban design implemented by the chief planner/ architect Oriol Bohigas were inspired by work in Berlin.

Monclús (2003) summed up the difficulties conceiving of a Barcelona model when he stated that it is unclear whether the formula was discovered by Barcelona, or whether Barcelona was the place where an existing formula had been applied most effectively. For Monclús (2007), the original feature of Barcelona's project was the quality of public leadership (see Chapter 4).

3 *The initiatives and their success were inseparable from the context in which they were implemented.* In the 1980s, Barcelona was a city facing severe de-industrialisation. The city lost 42 per cent of its manufacturing jobs and 69 per cent of its construction jobs between the 1960s and 1985 (McNeill, 1999). This decline was typical of many European cities that had been reliant on these sectors. However, there were also some very untypical characteris-tics of Barcelona in the 1980s. The city had recently emerged from almost forty years of repressive rule by Spain's leader General Franco. This national regime had deliberately tried to suppress Catalan identity and Barcelona was punished by years of neglect because of its role as the stronghold of the opposition movement. During the Franco era Barcelona became a grey city, even though it still boasted fine architecture dating from the Catalan

renaissance (1880–1929). The British statesman Roy Jenkins remembers a visit he made in 1953 and compares it to the recent changes made.

'It was dingy and dull. I find it almost impossible to reconcile the city then with the city I have known in the past 25 years' (Jenkins, 2002: 229).

When Franco died in 1975 a new democratic government was installed and Catalonia was granted an autonomous regional government. This meant Barcelona began to unfreeze. The new governments re-established at the regional and city levels were desperate to address issues that had been neglected for decades. These governments were also keen to restore Barcelona to its former status as a European regional capital. Spain entered the EU in 1986 and this provided funds and backing for new projects. Catalan nationalism flourished and there was civic support for major interventions in the urban sphere. Architects and urban designers were eager to install projects that they or others had been planning for decades. In short, Barcelona was a city waiting to be unlocked. This context helps to explain how such an impressive regeneration project was implemented and why it was so successful. As Garcia and Claver (2003: 123) confirm, it is clear that the 'Barcelona model of restructuring is historically contingent'. Unsurprisingly, other cities have found it difficult to emulate Barcelona's success.

Other events

Barcelona is a city that is obsessed with its own history and the 1992 Olympics was a project reminiscent of other major events staged during key periods in the city's past. Olympic projects were also assisted by smaller events. The swimming pools used for the Games were originally built for the European Swimming Championships in 1970 and the city was one of the hosts of the 1982 FIFA World Cup. Unrealised plans also contributed. Monclús (2007) cites the proposals for a World Expo in 1982 as something that laid the foundations for the Olympic project, and the city had previously bid for the 1972 Games which were staged in Munich. This ingrained culture of using major events to secure the city's regeneration dates back to a golden era for Barcelona and Catalonia (1888–1929). At this time, as in 1992, the resurgence of Catalan nationalism provided the impetus for staging other events that would leave a significant impression on the city.

The 1888 Universal Exhibition

Barcelona's use of events as a tool for urban transformation can be traced back to the 1888 Universal Exhibition. Although this was a second-tier World Expo overshadowed by the exhibitions in Paris, the event attracted 1.5 million visitors over thirty-five weeks (Hughes, R. 1999). Garcia-Espuche *et al.* (1991) argue that the event is best understood as one that changed the city's appearance, rather than its urban structure. In this sense it was a project designed to impress outsiders. McCully (1985: 16) suggests that the mayor used the Universal Exhibition to 'present an image of the city of Barcelona to the world as an independent, prosperous and industrially strong urban centre'. However, the event did result in some important physical changes including a new park built on the site of the abandoned citadel, new buildings (see Figure 5.8), new monuments (such as the Arc de Triomf and the Statue of Christopher Columbus) and improvements to the city's streets (paving and lighting). Many of these additions still attract people to the city today (see Figure 5.8). The number of architects involved in the preparations for the event prompted one journalist to write: 'in days of yore, our leaders surrounded themselves with jesters for amusement, modern day mayors surround themselves with architects' (cited in Rohrer, 1985: 97). This comment would not be out of place in contemporary media accounts of major events. As with the event projects conceived a century later, the Exhibition helped to accelerate

Figure 5.8 *The Castell dels Tres Dragons in Cuitadella Park, Barcelona. This building designed by Domènech was built as the restaurant for the 1888 Universal Exhibition*

existing development projects. Garcia-Espuche *et al.* (1991: 148) comment: 'the Exhibition probably functioned as a mechanism to accelerate work that had already started'.

The 1929 World Expo

A decade after the Universal Exhibition, Barcelona's city leaders were already preparing to stage another major event. However, it would be almost thirty years before their plans came to fruition. Like the 1888 Exhibition, the event was to be staged on a site of military repression. At the turn of the century (1901), Barcelona's ruling elite proposed to transform the central hillside of Montjuic from a military space into a public park. The long-held objective to stage a follow up to the 1888 Universal Exhibition provided an ideal opportunity to make this happen. As Roca (1985: 133) states, the plan to stage a World Expo was the 'moving force' in the transformation of Montjuic (see Figure 5.9). An organising committee was formed in 1907 and the original idea was to stage an exhibition of electrical industries in 1917. Even though some building work began, World War I and the turbulent political situation in Spain delayed the event.

Figure 5.9 *The view from the Palau Nacionale on Montjuic, Barcelona. This area was remodelled for the 1929 World Expo*

The Expo eventually opened in 1929. The design of the exhibition site reflected a divided Spain that was only a few years from civil war. Key features like the Palau Nacionale and Poble Espanyol (a model village) emphasised (Spanish) historicism and nationalism; whereas the futuristic design of some of the other structures (most notably the German pavilion designed by Mies van der Rohe) and the impressive light shows, symbolised a forward-thinking, international city. The 1929 Expo also instigated wider changes to Barcelona's urban landscape. According to Ganau (2008: 816), 'the greatest incentive for the new government to transform Barcelona was the celebration of the World's Fair of 1929'. As with the 1992 Olympic Games, the event was accompanied by 'parallel' elements in addition to the development of event venues. As well as the redevelopment of Montjuic as a public area, the event was associated with the enlargement of the port area between Montjuic and the Llobreget Delta (where the airport is currently located) and (as discussed below) the renovation of the historic centre (Roca, 1985).

According to Ganau (2008), the city's famous Barri Gotic area did not assume the importance it has now until the preparations for the 1929 World Expo. Up until the event, the term Barri Gotic was not used and the area had not previously featured in tourist guides. In the build-up to the Expo, a number of restorations and amendments were carried out (e.g. the façade of the Ajuntament) and a gothic-style bridge constructed (Ganau, 2008). The changes were driven by a nostalgic philosophy that aimed to recreate the city centre to reflect its appearance in the sixteenth and seventeenth centuries. This assisted politically motivated ambitions at that time to promote Spanish values by emphasising the nation's golden age.

Universal Forum of Cultures 2004

The success of the Olympic Games, and the way they pushed the city (and its leaders) into the international limelight, meant Barcelona was keen to repeat their success. By 2002, ten years had passed since the Olympic Games and the anniversary of the Games was used as the opportunity to launch the Universal Forum of Cultures: a new event which was staged in 2004. Barcelona had wanted to stage a World Expo, but the BIE refused to give permission to stage an officially registered event. Instead, city leaders decided to develop their own major event, in association with UNESCO. The idea was that Barcelona would stage the first edition, then allow other host cities to stage it in the future.

The 2004 Universal Forum of Cultures was a conference-style event that had three central themes: cultural diversity, sustainable development and conditions for peace. The event cost over €300 million to stage. Funding was derived from the public sector (60 per cent), but also private sources (20 per cent) and anticipated event revenues (20 per cent) (Benedicto and Carrasco, 2007).

Two large indoor auditoria were built – including one that accommodates 15,000 people – and two open air auditoria were also constructed. Parallel physical development projects included the creation of a yacht harbour, new beaches, new medical facilities and a shopping centre. Hundreds of new hotel rooms and private homes were also developed. The project included 800 new housing units, but only seventy of these were reserved as affordable homes for low-income residents (Benedicto and Carrasco, 2007).

Like the Olympic projects of the 1980s, the plan to stage the Forum was embedded within wider spatial strategies for the city. For a long time the city had wanted to extend a major artery (Diagonal) to the sea, thus completing the extension of the city. The Forum project was staged on a 214 ha waterfront site near Diagonal Mar, the point where Diagonal met the seafront. The site was a key node within the development of the city's northeast axis and the project was also linked to other major regeneration projects undertaken at this time, such as the new high-speed rail station at Sagrera and the 22@ creative cluster near Poblenou.

Rather than building on the success of the approach used in conjunction with the Olympic Games, the Universal Forum of Cultures project involved a much less impressive development model. The event site was located near to the disadvantaged districts of La Mina/La Catalana which were partially inhabited by marginal communities. This caused controversy. A neighbourhood consortium was established to negotiate local benefits, but a major criticism of the project was the way the event prioritised the construction of the event facilities at the expense of the wider interests of the area. Garcia and Claver (2003: 120) observe that 'unlike the redevelopment during and after the Olympics, there has been almost no consultation with neighbourhood associations'. Blanco (2009) suggested that the dominance of private interests resulted in opposition to the Forum from neighbourhood associations and social movements – something that was less apparent throughout the Olympic project. The Federation of Neighbourhood Associations (FAVB) withdrew its support for the event partly because it objected to the loss of land originally destined to house public facilities (Blakeley, 2005).

The event also experienced unfortunate public relations problems. For many observers, the main themes of the event were incompatible with the actions of the organisers and the companies who sponsored the Forum. The build-up coincided with protests against the second Iraq war – a US-led military intervention which the Spanish government supported. This was rather embarrassing for the organisers of the 2004 Forum, who could not officially denounce the war as the national government was one of the main sponsors. Several private sector sponsors were linked to the conflict and this, plus the feeling that the event was over-commercialised, led to scepticism amongst local people. The event failed to make much of an impression outside Spain, and the aim that the main Forum building (designed by Herzog and de Meuron) 'would become one of Barcelona's most emblematic buildings' (Benedicto and Carrasco, 2007: 102) never materialised.

The future?

The net outcomes of the 2004 Universal Forum of Cultures were rather disappointing, especially if we consider that the event was originally promoted as the worthy successor of previous major events staged in Barcelona. The rather underwhelming effects of this event may mean Barcelona moves away from event regeneration in the future. According to Blanco (2009: 362), because of the stark contrast between the outcomes of the Forum and people's needs, the project indicated 'the possible expiry of an urban development model based on major events'. This conclusion concurs with other critics who have commented that Barcelona's 'dependence on major events has led to an emphasis on style rather than substance, which hides an inability to tackle the day to day challenges of urban life' (Benedicto and Carrasco, 2007: 108).

Events and social regeneration

6 From social impacts to social leverage

INTRODUCTION

The previous two chapters focused mainly on physical changes made to cities in association with staging major events. Urban regeneration has traditionally been associated with these place-based transformations to improve infrastructure, housing and local environmental quality. But there is a growing realisation that physical change is not necessarily the best way to encourage wider social and economic development. This is related to the perceived failure of some high-profile property-led projects in the 1980s. There is now increasing pressure for more people-oriented regeneration strategies that focus more on education, work-lessness and health (Lawless, 2010). Greater appreciation of social issues is also something witnessed in the events sphere and more recognition is now given to the social outcomes of event strategies. As will become clear during this chapter, these social effects are not always positive. Initiatives are needed to maximise positive effects, minimise negative social impacts and embed positive changes so that they are sustained in the long term. The key aim of this chapter is to explore whether (and how) events can help to make a positive and sustained contribution to the social regeneration of urban areas.

Automatic impacts versus leveraged outcomes

To understand social regeneration and events, the difference between automatic impacts and leveraged outcomes first needs to be acknowledged. The social impacts of events are the effects of event projects on people. These impacts are different from effects that have been deliberately levered by attaching parallel initiatives to events so that they deliver more optimal outcomes. The latter are referred to as leverage initiatives, defined by Chalip (2004: 228) as 'those activities which need to be undertaken around the event itself which seek to maximise the long-term benefit from events'. Other researchers call this process 'activation' (TSE, 2010). The term of activation stresses that positive action needs to be taken in association with events to achieve desired effects. Using initiatives in conjunction with events can increase the temporal, geographical and demographic scope of an event and allow host cities to address a more diverse range of policy objectives (beyond sport and culture) including those related to health, education, crime prevention, community development and social justice.

This chapter is divided into four main sections. The first is a general introduction to some key concepts within social regeneration. In the second section, research on the social impacts of events is discussed. This is followed by a discussion of the importance of involvement in events to secure positive social effects. In the final section the content is focused on attempts to lever (or activate) wider outcomes.

SOCIAL REGENERATION

Social regeneration involves efforts to achieve 'softer' urban transformations, where people, rather than just places and businesses, are the focus of interventions. Social outcomes occur at a level somewhere between individual and cultural effects. Ohmann *et al.* (2006) make a distinction between social and cultural effects, suggesting that the latter are long-term because they involve a change in social relationships. It is rare for event organisers to advocate events as a way of changing the cultures of host cities. Instead, the aim is usually to achieve sustained improvements in social conditions; in others words, people's quality of life. Regeneration projects try to achieve social effects at the shared, collective level, rather than merely benefits for individuals. Examples of these types of effects are social cohesion, shared identity and pride in place. These social effects are often difficult to achieve. For example, Lawless (2010) suggests that regeneration projects configured outside local mainstream provision have a poor record of delivering collective benefits.

The concept which perhaps best helps us to understand the potential benefits is social capital – interpreted here as the networks, norms and trusts that enable people to work together to pursue shared objectives (Mohan and Mohan, 2002). Social capital is 'owned' by a group of people, rather than something which is made up of individuals' cultural knowledge (cultural capital) or skills/ competencies (human capital). Social capital is usually divided into bridging capital and bonding capital (Putnam, 2000). Bonding capital involves the everyday ties that exist between existing community members – including those that bind families and friendship groups – whereas bridging capital refers to links between community members and other individuals/agencies. The idea of building bridging social capital and achieving greater community cohesion are noted objectives of many event strategies.

Community

In some parts of the contemporary world people's sense that they belong to a community has been challenged by new mobilities and communications technologies. These factors have not necessarily resulted in the demise of communities, but they have resulted in the reconfiguration of communities and the emergence of communities that are not place-based. In this book, where the focus is on urban regeneration, a more conventional sense of community is used – one which is place-based. The cohesion of place-based communities has been challenged by people's increased mobility and by forces in contemporary society that reduce the amount of time people spend in the vicinity of their homes. Some commentators suggest the actions of governments and other influential stakeholders have contributed to the demise of community values. Neo-liberals (see Chapter 2) argue that intervention by governments has contributed to the demise of communities because the state has assumed the welfare roles that communities once performed themselves (Mohan and Mohan, 2002). Others suggest that destructive planning and urban regeneration projects introduced by municipal planners and private developers have caused similar negative effects. Reinstalling a sense of community and (re)building cohesive communities have now become key goals for many government authorities and NGOs at a variety of scales. These aims are also part of the rationale for staging major events. However, it could be argued that attempts to revive community spirit are based on a misconceived and 'rose-tinted' notion that communities in the past were always cohesive, interactive and fully functioning. It is also rather patronising to assume that there is a problem with community spirit in disadvantaged communities – in fact many affluent districts should be envious of this aspect of many working-class communities. And rather than building social capital in communities, authors such as Newman (1999) and Olds (1998) view major events as interventions that *break* social networks and create *distrust*.

A sense of community can be encouraged by allowing new or excluded members to feel part of a collective identity. This requires better relationships and more trust between members; in other words, more social capital. Misener and Mason (2006) argue that events can generate this social capital by generating increased participation and trust. If the local community is involved in the process of hosting events, and if those events embrace the core values of residents, they can assist community development (Misener and Mason, 2006). Misener and Mason also argue that important social networks are created thorough local people's participation in, and their planning and consumption of, events. Events can provide a shared mission – something that also assists community development. Even if some people are not interested in the events themselves, these occasions encourage reflection on the future direction of a place amongst the communities that live there. Discussions and – hopefully – some consensus regarding that direction can provide the basis for community development. Events can also generate a heightened sense of community on a more practical level by generating interactions that would not have taken place otherwise. Importantly, event interactions are often face to face – which are more likely to induce feelings of trust between members (Mohan and Mohan, 2002). These interactions can occur during the event itself or when people attend meetings regarding event preparations.

Events provide an opportunity for people to interact, but also to celebrate. This celebratory aspect explains why events are often credited with an increase in community spirit. Burgan and Mules (1992) use the term 'psychic income' to refer to this effect. This is not only an outcome of an event, but a possible explanation for the popularity of events. Ehrenreich (2007) uses Durkheim's notion of collective effervescence to explain the significance of events. The collective effervescence people feel during major events may have a residual effect where people experience an increase in shared morale or a heightened sense of belonging. This may be more important in a more mobile world where migration is common. The inclusion of new and previously excluded members can be encouraged if an event has an international dimension, or a theme which is not grounded in embedded in (potentially divisive) historic events. This is relevant to the one-off major events that provide the focus of this book. Nevertheless, there are some possible problems with using events to assist community development. Events can strengthen communities, but this may only happen where there is already sufficient social capital. This means they are perhaps less suited to dysfunctional communities – where social regeneration may be most needed. Furthermore, Olds (1998) suggests that major events merely create an 'artificial' sense of unity in communities – one that is deliberately engineered to sanction controversial developments that would not normally be allowed.

Civic pride

Pride in place or civic pride is strongly related to community consciousness. But civic pride is a looser concept than community (Wood, 2006). This looseness can be helpful in that cities with a diverse population can aspire to raising levels of pride without asking citizens to subscribe to a homogeneous identity. Pride in place is not merely something which is built from within: it is determined by how we see ourselves, but also by how others see us. Therefore, pride in place can be improved by enhancing external place image as well as by improving local perceptions. There are seemingly many benefits of civic pride. The more pride people take in where they live, the more likely they are to act as 'stewards' for their local environment. This can cause a virtuous circle of improvements. Furthermore, if people are proud of where they live, they are more likely to stay there, more likely to promote the place to others and more likely to participate in activities that contribute positively to a place's future. This can assist regeneration. Achieving more pride in place is a key objective of some event regeneration projects. For example, one of the main aims of the organisers of London's 2012 Olympic Games was to turn East London into a 'place of choice' – in other words one that people want to live in, not one that they reside in because of historical accident or economic circumstances.

Alongside feelings of community and pride, events can inspire people to participate more in certain activities. These activities range from greater participation in local organisations, to sport and cultural pursuits. Such activities may – directly or indirectly – contribute towards an individual's or a community's well-being. Events are often credited with generating a feel good factor, but they may make a more positive contribution to social regeneration if they also encourage a 'do-good factor' (Smith, 2009). Increased community spirit and civic pride can result in significant regeneration benefits if people are then inspired to engage in certain activities – either by helping others or by reducing the burden they themselves place on society. Of course, events are also associated with a series of negative social impacts. The most damaging of these is the displacement of existing residents (see Chapter 5), something that destroys networks and erodes people's attachment to and pride in places.

THE SOCIAL IMPACTS OF EVENTS

It is widely recognised that events can cause a range of social impacts; and various positive impacts may provide the basis for social regeneration. Whilst these social impacts are undoubtedly important, they are sometimes lazily cited by host cities to justify events when promised economic impacts have not materialised. Social impacts are hard to measure, allowing host cities to evade detailed assessment and scrutiny. Even when attempts have been made to assess these impacts, the quality of the research has been questionable. McCartney *et al.*'s (2010) meta-evaluation of fifty-four studies found that most impact studies used a basic cross-sectional design rather than a comparison group, suggesting that a large proportion of the research has a high risk of bias. Overall, the authors decided that there was insufficient evidence to confirm or refute the health and socio-economic benefits of major sport events.

Table 6.1 Research projects that address the social impacts of major events

Author(s)	Event	Sample size	When research undertaken	Main positive impacts	Main negative impacts
Ritchie and Lyons (1990)	1988 Winter Olympic Games, Calgary	400 residents	Immediately after event	Recognition for city (50%), reputation/image (14%), citizen pride (9%), community cohesion (5%)	Not enough community involvement (28%), commercialisation (23%)
Waitt (2003)	2000 Olympic Games, Sydney	658 residents before and 178 in 2000 (results here apply to 2000)	During event and two years before	Sense of community inspired by Olympic spirit (68%), international promotion	No personal rewards, opportunity costs
Nylund (2006)	2005 World Athletics Championships, Helsinki	1,000 residents	Immediately after event	International attention (61%), sports (26%), revitalisation (19%)	Traffic jams (47%), littering (11%), crime (8%)

Table 6.1 Continued

Author(s)	Event	Sample size	When research undertaken	Main positive impacts	Main negative impacts
Ohmann, Jones and Wilkes (2006)	2006 World Cup, Munich	130 residents	Immediately after event	Improved sense of community and improved relationships between people of different ethnic origin (88%), atmosphere (38%)	Increase in prostitution (21%), crime (12%), noise, bad fan behaviour (11%)
Bob and Swart(2009)	2010 World Cup, Cape Town	200 residents (results here apply to 100 in city only)	Five years before event	Training and skills (72%), community will benefit (68%)	Crime (65%), price increases (65%), congestion (46%), noise (43%)

Although they may be of comparatively low scientific quality there have been several empirical assessments of the social impacts of events. The key findings of some of this research are summarised in Table 6.1.

Attitudes towards major events

It is often said that the regenerative capacity of major events can be explained by the way they resonate with people. This suggests that it is people's positive attitude towards events that helps to provide the gateway for wider effects. According to empirical research undertaken in the immediate aftermath of major events, residents tend to have positive attitudes towards them. For example, Ritchie and Lyon's (1990) survey of 400 Calgary residents found that 98 per cent were supportive of the decision to stage the 1988 Winter Olympic Games. Interestingly, subsequent research published by Ritchie (2000) suggests that 90 per cent of residents continue to view the 1988 Games as a positive experience, for them personally and for the city. Attitudes have also been tracked in the period before an event takes place. This is important because several authors imply that the pre-event period (sometimes referred to as the pregnancy or sunrise of an event) is when positive impacts can occur. Longitudinal research by Waitt (2003), Ritchie and Aitken (1984, 1985) and Ritchie and Lyons (1987, 1990) suggests that residents' attitudes tend to become more positive as an event approaches. For example, support for the Calgary Games climbed steadily from an approval rating of 85 per cent in 1983 to 98 per cent (Ritchie and Lyons, 1990). Waitt's (2003) research (conducted in 1998 and 2000) found that during the Sydney Olympic Games local residents were much more enthusiastic about the event than they had been two years previously. Fears about negative impacts (e.g. cost of living increases) lessened 1998–2000 as the reality of hosting the event became apparent (Waitt, 2003).

Public support for a major event varies from example to example, but most research findings suggest a generally positive attitude. This contradicts critical accounts of major events that tend to represent them as dubious propaganda projects. Critical accounts tend to presume that any support for event projects is a result of some form of socialisation. Urban boosters are presumed to have somehow 'duped' residents through the hype and propaganda associated with an event. A slightly different interpretation is that events bewilder residents by throwing a range of discourses at them that people find hard to process; thus disabling them from opposing the event (Boyle, 1997). These critical accounts tend to discount the possibility that residents' responses can be both informed and positive. Attitudes may defy logical explanation but that does not mean they should be discounted. Some authors (e.g. Atkinson *et al.*, 2008; Walton *et al.*, 2008) have tried to estimate the monetary value of the social effects of staging events, but it is important not to be too obsessed with economic measures of value. This is emphasised by one of Waitt's (2003: 210) respondents who stated that even though the 2000 Olympic Games were an expensive project, this expense was justified in terms of the community spirit generated alone: 'yes, for the community spirit, even if it cost ten billion'. This feeling of pricelessness corresponds with MacRury and Poynter's (2008) notion that event legacies can be understood as 'gifts', which can be considered outside the framework of rational cost–benefit analyses.

Factors affecting attitudes

As well as monitoring overall resident attitudes towards major events, it is important to understand how attitudes vary amongst different groups. This is especially important if events are designed to assist particular sections of society – e.g. disadvantaged citizens. Dodouras and James (2007) state that although most Athenians were strongly positive about their city hosting the 2004 Olympic Games, levels of support for the Games were particularly high amongst low-income earners and pensioners. Waitt's (2003) research found that Sydney's 2000 Olympic Games were most positively regarded by younger adults, families with children and migrants from non-English speaking backgrounds. These are all groups targeted in social regeneration initiatives – highlighting the potential of events to engage target beneficiaries.

In Sydney, feelings of community and national spirit were deemed to be the most powerful psychological rewards of staging the Games. Waitt's (2003) research indicated that migrants held more positive views because the event encouraged them to feel part of an Olympic-inspired community. There was a slightly different explanation for positive attitudes amongst young parents. Adults with young children felt that the event helped to illustrate the principles of global citizenship, social equity and respect for cultural difference to their offspring (Waitt, 2003). These findings seem to demonstrate that, even though the media have become sceptical about Olympic values and the credibility of Olympism as a social movement, these notions still seem relevant to the residents of host cities that stage the event. This was also apparent in Ritchie and Lyons' (1990) research into the Calgary Olympics (1988) where 87.5 per cent of residents thought a positive aspect of the event was that it would help nations to understand each other better. Even in assessments of FIFA World Cups, where national rivalries tend to be greater, recent evidence suggests events can be a force for international understanding, rather than ethnic division (Ohmann et al., 2006).

The variables that affect the level of social impact in a host city seem to include where residents live. During the Sydney Olympic Games, the proximity of respondents' homes to the main site at Homebush Bay affected levels of enthusiasm – the nearer they lived the more positive they were (Waitt, 2003). Waitt (2003) attributes this to demographics and the expectation of material rewards: those living near Homebush Bay were more likely to be younger, and more likely to benefit from the legacy of new facilities provided (Waitt, 2003). This finding is not necessarily repeated elsewhere. In Helsinki, negative attitudes towards the 2005 World Athletics Championships were caused by feelings of irritation and inconvenience (particularly because of increased traffic) and these were more common amongst those living near to the stadium (Nylund, 2006). However, it should be noted that even amongst these people, attitudes to the event in general were still generally positive.

Specific social benefits

Whilst positive attitudes amongst residents can be deemed a positive social outcome in itself, it is also useful to explore the range of different social benefits deemed to have been generated by events. In Nylund's (2006) research into the World Athletics Championships, the main emotional responses were satisfaction (59 per cent), excitement (56 per cent), pride in Helsinki (52 per cent) and the creation of a special atmosphere (16 per cent). The pride generated in Helsinki links well to the discussion of civic pride above. In Ritchie and Lyons' (1990) research into the 1988 Calgary Winter Olympics, social benefits such as citizen pride (9 per cent), bringing people together (5 per cent), meeting other people (4 per cent) and excitement/atmosphere (3 per cent) were cited by fewer people than recognition for the city (50 per cent), tourism (36 per cent), economic benefits (34 per cent), Olympic facilities (21 per cent) and city image (14 per cent). This rather undermines Ritchie's (2000) subsequent conclusion that 'the most profound legacy' of the 1988 Games was the generation of feelings of civic pride and social cohesion.

Mechanisms for behavioural change

One of the most important social effects of events is inspiring behaviour change – in particular the way that they supposedly stimulate participation in cultural, sporting and community activities. This effect is commonly used as a key justification for staging major events, but there is little evidence that events cause increased levels of activity.

Events are supposed to help change behaviour in two ways:

- First, through the high-profile 'demonstration' of excellence that will inspire other people to take up cultural or sporting pursuits. In the UK, the example of tennis is often used to justify this 'demonstration effect'. After the annual

All England Championships at Wimbledon the nation's parks tend to be full of people playing tennis. The challenge is to sustain such effects so that they deliver long-term changes in behaviour.

- The second way that major events can generate behavioural effects is through what are termed 'festivalisation' effects (Weed *et al.*, 2009). This is when people are affected because of the excitement and positive associations attached to events. The hype before events and special atmosphere created during an event can encourage people to engage with certain programmes, behaviours and activities that they may otherwise have ignored. Festivalisation effects rely on the spirit of the event as the mechanism for the effects, rather than the specific activity on display. The idea is that these effects may deliver more participation in a range of activities, rather than just participation in a certain sport or cultural activity.

There are noted problems with both the mechanisms outlined above. Evidence suggests that the demonstration effect may only really work when people are already engaged with a certain activity. In a study of Helsinki's residents after the city staged the World Athletics Championships, 72 per cent of those who undertook regular exercise found the Games inspiring, whilst amongst occasional participants the proportion was only 43 per cent (Nylund, 2006). This raises an important question. Do events merely inspire the already inspired? Events seem to have the most obvious effects on those people who are already involved in a sport or cultural activity, or lapsed participants who were previously involved and who have stopped for some reason. An event may rekindle their interest, but major events do not have a strong record of inspiring *new* participants.

Furthermore, with respect to sport events, researchers have noted that certain events may lead to a *switching effect*: people who participate in one sport may switch to another activity because of their exposure to an inspiring event (Weed *et al.*, 2009). Again, this doesn't add to the overall number of people participating in sport/activity. A more fundamental problem with the demonstration effect is that elite performances may actually dissuade amateur enthusiasts from attempting to emulate performers/athletes. This is known as the *aversion effect*. People may be intimidated by exceptional talent and feel that they would never be able to reach such standards, so don't bother trying. This is why some researchers think events have actually led to decreased participation rates following an event (Coalter, 2004).

The available evidence suggests that major sport events do not tend to cause increases in participation rates. A good example is the 2002 Manchester Commonwealth Games. Even though the event was generally deemed to be a success, overall sports participation (defined as one activity per week, excluding walking) decreased by 2 per cent in the area after the city staged the event (MORI, 2004). Coalter (2004) outlines how sports participation also declined after the Sydney Olympic Games. He concluded that staging displays of excellence may not be a very effective method to increase participation. Instead of staging major events he recommends investing directly in local facilities. Indeed, major events may be detrimental to levels of activity because they are often used as an excuse to reduce public sector investment. Rather than generating new investment, funding is shifted from grassroots activities to event budgets. This highlights another important point – there is no point inspiring people to take up cultural or sporting activity if the provision of tuition and facilities remains deficient. Even if events do inspire participation, allowing people to act on this is something that needs to be considered by event hosts. This highlights the importance of considering social regeneration initiatives alongside more conventional physical projects.

Negative impacts

Whilst overall assessments of social impacts tend to be positive or neutral, most events are still responsible for causing some negative effects. The most damaging impacts are those involving the displacement of people from their homes – these are dealt with in Chapter 5. Displacement can also occur on a more temporary basis. In Ohmann *et al.*'s (2006) research, 39 per cent of residents surveyed in Munich tended to stay away from local facilities and amenities during the 2006 FIFA World Cup. And in the build-up to the Athens Olympic Games people were worried that the Games would exacerbate problems of overcrowding, violence, poor planning and environmental degradation (Dodouras and James, 2007). Other negative impacts that frequently occur include the temporary problems regarding the inconvenience, extra traffic and noise generated in the period when construction works are being completed and during events.

More worrying social impacts associated with major events are increases in crime, prostitution and heightened fears for personal safety. Crime and security risks were noted by 8 per cent of the population as a key disadvantage of the 2005 IAAF World Athletics Championships in Helsinki (Nylund, 2006). Trying to prove any causal relationship between major events and rates of crime is difficult, particularly as the population of any city tends to rise during the time of an event, which makes more crime inevitable (Barker *et al.*, 2002). Events attract tourists, and this raises the number of potential victims (and criminals), particularly as tourists are regarded as soft targets for petty crime. Barker *et al.*'s (2002: 779) study of crime levels during the America's Cup in Auckland (October 1999–March 2000) concluded that the variables associated with the event 'were more favourable in deterring crime than increasing it at a rate greater than the proportional increase in population'. In other words, crime was not as much of a problem as one might have expected.

If events are a source of civic pride and community spirit then one might expect levels of crime and anti-social behaviour committed by residents to fall in the aftermath of an event. Reported vandalism in Manchester decreased after the 2002 Commonwealth Games (Newby, 2003). Ohmann *et al*.'s (2006) research into the 2006 World Cup dealt with perceptions of crime and this study also provides evidence that the commonly held belief that events expose communities to increased levels of crime is overstated. A large majority (88 per cent) of respondents (in Munich) disagreed with the statement that hosting the 2006 World Cup resulted in an increase in crime. There were other interesting aspects of Ohmann *et al*.'s (2006) research findings. When respondents were given a chance to voluntarily offer other comments, fifty-one respondents (out of 130) said that they felt an increased sense of security during the event and that this was a positive effect for them. This shows that major events – and the security arrangements that now surround them – may actually make people safer. Events are often criticised for over-zealous security measures, but it is interesting to note that some urban communities may actually appreciate them.

THE IMPORTANCE OF INVOLVEMENT

The degree to which increased involvement in an event increases positive social impacts and restricts negative social impacts is an important issue. A particularly interesting question is what level of engagement is needed to optimise social impacts. There are different ways that people are involved in events and this means different levels of engagement with an event. These include:

- Performing
- Volunteering
- Spectating
- Watching on television
- Reading about events in the media
- Knowing about events within your locality.

More research is needed on how these different types of engagement influence the social outcomes of event projects – in particular how they affect the likelihood of a demonstration effect. The proximity of target beneficiaries to an event is also an interesting issue. Even if some of the demonstration effects of events could be proved, with modern communication technologies such effects could be felt anywhere in the world. Most people 'experience' major events via television and newspaper coverage. This may lead to certain social effects. For example, Pillay and Bass (2008) cite a study that found that the place most significantly affected by the 1998 FIFA World Cup (staged in France) was Brazil. Similarly, one of the most successful examples of an event inspiring people to take up sport was the 2003 Rugby World Cup in Australia. This encouraged more young people to play the sport in England – the nation that won the tournament. If events are staged and funded at the city level, there needs to be more evidence that they will inspire local people. Otherwise, it may be more expedient for governments to leverage effects from events staged elsewhere.

As well as the different types of engagement listed above, residents in host cities can be involved in the planning and operation of events. Involvement can take various forms and can take place at different stages of the event lifecycle. Community-based initiatives can integrate local people within the planning, delivery and impacts of projects – depending on the approach of event organisers and the levels of interest and capabilities of community members. The most common forms of community involvement in event projects are:

- Consultation on key decisions
- Delivery roles such as workers/volunteers
- Attending events or subsidiary events.

The ultimate aim should be to encourage a sense of local ownership, which Raco (2004) describes as a key factor that affects the success of any event project. This means removing practical constraints to community participation – which in turn can leave a positive legacy of community capacity building. As Raco (2004) suggests, despite the pressures at the early stage of event projects to justify plans to rights holders and other stakeholders, organisers need to promote realistic expectations of what could be achieved. Ideally, community involvement in event projects should start before the bidding stage, because once events have been bid for, and won, event projects gain momentum and it is difficult to make anything but cosmetic changes. Some good practice has emerged from Canada. In one of the more enlightened major event bids, Toronto's authorities approved the provision of funding to allow community groups to participate more meaningfully in the discussion and evaluation of the city's bid for the 2008 Olympic Games (Olds, 1998).

There have been several high-profile instances of events where public engagement has been notably poor. Tokenistic involvement of communities is common, and Lowes (2002) describes how organisers of an Indy Car Race in Vancouver tried to use free tickets and vague promises of job opportunities to convince the local community to develop a new circuit in a public park. Attendance at events, or at subsidiary events, is a slightly different type of involvement. At some events the proportion of attendees that are local people is very low – a problem exacerbated by regulatory and commercial pressures that mean privileging local/ disadvantaged people in ticket distribution systems is difficult. Whilst some tickets may be promised to local people, or low-income groups, these commitments are not always kept. Even when they are offered, these tickets are often for the least popular days/events, making them unattractive to target beneficiaries. This was the case in Sydney in the run-up to the 2000 Olympic Games where the take-up of 'social inclusion' tickets was very poor. The organisers promised 1.5 million tickets to schools and disadvantaged people. This was later reduced to 735,000, but only 20 per cent of these were actually sold (Thamnopoulos and Gargalianos, 2002).

It is debatable whether it is more ethical to offer subsidised tickets to deserving beneficiaries or to minimise negative financial legacies by maximising the commercial potential of an event. The solution to this conundrum depends largely on the destination of ticket revenues. For expensive event projects funded and managed by public sector agencies, attempts to maximise the revenues earned seem justified as long as monies are not siphoned off by rights holders. If the local area is paying for an event, or underwriting losses, then maximising revenues may actually work in the best interests of vulnerable community members who may rely on welfare services.

In this section we are most concerned with social effects and so a critical issue is whether effects envisaged from events – such as community development, civic pride and inspiration – require attendance or are amplified by attendance. If so, then there would seem to be a strong justification for improving access for local people, particularly target beneficiaries. However, there is some evidence that attendance is not a critical factor in delivering social benefits. In Ohmann *et al.*'s (2006) research there was no significant difference between the views of those residents who attended public screenings of the 2006 FIFA World Cup and those who did not (Figure 6.1). Both sample groups felt the event strengthened the sense of community and improved relationships between different ethnic groups. This suggests social impacts rely more on the general hype and atmosphere surrounding events than the 'action' itself. This corresponds with the idea of festivalisation effects (see above), and the view that much of the positive social impact of events occurs in the build-up and anticipation of an event, rather than its actual manifestation (Anderson and Holden, 2008).

There is evidence that residents would like to be involved more in major events and that when they are more involved they tend to get more from them. After the 1988 Winter Olympics, 64 per cent of Calgary's residents thought there had not been not enough community activities for city residents prior to and during the Games (Ritchie and Lyons, 1990). This involvement – particularly that which takes place at higher levels – is deemed to be a key factor in determining overall attitudes to events. This was the conclusion of research by Lim and Lee (2006). Their survey of 1,204 residents revealed that the main factor determining

Figure 6.1 *Hernan Crespo, Javier Mascherano and the Brandenburg Gate tower above the FIFA FanFest staged in Berlin during the 2006 FIFA World Cup*

residents' attitudes to Korean Expo events was their willingness to collaborate. The authors conclude that 'event organisers need to induce community members to participate more actively' by encouraging them to attend events and act as volunteers (Lim and Lee, 2006: 419). Waitt (2003) suggests people are more likely to be positive if they have participated in an event's planning.

It seems logical that the more citizens are involved in the planning, management and outcomes of an event, the more supportive they are likely to be. But the cause and effect relationship here is not clear. We are not sure whether a positive attitude follows from involvement in an event, or whether a positive attitude to an event encourages involvement in the first instance. If we accept the former explanation then this may be because community groups have influenced key decisions that direct events and their legacies towards their own needs. But often involvement is encouraged simply to legitimise events by 'co-opting' community support. Boyle (1997) thinks the co-option of community groups is one way that legitimacy is achieved by urban propaganda projects.

Individual versus social benefits

The notion of individual versus community-wide benefits also deserves consideration. When asked what the main benefits of staging an event are, many residents reply that it is good for the image, profile and/or economy of the area. These are public benefits, rather than individual ones. As Waitt's (2003) research suggests, there does seem to be a willingness to accept public expenditure on events. Overall attitudes towards events still seem to be positive, even if personal benefits are minimal. However, when there are perceived to be significant personal costs with few benefits, residents are likely to be negative about events. This conforms to the principles of social exchange theory. This theory postulates that those who perceive to have gained net benefits from an intervention will think positively and vice versa. Therefore, it is interesting to consider perceptions of residents regarding who benefited from a major event. Nylund (2006) conducted 1,000 interviews with residents immediately after the 2005 World Championships in Helsinki. Whilst most people (c.58 per cent) were generally satisfied with the event, residents felt the main beneficiaries were the sports community (40 per cent), the whole nation (34 per cent), companies (25 per cent), with only 22 per cent citing that Helsinki was a principal beneficiary.

Unfortunately, it seems that where no efforts are made to direct the effects of events, they may gravitate to those who *least* need them. Evidence suggests that areas already exhibiting high social capital and a strong sense of community are more likely to benefit from major events. For example, research into the 2002 Winter Olympics in Salt Lake City concluded that 'residents who expressed a high level of attachment to their communities are more likely to view hosting a mega event as beneficial' (Gursoy and Kendall, 2006: 618). The event may have helped to encourage community affiliation, but it is more likely that this affiliation existed prior to the event. This suggests that, rather than being an outcome of events, social capital is an important prerequisite that influences attitudes/ benefits (Smith, 2009). More conventional forms of capital may also be required to unlock social development opportunities. Those able to access events, and any social benefits that come from attendance, are perhaps more likely to view them positively. If public funds are used this represents a significant opportunity cost for excluded groups. As Tranter and Keefe (2004: 182) remind us, adopting an event strategy 'typically marginalises significant sections of society that are not interested in the events or lack the financial means to experience them'. This position contradicts the notion that major events are useful regeneration tools because they mobilise engagement from disadvantaged urban citizens.

If events are to deliver regeneration, then social impacts not only need to be observed but they need to be sustained in the post-event era. There is some evidence to suggest that the opposite effects can occur – when an event has finished there may be an anti-climactic 'hangover'. An extreme example is provided by Clark (2008), who suggests that local suicide rates in Sydney declined in the run-up to the 2000 Olympic Games, but increased in the post-event period.

LEVERED OUTCOMES

One of the central principles that recurs consistently in this book is that it is inadvisable to rely on major events to automatically assist the regeneration of urban areas. Events should not be seen as interventions in themselves, but as opportunities to achieve progress using initiatives timed to coincide with an event. To achieve social regeneration via events, relevant authorities can intro-duce supplementary initiatives and policies. These help to lever positive social outcomes from the event – using the publicity and 'hook' of the event to bolster social initiatives. Just like well-planned physical regeneration projects that use events to help achieve established urban objectives, major events can be levered to achieve existing social policy ambitions. Successful initiatives are often those designed around social regeneration objectives – rather than led by the requirements and characteristics of the event itself. The event becomes the 'lever' with which wider ambitions are achieved. Leverage pursued alongside events can deliver more diverse effects and they may help any positive effects to be sustained.

Unfortunately, an emerging role of event leverage is as a form of justification for the event itself. Social leverage initiatives have become part of the official response to criticisms that large investments in event venues are not helping people in need. The budgets for leverage projects are usually disproportionately small compared to the amount of publicity they receive (and tiny compared to the overall costs of staging events). Accordingly, there is a need to ensure social initiatives are not merely used as PR tools to deflect criticisms about poor returns from event spending.

Although the cost of social leverage initiatives may be minimal compared to the overall costs of staging a major event, they do add to the overall financial burden. The idea is to make the most of the opportunity. But if projects are unsuccessful or if they rely too heavily on events that are unsuccessful, host cities can be accused of unnecessarily adding to the costs of an event. For example, one high-profile critic of the London 2012 Olympic Games suggested that the organisers' 'big mistake' … 'was to tip into their budget a mass of feel-good junk about legacy' (Jenkins, 2007). Social leverage initiatives also make the task of evaluat-ing the social impacts of events more difficult. Researchers now find it hard to separate the outcomes of the event from the effects of supplementary initiatives undertaken in association with events.

Management issues

One of the interesting aspects of social leverage initiatives is who should design and implement them. In practice, there are four stakeholders who normally take on this responsibility:

- Event managers (LOCs)
- Local governments
- Voluntary organisations/community groups
- Event rights holders and their sponsors.

Experience suggests that the optimal arrangement involves funding and co-ordination at the event management level, with local stakeholders in the public and voluntary sectors encouraged to design and tailor initiatives to suit target beneficiaries (Smith, 2008). Initiatives introduced by rights holders (e.g. IOC, FIFA) tend to be those aiming to legitimise the event, rather than satisfying local long-term policy objectives.

The different objectives of event-themed social regeneration projects

Social regeneration initiatives often try to capitalise on some of the essential features of events – their popularity, their international significance and related thematic associations. This suggests close parallels with the festivalisation effect noted above – where effects rely on the wider emotional pull of an event rather than a specific activity. Thematic associations have been used to help achieve a number of social policy goals, including:

1 Enhancing community cohesion
2 Encouraging local involvement and civic responsibility
3 Increasing employability
4 Assisting education
5 Encouraging healthier lifestyles
6 Improving attitudes towards, and experiences of, persons with a disability.

These objectives are reviewed in more detail below.

Community cohesion

Many contemporary cities are extremely diverse, and they are likely to become even more diverse in the future. Making migrant communities feel welcome, whilst building a wider collective identity, is difficult. One way that events can be used to assist community cohesion is by providing an institution around which a range of social groups can coalesce. Most major events only interest a specific part of a community. However, leverage initiatives can be introduced to assist broader effects. Effective social leverage initiatives often draw upon one element of an event and use this to achieve broader policy aims. In the example of an international sport event, rather than merely focusing on a particular sport, host cities can focus attention on an event's international dimension. This can help to engage international communities.

Interestingly, some evidence suggests that migrant communities are often the most positive about staging international events. Relevant research has found that 'global sporting events can operate to help ethnic minorities recognise themselves as wider of a wider national community' (Waitt, 2003: 207). Waitt's research was based on the social impacts of Sydney's Olympic Games. The view amongst the local population was that the event helped to dissipate perceived differences between people of different ethnic groups (Waitt, 2003). Some host cities have decided to capitalise on this outcome of international events and try to lever more pronounced – and longer lasting – effects. A good example is the 2006 Commonwealth Games in Melbourne, Victoria where an 'Equal First' legacy programme was implemented. This strategy focused on five key priorities: diversity, accessibility, inclusive employment opportunities, connecting and celebrating cultures and active/inclusive communities. As this list emphasises, a key aim was to develop tolerance and cohesion amongst the highly diverse communities that live in Victoria State. More than 44.5 per cent of Victorians were born overseas or have at least one parent born overseas, and 20 per cent originate from countries where English is not the main or official language (Renzaho, 2008).

One of the main vehicles for delivering community cohesion in Victoria was the 'adopt a second team initiative'. Each of the seventy-nine municipalities in the state was assigned one of the competing national teams. Municipalities were encouraged to develop projects – workshops, schools initiatives and events – to forge links with the respective nation (Kellett *et al.*, 2008). As well as the benefits of increased tolerance and awareness of other cultures, the initiative delivered other positive outcomes. Working relationships between some local governments and schools were enhanced and the projects helped to make the Commonwealth Games a more meaningful event for local people in peripheral parts of the region (Kellett *et al.*, 2008). For inherently multinational events like the Commonwealth Games, adopting diversity initiatives seems particularly appropriate. Visiting competitors or teams from abroad can be used as the fulcrum for these projects. As Kellett *et al.* (2008: 103) identify, 'from the standpoint of fostering relationship and cultural learning while building a sense of excitement and community pride visiting teams seem an ideal resource'.

Encouraging local involvement and civic responsibility

The perceived failure of interventionist government means that many politicians and commentators suggest that the solution to society's social problems lies within communities themselves. Hence the rise of the localism and big society agendas in the UK and other developed countries. Whilst major events may be seen as the antithesis of local action, in some cases they may inspire people to take a more active role in their communities. This may be one of the positive outcomes of heightened civic pride caused by a major event. Volunteering programmes are good examples of projects that help to link events to community objectives. Experiencing what can be achieved when volunteers work together may inspire people to offer their services for other types of community work. Volunteering for events gives people access to training and work experience and it allows them to experience the sense of fulfilment that can result from contributing positively to their community.

To achieve long-term benefits for communities, event volunteers need to become regular volunteers. Several studies suggest that volunteers may continue to offer their services after an event has finished. Over half of the volunteers for the Melbourne 2006 Commonwealth Games stated that they wanted to keep volunteering (Insight Economics, 2006). Similar figures were revealed by Ralston et al.'s (2005) research into the 2002 Commonwealth Games where c.42 per cent of the 698 volunteers surveyed stated that the Games made them more inclined to offer their services as a volunteer in the future. Interestingly, this figure was similar for those with (40.9 per cent) and without previous volunteering experience (42.7 per cent) (Ralston et al., 2005). However, there are doubts about whether these good intentions are carried out. This reticence has prompted radical suggestions. During the build-up to the 2012 London Olympic Games, eminent sports coach Tom McNab suggested to the local organising committee (LOCOG) that 'all of the 80,000 Olympic volunteers be required as part of their contract to serve another year of voluntary activity' (McNab, 2010). McNab (2010) believed that this was a way to provide a 'guaranteed Olympic legacy'.

In volunteering projects, the priority for event organisers is usually to recruit the required numbers and the best candidates. This may mean hiring people who are already active volunteers. More enlightened host cities have tried to find ways to ensure that people who don't usually volunteer are included. This is a way to expand the number of volunteers in communities. Thinking more carefully about who can access opportunities means places can be allocated to help people who need them most. If people from disadvantaged areas can access volunteer placements, this provides valuable work experience and may encourage them to take a role in assisting their own community in the future. And if volunteering projects are designed with extra training, associated qualifications and places for disadvantaged people they become less like cost-effective management tactics and more like social regeneration projects. One of the most positive developments in recent years is the rise of pre-volunteering programmes (PVPs). These aim to train volunteers from disadvantaged areas/groups to help them access volunteer placements when they become available. This ensures that a proportion of the overall volunteer force is drawn from disadvantaged groups.

Other community regeneration initiatives include projects that seek to support groups who want to enhance their own neighbourhoods in advance of an event. Funding is provided for small-scale projects that focus on environmental improvements. Projects such as these have two main benefits. First, they guarantee that at least some community-based regeneration is pursued in association with events. This helps to assuage criticism that event regeneration is a top-down process which is imposed on communities. Second, encouraging communities to take on their own projects helps to build capacity and this means local groups may be able to lead future community-based regeneration projects. An example of this type of scheme was the London 2012 'Changing Places' programme that ran 2009–2011. This fund helped communities surrounding the Olympic Park to undertake small projects that enhanced their local area during the run-up to the Games in London. Applications for up to £1,000 could be made and the scheme was restricted to not-for profit organisations based in Olympic boroughs. Whilst this type of project seems laudable, the amount of funding involved (especially when compared to the budgets for the main venues) suggests it is best understood as a form of tokenism, rather than a shift towards a genuine community-based approach.

Pre-employment schemes for disadvantaged individuals

Many social regeneration projects aim to help individuals who need assistance to get their lives 'back on track'. This benefits them individually, but it also means that their net contribution to society is more positive. These individuals are sometimes hard to reach via conventional social policy and one advantage of event projects is that they can engage people who may have previously been reluctant to get involved (e.g. young men). As Coalter (2010) states, one way of using sport events strategically is by deploying them as a type of 'fly paper' to get young people into education and training. Schemes usually involve some form of pre-employment assistance. Training (both informal and formal), work placements, personal support and taster sessions can be provided to get people in a position where they can apply for jobs. These projects are often undertaken in conjunction with volunteering programmes. Shaw's (2009) research into an event in Dunedin, New Zealand, showed how this process might work. One of the volunteers was a woman who had lost confidence in her ability to find and do paid work. According to Shaw's (2009: 32) interviews: 'She did a little bit of work pre-Games and then she worked during the Games. And now she's back to the stage where she's applying for jobs.'

Pre-employment initiatives associated with events can be linked directly to event-related employment. For example, there have been projects that provide pre-employment training for the construction, media, hospitality, sports and cultural industries sectors. In some instances these schemes allow people to apply for work that is linked to a specific event, but normally projects are set up so that people can enter the employment market more generally. The event merely provides the inspiration for the target beneficiary and a 'hook' to get them interested in the scheme. The main difficulty with getting unemployed people involved directly in event-related employment in the pre-event period is the tight timescale involved. Projects need to be set up very early if they are to provide pre-employment training for work that needs to be completed before an event takes place. Because of time pressures, event delivery agencies tend to be more obsessed with the efficiency of their work rather than the wider social benefits of employment. Nevertheless, proactive event organisers have set up dedicated academies which aim to train people to work on event projects. The confidence, contacts, experience and cv points gained by working on high-profile event projects makes it more likely that these people will gain permanent employment after the event.

Pre-employment schemes are often dedicated to specific disadvantaged groups. This ensures target beneficiaries are assisted. The range of groups that can be engaged by one major event is demonstrated by the projects funded by the London 2012 Opportunities Fund set up in the run-up to the 2012 Olympic Games. This £30 million fund was established by the London Development Agency and it assisted a range of social projects. These were generally led by third-sector agencies. A selection of pre-employment projects that were funded is listed in Table 6.2 (LDA, 2007). This table demonstrates the range of groups that can be targeted by event schemes and the range of employment sectors that disadvantaged people can be helped into.

Education programmes

If long-term societal change in disadvantaged areas is the aim, then it makes sense to engage young people. Targeting young people can help them to develop good habits at an early age and educate them more generally. The more people engage with learning at a young age, the more likely they are to stay in education and achieve their objectives in life. Educational engagement and attainment can be assisted by event-themed initiatives. Major events can be linked to a range of academic subjects and their popularity may make learning more interesting – especially for disaffected students who are turned off by 'dry'

Table 6.2 Pre-employment projects funded through the London 2012 Opportunities Fund

Name of project	Target group	Employment sector
Lansbury Lodge Women's project	Women	General
Choice Pathways	'At risk' young people	General
New Horizons	People on incapacity benefit	General
Enterprise in Sight	Visually impaired people	General
Real Life London	Ethnic minorities	General
Pathways for Disabled People as Coaches	Disabled people	Sport
Deaf Active	Deaf people	General
Morph Carpentry	16–18 year olds not in employment, education or training	Carpentry and joinery
Skills for Working with Food	Deprived communities	Food and hospitality
Cultivating Skills	Homeless people	Horticulture
Sporting Chance	Unemployed people	General
New Steps	Mentally ill people	Office work, gardening, painting/decorating
Employ your Languages	Refugees	Language related work

academic subjects. This means they may be useful in under-performing schools in disadvantaged areas. There is a useful knock-on effect in that event-themed education also helps to build anticipation amongst young people for the event. This is helpful but it also raises the possibility that event education initiatives become little more than extensions of event propaganda into the educational sphere.

Event-themed educational initiatives usually involve the production of educational resources. These are often specific materials – including lesson plans, suggestions for links to school curricula, as well as multi-media materials to support learning. The resources are primarily aimed at teachers who may be able to include them in conventional sessions or in dedicated classes. Some host cities like Vancouver (host city of the 2010 Winter Olympic Games) have developed online forums that allow teachers to share ideas and resources. This helps to build on good ideas from within the teaching profession, rather than patronising teachers by telling them what they should be doing/how to do their jobs.

One way to ensure that schoolchildren engage with this learning is to ensure it culminates with (or includes) a visit to the event itself (or at least the event site). Many host cities have provided reduced rates or free tickets for certain schools. It is also common for event organisers to co-ordinate visits of performers/athletes into schools to support event-themed learning. Others have sent certain students to conferences in advance of an event to encourage them to lead event-themed projects of their own. For example, in advance of the 2014 Commonwealth Games in Glasgow, the event organisers (in conjunction with the Sports Council and Youth Sport Trust) aimed to send some pupils from every secondary school in Scotland to specially arranged conferences at leading universities. The basic aim was that participating students would return to their schools to inspire younger students to stage Commonwealth Games festivals within their own communities.

Olympic Games hosts have been particularly proactive in using educational initiatives. This is perhaps because of the strong educational mission of the IOC and its aim to promote Olympic values. According to Grammatikopoulos *et al.* (2004), Olympic hosts since Los Angeles (1984) have tried to integrate the Games into school curricula. These projects can provide a basis for other social effects discussed elsewhere in this chapter. Learning initiatives often focus on healthier lifestyles, environmental issues and personal development – all of which feed into wider programmes of social regeneration. For example, 'Get Set' programme developed for the London 2012 Olympic Games involved resources that taught children abut the importance of exercise and healthy lifestyles; raised awareness of environmental issues; and developed the personal skills of youngsters. Athens's initiatives (adopted in 2000) in advance of the 2004 Games were focused on the history, values and impacts associated with the Games but, like London's subsequent project, they emphasised the importance of exercise and the development of personal skills (Grammatikopoulos *et al.*, 2004). Vancouver's programme for the 2010 Winter Games was even more ambitious. One strand of its educational programme was the 'Make Your Peace' initiative that included the production of a 'Truce Guide' which teachers could use to promote tolerance, peace and conflict resolution.

Grammatikpoulos *et al.* (2004) concluded that the Athens 2004 educational programmes resonated with teachers, but they felt they were not properly evaluated. This conclusion seems relevant to event-themed education programmes in general. Host cities have tried hard to develop imaginative educational initiatives in association with events. However, proper evaluations of these projects are rare and we do not have clear evidence whether they work.

Initiatives to promote healthier lifestyles

One of the biggest problems in disadvantaged urban areas is obesity. This is not only a social problem that can lead to depression, dependency and poor life quality. It is also a financial one: there are huge costs associated with caring for people who develop medical conditions caused by inactivity and poor diet. Accordingly, there is a strong incentive to use events in conjunction with initiatives to get people to lead healthier lifestyles. This obviously applies more to sport events, where there is a strong thematic connection between the events and activity/diet. However, it is also something linked to creative activities such as dance and drama that have an active dimension.

Initiatives adopted by host cities can take various forms. Often these involve attempts to 'activate' the demonstration effect and festivalisation effect mentioned earlier. Sport participation programmes can be set up pre-event, with the event used to help support recruitment. If people who don't engage with sport are turned off by sport events, one option is to de-emphasise sport in relevant promotions and encourage other forms of physical activity using the event theme. For example, when London staged the opening stages of the 2007 Tour de France, the aim was not to promote competitive cycling, it was to get people to ride bikes more generally. A cycling festival was staged in one of the city's main parks and local boroughs were encouraged to stage cycling demonstrations and workshops. As this example demonstrates, a common approach is to stage multiple participatory events in the run-up to major events. These events are known as augmentations. Amateur tournaments, schools events, fun-runs, taster sessions and demonstrations are common examples. The hope is that the augmentation of events in combination with the excitement generated by the events themselves leads to regular exercise and good habits that last.

Another option for event organisers is to offer grants to sports/cultural organisations who propose viable ways of increasing their membership, especially if that includes widening access to disadvantaged groups. Existing facilities can stage open days and other outreach programmes in the period before, during and after events to encourage local people to use local resources. Extra funding can be provided for new community sports facilities. These venues can also use event links to help gain interest and visibility. In a more limited sense, host cities can try to ensure that volunteers and those directly associated with the event are encouraged to take up healthier lifestyles and exercise.

Initiatives to assist persons with disability

Initiatives to assist persons with disability (PwD) – and to change societal attitudes towards disabilities – have also been introduced in association with

BOX 6.1 THE 2005 UEFA WOMEN'S FOOTBALL CHAMPIONSHIPS

Potter (2009) analysed the event-themed projects developed in conjunction with the 2005 UEFA Women's Football Championships (WFC) – a tournament that was staged in northwest England (Blackpool, Blackburn, Manchester, Preston, Warrington). The northwest region contains many of England's most deprived neighbourhoods. The 2005 UEFA WFC legacy programme was an interesting example of how event-themed initiatives can be developed around a smaller event. Initiatives were attached to the tournament so that it could achieve a broader range of effects. The aim was to lever the event to increase women's participation in football and other sports, as well as to improve women's overall levels of health and fitness (Potter, 2009). Specific target groups were identified and separate projects were developed to promote engagement amongst homeless women (Big Health Kick), young women (Off the Couch) and ethnic minorities (One Culture). The case highlighted two interesting issues about these types of projects. First, there was a noted conflict between the main sponsors of the event and health authorities. Major events continue to rely on funding from soft drinks companies, fast food corporations and computer games manufacturers. These associations somewhat undermine messages about healthier lifestyles. Second, Potter (2009) notes how the support for the initiatives waned within weeks of the tournament's close. The longevity of effects is a key issue, and a problem that affects many of the social leverage projects examined in the chapter.

major events. These link to regeneration in several ways: if PwD are taken into consideration, the physical regeneration of cities can be undertaken in an accessible way. PwD are also some of the most disadvantaged urban citizens, and therefore direct assistance, as well as improvements in society's attitudes towards disability, can improve quality of life levels for this group of people. Some events such as the Olympic Games include a parallel event for PwD and this provides an obvious opportunity to pursue related initiatives. The Paralympic Games 'has the potential to act both as a symbolic event that challenges dominant negative perceptions about PwD and as an opportunity to launch new programmes that break down barriers of social exclusion' (Raco, 2004: 44).

The lack of solid evidence regarding the legacy of the Paralympics generally, and on disability awareness levels in particular, makes establishing the specific contribution of major events difficult (UEL, 2007). The very poor levels of provision for PwD in the developing world demonstrate that different initiatives are needed for different contexts. Accordingly, 'cities such as Sydney, Turin and London could build on their existing practices which were already enshrined in legislation, whereas the Games in Athens and Beijing were the catalysts for initiating the disability agenda' (Gold and Gold, 2007b: 94). In some instances, Paralympic events have been supported by leverage initiatives to promote awareness of disabled issues more generally. Ray and Ryder (2003: 58) highlight a promotional campaign run by the organisers of the Sydney Paralympics that used a provocative slogan aimed at the able-bodied world: 'What's Your Excuse?'

The 2000 Sydney Olympic Games involved some commendable initiatives for PwD. Disabled people took part in an access advisory committee for the Paralympics in 2000 (UEL, 2007). Sydney's Paralympians received good support from the host city and sponsors; and the event advanced disability education in schools (Cashman and Darcy, 2008). Higher levels of disability awareness were supposedly achieved in Sydney but, as in other examples, the benefits disappeared rapidly in the years after the Games (UEL, 2007). Australia boasts other examples of good practice. The Melbourne Commonwealth Games in 2006 was one of the first events to place accessibility issues at the forefront of event legacy priorities. The Commonwealth Games is unique in that it integrates athletes with disabilities into the core programme (Smith and Thomas, 2005). This makes it a good vehicle for leveraging benefits for PwD. Disability objectives were a key part of Victoria State's Equal First legacy programme that aimed to use the 2006 Games to promote inclusion for all groups. Provision was made for PwD at Games facilities and the idea was that the Games would leave behind more accessible venues, hotels, restaurants, shops, and streetscapes; but also knowledge about how best to provide for PwD.

Despite some progress in leveraging events to assist PwD, there are still few solid examples of good practice that future event hosts can learn from. When members of the Canadian Paralympic Committee (CPC) asked previous hosts to identify the best ways to welcome paralympic athletes and other PwD to the 2010 Olympic and Paralympic Winter Games in Vancouver they were told that no guidelines existed and that the hosts should do whatever they could afford (VANOC, 2010a). Some of the projects that Vancouver did develop may provide some useful lessons for future hosts. VANOC developed six sustainability objectives for the Games, one of which was to convene an accessible Games that had a positive impact on socially and economically disadvantaged groups that otherwise might not have benefited (VANOC, 2010a, 2010b). The planned legacies included good consideration of disability issues, including accessible playgrounds that would allow children of all abilities to play together, barrier-free guidelines for accessible events and accommodation, and an educational programme dedicated to the Paralympic movement. Another Vancouver 2010 project was the Measuring Up programme supported by LegaciesNow and the Province of British Columbia that helped more than 100 communities to assess and improve accessibility for PwD. There were several projects supported by Measuring Up, including enhancing pavements, making parks more accessible and improving transit options. An Accessible Tourism initiative helped 3,600 tourism businesses to measure their accessibility provision, and learn how to improve it, so they could attract and serve PwD (VANOC, 2010a).

Social leverage initiatives: key issues

Developing event-themed initiatives to pursue social objectives helps to deliver social regeneration, but there are problems and disadvantages associated with these initiatives. Aside from the extra costs involved and the lack of solid empirical evidence that they work, there are other concerns that need to be highlighted. One major issue is the restrictions placed on using event brands. All the social initiatives mentioned above rely on the 'hook' of the event to drive engagement. But to protect event brands and sponsorship revenues, rights holders and local organising committees have a tendency to prohibit the use of official logos, certain wording and event associations. This means that projects led by organisations other than local organising committees (and their sponsors) are often unable to make official connections to events. For example, in the aforementioned London 2012 Changing Places programme, those submitting grant applications were instructed that the name of their project should not include any of the following: Olympic, Olympian, Olympiad, Paralympic, Paralympian, London 2012 or 2012. These restrictions make it very difficult to use the hook of the Games to frame 'unofficial' projects. This is not merely an Olympic Games problem. In research regarding the opening stages of the 2007 Tour de France (staged in London), local areas found it difficult to promote various social initiatives because of the limits placed on the use of the race brand (Smith, 2008).

Problems regarding branding restrictions are not insurmountable. Compromises have been reached that protect the interests of sponsors, but which allow other organisations to use event associations to theme social regeneration projects. In the case of the London 2012 Olympic Games, the Inspire Programme was adopted for this purpose. Non-commercial organisations that had developed Games-inspired projects were invited to apply to the scheme. Successful applicants were able to use a specified logo – a subsidiary version of the 2012 logo that indicated that a project had been 'Inspired' by the Games. One of the beneficiaries was the 'Gateway to the Games Volunteer Programme' – a pre-volunteer programme for the Barking and Dagenham area (an area outside the five original Olympic boroughs in which a major urban regeneration programme has been proposed). If organisations cannot access either official or subsidiary branding they can still allude to event links without contravening licensing restrictions. In the case of the 2007 Tour de France mentioned previously, local authorities were given advice by the local organisers about using cycling imagery and colouring that inferred a connection with the event, but which used neither official logos nor wording (Smith, 2008).

Sponsors can challenge event-themed initiatives in other ways too. Funding from sponsors is often used to pay for official event-themed initiatives. In an era when corporate social responsibility is supposedly a priority, companies like to be associated with social initiatives and so individual projects are often paired with specific sponsors. Unfortunately, large corporate sponsors are not usually very appropriate partners of social programmes and this problem is exacerbated when the companies try to influence the direction of these programmes. A good example was the Young Leaders initiative – part of LOCOG's 'Get Set' Olympic-themed education project. This was sponsored by BP. The idea was to give 100 young people from disadvantaged backgrounds the chance to participate in an intensive 18-month personal development programme. This would allow them to play an active role in leading and promoting Olympic projects within their own communities. However, when one analyses the programme more closely it appears that candidates were selected based on the basis that they lived close to one of BP's four hub locations: Hull, Aberdeen, Canary Wharf or Sudbury on Thames. Therefore, aside from the ethical dilemmas associated with connecting social programmes to discredited oil companies, sponsors tend to want to direct schemes rather than simply fund them. There remains the danger that these schemes do more to improve the reputations of the companies that sponsor them than they do to improve the lives of disadvantaged people.

A further problem with event-themed projects is that they are often jettisoned if there are budgetary problems. Events are infamous for their tendency to go over-budget and this means that some well designed social regeneration projects are never implemented. Again, the preparations for the London 2012 Olympic Games provide a useful example. In 2011, the Department for Culture, Media and Sport announced that a scheme to use the Olympics to inspire people to volunteer to do unpaid work in their community was to be scrapped. The incentive for participation was the possibility of attending a rehearsal for the opening ceremony. However, the project – called the 25th Hour – was discontinued (at the 11th hour!) because it was considered to be 'too expensive and lacking focus'.

A final problem associated with event-themed social regeneration initiatives is the danger that they are adopted merely for public relations reasons to fend off criticism about event projects more generally. Spending on these projects is usually dwarfed by the spending on event venues and physical regeneration. Social projects are often adopted because of the need to bring local communities 'onside' and they are cited by event organisers when criticism is forthcoming about the lack of consultation, wasteful spending on facilities or the lack of local benefits. Regeneration is used as a key part of the rationale for many events, and social regeneration is now accepted as a key objective. This means that event hosts of the future may need to take event-themed projects more seriously and start to formulate events strategies that address social needs, rather than retrofitting social provision into physical regeneration projects.

SUMMARY

This chapter has examined the different dimensions of event-related social regeneration. The discussion highlights how events have been allocated a role in delivering community cohesion, civic pride, inspiration for people to engage in various positive activities and help for those in need. Evidence regarding the social impacts of major events is also provided. This evidence suggests it is not enough for host cities to rely on the automatic effects of the events they host. To activate desired effects, leverage initiatives need to be employed. These projects rely on the wider associations and popularity of events – rather than the automatic effects of an event itself. Projects vary considerably and there are not enough rigorous evaluations of them, but some evidence suggests that event-themed social regeneration initiatives can be useful tools within regeneration.

The contents of the chapter illustrate several advantages of socially oriented event projects. First, they can be pursued in association with events that do not necessarily have a hard legacy of new facilities and infrastructure. This means regeneration could be achieved in association with parades, carnivals and other events that take place in public spaces. Second, they can be pursued in a range of geographical areas as they do not necessarily rely on the physical proximity of events. This means an event staged in one part of a city could be used to help those in a remote district. Finally, and perhaps most importantly, these initiatives can be aimed at disadvantaged people. This means that they can escape the recurring criticism of physical regeneration projects – that they do not assist those most in need. The major criticism of these projects is that they simply provide convenient ways to justify wider event projects, rather than comprising integral parts of event strategies. This criticism can be countered only by designing a new generation of event projects that are driven by a people-oriented agenda, and by ring-fencing the funding for social initiatives to ensure they are not cancelled when event projects go over-budget.

EXTENDED CASE STUDY 3: THE 2002 COMMONWEALTH GAMES LEGACY PROGRAMME

The 2002 Commonwealth Games in Manchester were delivered in association with an event legacy project in which social and economic regeneration objectives were prioritised. A summary of this case is provided here, but for the fuller version please consult Smith and Fox (2007). The Legacy Programme adopted by organisers was innovative as it aimed to achieve 'bottom-up' and socially oriented regeneration, rather than assuming that the benefits would 'trickle-down' to the most needy. A range of social and economic projects was pursued that were indirectly linked to the Games. This 'event-themed' approach had several benefits: it encouraged more dispersed effects, and encouraged more diverse impacts, as educational, health, cultural and skills projects were pursued alongside those directly associated with sport (Smith and Fox, 2007). The seven projects incorporated into the £17.7 million programme are detailed in Figure 6.2. Several of these can be linked to the social agenda previously outlined. For example, the Pre Volunteer Programme (PVP) project aimed to provide useful experiences of work for disadvantaged individuals; Passport 2K was designed to increase confidence, engagement and integration amongst young people; and Let's Celebrate was intended as a way of increasing participation in cultural festivals. Other projects had a more economic focus: for example Prosperity involved establishing a business network (see Chapter 4) and Games XChange was designed to promote tourism to the region (see Chapter 8).

One of the Legacy Programme's most notable achievements was its success in engaging and benefiting individuals from disadvantaged groups. This was attributed to the branding and 'hook' of the Commonwealth Games. The PVP, for example, was successful in engaging 16–19 year olds, ethnic minorities, people with special needs and the retired. This helped to address social equity issues, and the focus on disadvantaged parts of the region meant that the programme contributed to greater spatial equity. Another positive outcome was the provision of new opportunities for gaining qualifications and employment. The training provided as part of the PVP enabled 2,134 individuals to gain one of the two qualifications offered as part of the project (Smith and Fox, 2007). Other 'human impacts' were also noted. A range of feedback from participants, youth workers and activity co-ordinators indicated that the Passport 2K project raised the confidence and self-esteem of participants (Smith and Fox, 2007).

In addition to helping disadvantaged individuals, the Legacy Programme seemed to provide social assistance for targeted communities. The Passport 2K project helped to achieve reductions in youth nuisance, greater access to sports/arts activities and the recruitment of volunteer mentors to support the young people participating. Let's Celebrate allowed more representative and more

Commonwealth Curriculum Pack - Used interest in the Commonwealth Games to motivate children and teachers at school to enhance their information and communications technology skills. This was encouraged through the development of new curriculum materials and a website. These new learning resources also aimed to stimulate learning about the Games, and Commonwealth countries in general.

Games Xchange - Provided the opportunity to promote and market Manchester and the North West region. This was achieved by providing information about the city/region to local people and visitors through a range of accessible, informative anf innovative methods. An event information centre set up as part of this project aimed to train and give employment experience to disadvantaged individuals.

Pre Volunteer Programme (PVP) - An opportunity for people from specific disadvantaged groups throughout the North West to undertake accredited training and to gain experience through volunteering at the Commonwealth Games. This training was in addition to the instruction given to conventional volunteers. Those involved were not guaranteed roles at the Games, but the aim was to encourage PVP graduates to apply for positions and, if successful, to give them extra support and guidance if they experienced difficulties fulfilling their roles.

Healthier Communities - Provided healthier living initiatives throughout the region before, during and after the Commonwealth Games. The project provided assistance to health services in disadvantaged communities, primarily through providing community representatives with new skills, contacts and opportunities to gain further funds. It also aimed to develop more coherent links between sport and health initiatives. More specifically, the project was intended to provide support for the elderly and those with learning difficulties, and to encourage young people to make healthy lifestyle choices.

Prosperity - Aimed to ensure businesses in the region benefited from the Commonwealth Games by forming strategic alliances between regional and Commonwealth organisations. It provided opportunities for local businesses to create sustainable trade links with Commonwealth countries. More specifically the project aimed to identify, and disseminate information about, business opportunities relating to the Games. A business club was established and administered in the run-up to Games to assist this endeavour.

Passport 2K - Provided out of school activities for young people aged 11–18 across the North West who took part in a range of outdoors activities incorporating sport and the arts. The project combined a series of local activity programmes, with a number of regional events. The latter aimed to enable young people from a range of backgrounds and locations to meet up and participate in activities on a regional basis.

Let's Celebrate - Used celebratory arts including carnivals and mela to build the capacity of South Asian, African and African Caribbean communities and representative organisations in the North West. The idea was to award franchises of varying lengths to new and existing groups who had aspirations to develop their own events. The overarching aim was to promote long-term social cohesion, cultural diversity, local employment and the development of community-led cultural infrastructure.

Figure 6.2 The seven projects that formed the Legacy Programme for the 2002 Commonwealth Games

effective community-based leadership of cultural festivals to be established. The Healthier Communities project helped to establish a number of Healthy Living Centres (HLCs). These centres now complement existing health provision and aim to reduce health inequalities in deprived areas. Although these HLCs and other Legacy Programme initiatives were only loosely linked to the

Commonwealth Games, event associations were crucial to their implementation (Smith and Fox, 2007).

Social regeneration is a long-term objective, and it can be advanced only if projects have long-term effects. One possible danger of using events as a lever is their temporal nature, which may result in merely short-term benefits. Encouragingly, four of the seven projects that were supported by the Legacy Programme continued to deliver even when their funding ceased. For example, Healthier Communities part-funded someone to support the creation and development of other HLCs. More HLCs consequently satisfied the UK government's 'New Opportunities Fund' criteria and provided services to communities as a result. Healthier Communities also established a regional sport partnership of health, sport and learning representatives and this continued to operate successfully post-2004. A regional forum for local groups concerned with provision for the elderly was one of the legacies of the Healthier Communities project.

There are numerous examples of seemingly sustainable impacts achieved by the Legacy Programme, but there are also instances where projects were less successful. There was a conspicuous failure to involve local communities in the planning and implementation of projects associated with the Legacy Programme. This was partly a result of the tight deadlines and competing priorities associated with event planning. There were other problems caused by having an event as the cornerstone of the regeneration scheme. Despite the programme's life officially running from 1999 to 2004, many of those involved doubted whether enough emphasis was placed on project activity and spend after the Commonwealth Games took place (in 2002). The perception was that much of the effort and project delivery was undertaken *before* the Games, with levels of interest and impact consequently dropping off after the event had finished. The majority of positive effects occurred prior to the Games and this had negative implications for the long-term impact of the Legacy Programme. There is also evidence that the post-event period was neglected at institutional level. The frequency of attendance at board meetings dwindled after the Games. This, plus the premature departure of the many staff (including the Legacy Programme's co-ordinator), meant that the programme underperformed during its post-event life (2002–2004).

Overall, the Manchester case is now cited as an exemplar of good practice with respect to social and economic legacy planning. In terms of the intangible characteristics of sustainable communities (defined by the ODPM in 2003 as those with jobs, leaders, community involvement, cultural provision, integration and a strong sense of place), then the Legacy Programme associated with the 2002 Commonwealth Games performs well. These outcomes were not derived from the Games themselves, but were mainly the product of more general social initiatives aligned to the Games to lever funding, participation and support. Ultimately the event acted as a potent theme for social initiatives, rather than an active agent of social change in itself (Smith and Fox, 2007). This made it an interesting example which other host cities could learn from.

Events and new directions
for post-industrial cities

Events can be part of localised regeneration (see Chapter 4) or wider physical regeneration projects (Chapter 5) in urban areas, and they can be used to assist social aims and disadvantaged groups (Chapter 6). They can also be deployed in more general efforts to change the direction of development in cities that have endured de-industrialisation. The redirection of post-industrial cities using events is the focus of this chapter. The discussion explores the different ways events can be used as part of general attempts to revitalise urban economies. Event projects can be the inspiration or stimulus for a change in direction and/or they can be used to symbolise and communicate shifts. On a more practical level, events can be used as vehicles for nurturing new industries. Emerging industries can benefit from the sites and structures developed for events, but also from more intangible resources that events have helped to develop – including networks, contacts and expertise. Perhaps the most important intangible resource for a contemporary city is its image, and events have been used to assist the re-imaging of post-industrial cities. These different roles of major events are discussed in this chapter.

Events and post-industrial cities

Since the 1970s many cities have used events to reorient their economies, shifting from production to consumption/service oriented industries. Cities with reputations for industrial production have used major events to assist their reconfiguration. Famous examples include Genoa, Glasgow, Rotterdam, Liverpool, Sheffield and Turin, plus some of the extended case studies included in this book: Barcelona, Gothenburg, Manchester and New Orleans. Although traditional industries remain important to the economies of these cities, city leaders felt that the relocation of manufacturing employment to newly industrial-ising countries meant they needed to plot a new direction. Major events have been used as part of this process: to symbolise the change, but also to try to instigate and accelerate that change.

As discussed in Chapter 2, events can provide 'fateful' moments in the life of a city from which there is no turning back. Major events provoke enormous amounts of discussion, debate and future-oriented thinking and can symbolise and lead fundamental changes in the direction of urban development. As Glynn (2008) notes, cities often use the symbolism of events to distance themselves from a troubled past and to aspire to a new future. This can cause great controversy. Glasgow's European City of Culture event (1990) and the city's subsequent attempt to position itself as a centre of 'high culture' is a good example. Working-class organisations within the city felt aggrieved that the city was being portrayed in a way not 'sedimented down the years in Glaswegian consciousness – but in new terms without direct reference to any external reality' (Boyle and Hughes, 1991: 221). As this case shows, changes in direction can mean that some people and some aspects of a city's heritage are neglected.

There are different ways that events have been used to provide new directions for cities. These include:

- Inspiration for new ideas
- New sectors linked to the theme of events: sport, cultural and ICT sectors
- Re-imaging and branding.

These different aspects are used to provide the overriding structure for the main sections in this chapter.

INSPIRATION FOR NEW IDEAS

One of the more interesting ways that events have inspired a new direction for cities is by highlighting possibilities for new models of urban development. Using events to trial or promote experimental models of urbanism (that can be adopted more widely after an event) is an established tradition. It is particularly relevant to World Expos – occasions that have often involved the production of innovative urban models at different spatial scales. Innovative architectural ideas and proto-type urban designs have been displayed at many events: the 1939/40 New York World Expo is perhaps the most notable example. This event displayed exhibits by famous urbanists such as Lewis Mumford and Norman Bel Geddes, who were very influential in the design of US cities (Ellis, 2005). Bel Geddes's Futurama exhibit was located in the General Motors pavilion. This was no coincidence as he advocated radical changes in cities to facilitate smooth traffic flow.

Bel Geddes's vision was never fully adopted, but his ideas contributed to the construction of large-scale freeways in US city centres (Elliss, 2005).

In later examples of World Expos (e.g. Montreal 1967, Osaka 1970), whole Expo sites were designed as self-contained cities (Gold and Gold, 2005). These event sites were often arranged as models of 'a city of tomorrow' to demonstrate different forms of urbanism. For example, Montreal's Expo (1967) used a 'mega-structure', an idealised urban form involving large grids capable of extension to which modular units could be attached. The Osaka Expo of 1970 was also laid out as an experimental plan for a new city structure. Although this model city was converted into a cultural and natural park after the event, the associated planning ideas were influential and the event provided a platform on which to test, communicate and exchange new forms of city planning (Lockyer, 2007). This highlights the normative function of World Expos and similar events. Rather than simply being events which reflected societies, Expos were always intended as ways of shaping those societies (Roche, 2000). Unfortunately, as Gold and Gold (2005) recognise, it was not always easy to convert the sites to form 'real' urban areas. But the sites did provide a vision of what cities might do to address emerging urban problems.

Since their reintroduction in 1896, the Olympic Games have also provided cities with an opportunity to establish prototype urban areas. This trend can be traced back to Pierre de Coubertin's (the founder of the modern Olympic Games) desire to create a modern version of Olympia in which to host the Games. Pierre de Coubertin stated that he wanted a modern Olympia to be a grandiose and digni-fied ensemble; which was designed in relation to its role; which fitted in with the surrounding area; and which was neither too concentrated nor too diffuse (Liao and Pitts, 2006). These criteria seemingly influenced the design of subsequent Olympic sites, some of which remain as successful residential areas (e.g. in Munich and Helsinki). Inspired by these precedents, Olympic Villages are now designed as prototypes of more sustainable urban living, including models of 'ecotowns' such as the one built for the 2000 Sydney Games. The Sydney eco-village was innovative in several ways: each house featured passive thermal strategies for cooling, heating and ventilation; photovoltaic cells were used to produce electricity; and the units featured efficient use and recycling of water (Liao and Pitts, 2006). The Sydney and Athens Olympic Villages were also inno-vative in that they illustrated how suburban-style housing could be laid out in a way that achieved high levels of urban density compatible with the principles of sustainable communities (see Figure 7.1).

Trialling and showcasing more sustainable forms of urbanism is something that has characterised major events since the 1970s. Since then many World Expo events have adopted an environmental focus; this is illustrated by the post-1970

Figure 7.1 *Suburban housing in Newington – the athletes' accommodation for the 2000 Olympic Games in Sydney*

World Expo themes listed in Table 7.1. However, there are some disadvantages with this approach. As those involved in Zaragoza's Expo in 2008 found, dedicating an event to an environmental theme (in this case sustainable water resources) can invite accusations of hypocrisy as organisers can be held to account for failing to live up to their own environmental credentials. Other host cities have also been keen to use events to develop cutting-edge environmental technologies. For example, Vancouver, host of the 2010 Winter Olympic Games, tried to use the event to further its ambitious plan to be the 'Greenest City in the World' by 2020 (City of Vancouver, 2010). Host cities of the Winter Games have always been more environmentally conscious because events take place in more rural, natural settings. However, Vancouver demonstrated a commitment to environmental sustainability in urban contexts too. Many of the projects, including the Olympic Village, qualified for Leadership in Energy and Environmental Design (LEED) status. The US Green Building Council indicated that the Olympic Village was not only the greenest in Olympic history, but 'the most energy efficient and sustainable neighbourhood in the world' (City of Vancouver, 2010). Other aspects of the event were used to showcase new environmental technologies such as hydrogen fuelled vehicles. The associated travel and intensive use of resources mean that events

Table 7.1 *The headline themes of World Expos since 1970*

World Expo event	Theme
Osaka 1970	Progress and Harmony for Mankind
Spokane 1974	Celebrating Tomorrow's Fresh New Environment
Okinawa 1975	The Sea We Would Like to See
Knoxville 1982	Energy Turns the World
Louisiana 1984	The World of Rivers: Fresh Water as a Source of Life
Tsukuba 1985	Dwellings and Surroundings: Science and Technology for Man at Home
Vancouver 1986	World in Motion – World in Touch
Brisbane 1988	Leisure in the Age of Technology
Seville 1992	The Era of Discovery
Genoa 1992	Ships and the Sea
Taejon/Daejon 1995	The Challenge of a New Road to Development
Lisbon 1998	The Oceans, a Heritage for the Future
Hannover 2000	Man, Nature, Technology
Aichi 2005	Nature's Wisdom
Zaragoza 2008	Water and Sustainable Development
Shanghai 2010	Better City, Better Life

cannot claim to be sustainable in themselves, but their sustainable credentials are salvaged to some extent by the number of experimental design and ideas that have been introduced in association with events. This fits well with the idea of using major events as the inspiration for new modes of development.

NEW INDUSTRIES

As well as inspiring new forms of urban development, major events may provide opportunities to develop industries that are linked (directly and indirectly) to the event. Many cities have tried to develop spatially concentrated clusters of new industries on or near to event sites. The benefits of clustering are well known: firms benefits from knowledge transfer, the availability of shared resources, better access to workers, suppliers and customers, and value added by the reputation of their location. These advantages seem to have endured despite claims that new technologies have rendered spatial proximity less relevant for contemporary firms. However, successful clusters often emerge organically, rather than by design, and commentators such as Nordin (2003: 34) have suggested that 'clusters cannot be created, particularly not by governments'. Despite this, host cities have attempted to use events to develop clusters of sports, cultural and IT industries (depending on the theme of the event). These sectors are highly important to new urban economies. As Gospodini (2009: 1158) argues, the leisure, culture and information technology industries are both 'the most visible manifestation of economic novelty in cities' and 'the growth engines of the post-industrial city'.

Sports industries

Some sport event hosts have attempted to develop a sport industry in the aftermath of staging a major event. The idea is that sports manufacturers, sports retailers, sports science/medicine providers and sports federations, as well as sports spectators, could be attracted to a city because of the city's reputation and facilities for sport. New facilities can be turned into elite training or product testing centres to support these activities. Some event hosts have been relatively successful at persuading sports federations to relocate. For example, Sydney's Olympic Park now hosts the offices of Swimming Australia, Tennis NSW, Tennis Australia, the Australian Paralympic Committee and the Rugby League Professionals' Association within the buildings that used to house an abattoir. However, there are fewer examples where sports manufacturers or retailers have relocated facilities or opened new premises in the aftermath of a major event.

Indianapolis in the USA (Rosentraub, 2003) and Sheffield, UK, are both cities that have staged major sport events and then tried to use this reputation to attract sports industries. Both have deployed a broad interpretation of sport. Rather than merely providing spectator sport events, provision has been made to cater for mass participation, amateur sport and elite training. Indianapolis's strategy was innovative in that it focused on sport and sport events as an 'export component' of the city, rather than merely a way of attracting revenue from tourists (Rosentraub, 2003). In other words, Indianapolis aimed to be a producer of sport, as well as a site for its consumption. Indianapolis is usually championed as a successful example, but it is interesting to note that Euchner (1999: 228) attributes this alleged success to the city's 'early commitment to the sports strategy'. This implies other cities may find it difficult to emulate this approach. That has not stopped other cities trying. In Doha, Qatar, authorities used the 2006 Asian Games to develop facilities that have been subsequently used as an Academy of Sports Excellence. The 'Aspire Zone' developed on the main site includes twenty classrooms, eight football pitches, swimming pools, athletics track, diving pool, gymnastics hall, other halls, a table tennis area and squash courts (Amara, 2005).

Creative and cultural industries

Just as major sport event hosts have targeted sports industries, hosts of major cultural events have aimed to nurture cultural/creative industries. According to the UK government, creative industries are 'those activities which have their origin in individual creativity, skill and talent and which have a potential for wealth and job creation through the generation and exploitation of intellectual property' (DCMS, 2001: 5). This includes sectors such as advertising, architecture, art, crafts, design, designer fashion, film and video, interactive leisure software, music, the performing arts, publishing, software and computer services, television and radio (DCMS, 2001). Richards and Wilson (2007) note the differences between culture and creativity, with the former rooted in the past, and the latter about skill, talent and exploiting intellectual property. The same principles could be used to help distinguish between the cultural and creative industries. However, in urban policy literature, cultural industries and creative industries are terms that are often used interchangeably.

Some efforts to use events to inspire the development of cultural and creative industries seem to have worked. For example, in the four years prior to Glasgow's City of Culture event (1990) the cultural industries sector (art, music, design, film and television) grew by 3.9 per cent in the city (CCPR, cited in Johnson, 2009). In Liverpool – European Capital of Culture 2008 – the number of creative industry enterprises grew by 8 per cent over the equivalent period (2004–2008) (Garcia *et al.*, 2010). It is difficult to establish a direct cause-and-effect relationship, but these events seem to have stimulated growth in these cities. Major events staged regularly have an even greater potential for helping to nurture cultural and creative industries. In Valencia a cultural quarter has emerged that specialises in producing items related to the city's hallmark event, Las Fallas. A similar effect is apparent in Edinburgh where the annual Edinburgh Festival is credited by Turok (2003) with contributing to the local concentration of TV/media producers – the UK's largest outside London.

Clusters of creative and cultural industries are said to flourish where there are strong networks and pivotal institutions (Scott, 1999). This may help to justify event projects. Major events can assist with the development of networks and act as institutions around which activity can coalesce. Events with a cultural focus can play a significant role in providing new contacts, inspiration, creative activity, visibility and consumption opportunities for emerging creative clusters. Most creative clusters have associated arts festivals, demonstrating the importance of events to these areas. These events are often one of the few occasions during the year when creative firms become visible to the outside world. Events are also useful ways to connect clusters to sources of inspiration and business. Bathelt and Graf (2008) emphasise the importance of 'global pipelines' to the success of creative clusters. These pump contacts into a cluster and facilitate learning, knowledge production and innovation. Following Bathelt and Graf's logic, it is possible to conceive of major events as global pipelines.

Cultural clusters often stage regular events (shows, launches, exhibitions, festivals). Positive effects are more difficult to achieve when an event is a one-off event. This was illustrated when Edinburgh staged the 2003 MTV music awards. The event was heavily criticised because people felt that it did not allow enough opportunities to support the development of the local music industry (Reid, 2007). Similar criticisms were levelled at the Cork European Capital of Culture event in 2005, which neglected the local music scene within the official programme (O'Callaghan and Linehan, 2007). Pappalepore's (2011) and Vanolo's (2007) research into the Cultural Olympiad staged in association with the 2006 Winter Games in Turin suggests that staging major events in creative cities is more beneficial to the *event* than local industries. Vanolo (2007) notes that two creative areas (Murazzi and Quadilatero) were the focus of media attention – helping to present attractive images and adding to the buzz of the event. However, Pappalepore's (2011) research showed no evidence that creative clusters developed further as a result of the event.

One concern about focusing on the potential of major events to leave a legacy of cultural or creative industries is the danger that economic priorities usurp other objectives. Harcup (2000) worries that local authorities' use of cultural events now has more to do with attracting mobile capital than it does with the social life of communities. Cork's European Capital of Culture event in 2005 made an explicit attempted to leave a legacy of new art and cultural spaces within the regenerated Docklands area. State aid for small and medium-sized enterprises (SMEs) locating in this area was expected to continue to 2013. But O'Callaghan and Linehan (2007) suggest that tying in these projects left community participation and social equity goals neglected. Other authors are more positive and suggest that economic and social objectives are not necessarily contradictory. Quinn (2005: 935) asserts that in Caribbean carnivals 'the substantial tourism and economic activity dimensions do not overshadow the profound social meanings of these festivities'.

High-tech industries

Hosts of events such as World Expos (and garden festivals – see Chapter 3) have tried to attract high-tech industries in the post-event era. The most notable example is perhaps Seville's attempt to use the 1992 Expo to provide a new direction for the city. Although Seville's Expo is usually considered to be an example of an event associated with a disappointing legacy, the IT cluster that was founded on Cartuja Island in the event's aftermath has recently emerged as a success. The original intention was to host research agencies and public institutions – again, using a model based on California's Silicon Valley. Once the authorities involved had accepted the need to adopt a more flexible, commercially oriented vision, the

---

BOX 7.1 ROSKILDE

Roskilde, Denmark, is the host of a successful rock music festival which was established in 1971. The event has grown into one of Europe's biggest and it is an important case to acknowledge here because the city has tried to secure a more permanent legacy of creative industries from the event. As Hjalager (2009) states, the festival has not only increased in size, it has increased in scope: with spin-offs created and wider networks established. The festival has been used as a test-bench for new technologies; networks of music professionals have been established; emerging young bands have been supported; and successful relationships have been developed with local training providers (Hjalager, 2009). These initiatives have been consolidated into plans for a growth pole – Musicon Valley – a physical cluster of music-related industries. This is a novel version of the kind of technology clusters that have been developed in California and parts of Europe. The philosophy adopted by officials in Roskilde is that the city can use the expertise and contacts that have been built up by the event to provide a more tangible and permanent zone that can assist local economic development. Future plans include more exploitation of the tourism potential of the site – including a rock-themed hotel and museum.

Park began to establish itself. By 2000 it hosted 187 enterprises and 6,000 jobs (Maddox, 2004). Growth continued after the Millennium and Monclús (2009) reports that by 2003 (ten years after it opened) Parque Cientifico y Tecnologico Cartuja was home to 245 companies and 10,000 jobs. Interestingly, this site now contains an ICT cluster, but also zones that host the other key sectors discussed in this chapter (sport and culture – see Figure 7.2).

Hannover hosted a Universal Exhibition in 2000 and it too aimed to develop an IT cluster on a site that already had an exhibition centre. Universal Exhibitions are sometimes more restrictive because they involve participating nations building their own pavilions – a feature that doesn't always lead to a coherent site post-event. Hannover's 57 ha Expo Park was planned as an ICT cluster from the outset. Some of the pavilions now house IT and multimedia companies, and one hosts a local university. However, the site is still under-utilised. Diez's (2003) research revealed that firms appeared to appreciate the infrastructure and location of the park, but concerns were expressed about the lack of qualified staff in the surrounding area and the absence of supporting industries locally.

The Cartuja Science and Technology Park now consists of four main clusters:

Scientific-business zone: this hosts advanced technologies companies, research centres, business schools and public institutions that support innovation. This area, together with the University, takes up the majority of the Park and it is located in the central section.

Education zone: this hosts the School of Engineering and the Telecommunications Faculty, both attached to the University of Seville.

Cultural zone: buildings used for cultural performance are here: the Central Theatre, the Andalusian Contemporary Art Centre, the Foundation for the Brotherhood of Mediterranean Cultures and the Rocio Jurado Auditoriu.

Sports and leisure zone: this hosts the Olympic Stadium, and facilities for tennis, indoor football, athletics, rugby, rowing and golf. This part of the Park also hosts the Isla Mágica Theme Park.

Source: http://pctcartuja.es/Home/tabid/77/language/en-GB/Default.aspx

Figure 7.2 *The different zones within the Cartuja Science and Technology Park, Seville*

The Hannover region was not known for ICT/media industries before 2000 and it may take time for this cluster to emerge. This is a useful reminder that there is no guarantee that staging an event will result in the emergence of a successful cluster.

The Hannover project also aimed to give a boost to the city's exhibition centre and the MICE (meetings, incentives, conferences and exhibitions) sector is another industry that event hosts can target. Several Expo hosts have used pavilions as exhibition centres in the post-event era, including Vancouver (1986), Lisbon (1998), Barcelona (2004) and Zaragoza (2008). Olympic venues have also been converted into conference centres – including Athens's Olympic Tae Kwon Do hall. New industries only indirectly linked to the theme of an event may also flourish after an event. As major events now require media companies to be hosted and the use of sustainable technologies, these sectors may be prioritised. Here it is the knowledge gained, contacts made, and reputation earned, rather than the venues themselves that provide the basis for new clusters of industries.

IMAGE DEVELOPMENT

Many cities come to the conclusion that a new direction requires a new image. According to the rhetoric contained within many event strategies, a key mechanism for securing new industries, new residents and more visitors is image enhancement. Events are regarded as potent vehicles with which to enhance place images. Indeed, Hall (1992) asserts that events are the image builders of the modern world. Image objectives are particularly important for cities aiming to address perpetual associations with industrial decline and social problems. Although marketing theory recommends targeted messages, many cities have adopted generic approaches that are attractive to a number of audiences. Madsen (1992) identifies the predominant way in which industrial cities have tried to accomplish re-imaging. Using the example of Liverpool in the 1980s, Madsen (1992: 636) suggests that this city attempted to use and communicate a 'post-industrial business location image'. This image supposedly involves all of the three important types of place image identified by Ashworth and Voogd (1990) – the entrepreneurial, the residential and the tourist image.

One of the main reasons cities host major events is to try to enhance their image(s). Specific image objectives include awareness building (making more people aware of the city), cognitive image development (what people know about a city) and evaluative image enhancement (what people think about a city). Cities may also try to change conative images – those that affect the decisions we make. Events can be used to assist attribute-based image development, in other words what people think about certain qualities of the city (e.g. its image as an events venue). They can also be used for a more fundamental objective: holistic city image change. This means changing the way that people think about a city as a whole. To fully comprehend the processes via which events affect images of holistic city destinations, it is possible to consider image enhancement as involving two key elements (Smith, 2005b). First, a 'synecdochical' impact where specific events are used to represent the city as a whole. Second, a more subtle influence, where the events connote, infer or symbolise values and associations which may become attached to the city and thus influence how the city is imagined. These mechanisms are explored further below.

'Synecdoche' is the rather ugly linguistic term for instances where a part of something is used to stand for the whole (or where the whole is used to stand for a part). A number of authors refer to this process as metonymy (e.g. Laurier, 1993), but metonymy is a broader concept that refers to instances when one name for something is substituted for another. Synecdoche is a specific metonymic process and it has particular resonance for cities and city images (Smith, 2005b). The construction of holistic images involves reducing the complexity of an urban area into simplified representations that encapsulate the whole city (Tuan, 1977). Tuan cites monuments such as the Eiffel Tower, or silhouettes such as the famous skyline of New York, as examples of this phenomenon. Because of their media exposure, contemporary significance and popular acclaim, major events may provide such imagery (Smith, 2005a). For example, Stevens and Wootton (1997: 52) suggest that sport venues can provide 'potent landscape features' and this view is echoed by Bale (1993: 3) who observes that 'it is the floodlights of the stadium, not the spire of the cathedral that more often than not act as urban landmarks and points of reference'. Accordingly, staging sport events in extravagant arenas, building experimental viewing towers for World Expos, or developing impressive theatres for cultural events may allow cities to develop new synecdochical images. Event projects often include the conscious production of structures that will provide a new visual symbol for a city; that is why Broudehoux (2007, 2010) classifies event projects as examples of 'conspicuous construction'. This approach reflects the noted tendency in the contemporary era for 'emblematic projects'; major urban development projects that 'capture a segment of the city and turn it into the symbol of the new restructured/revitalised metropolis' (Swyngedouw *et al.*, 2002: 562).

Alongside possessing the capacity to become a component of city images through synecdochical processes, it is proposed that certain connotations generated by event initiatives can influence holistic images (Smith, 2005b). Therefore, although holistic images held by potential tourists may not include events imagery, they may be influenced significantly by certain connotations generated by them. If, again, we take the example of sport events, sport has come to symbolise abstract concepts such as modernity (Nielsen, 1995), progress (Rowe, 1995) and national identity (Blain *et al.*, 1993). Raitz (1987) is confident that sport has the capacity to influence perceptions of cities via symbolic associations. According to Raitz (1987: 7), sport events venues may become a symbol of imagined ideals, for example 'the pastoral in the midst of a gritty city'. However, it would appear that many post-industrial cities use sport events to generate more dynamic meanings such as the 'transcendence of the old' (Rowe, 1995: 137) and to 'popularise sometimes obscure notions of progress' (Rowe, 1995: 138). This fits with the idea of events as agents of modernity discussed in Chapter 2. Cultural festivals are also thought to generate positive connotations. The City of Edinburgh justifies the prominence of festivals within its marketing by noting that festivals connote 'sophistication, modernity, civilization and attractiveness' (Jamieson, 2004). Indeed, the idea of a festival is thought to be so attractive that other types of events try to use the term to make them sound more exciting. This includes sport events, business events and even academic conferences. There is now even a Festival of Social Science!

Although event hosts often assume that the image effects of events will always be positive, it is important to acknowledge the possibility that major events could connote negative associations. Sport events can promote a range of problematic associations: for example, machismo (Schimmel, 1995) and violence (Baudrillard, 1993). Tranter and Lowes's (2009) research focuses on motor sport events, occasions that may generate particularly unhelpful connotations. The authors suggest that these events convey messages about excessive energy consumption, pollution, alcohol use and unhealthy diets. These contradict many of the key messages promoted by government authorities. Similarly, cultural festivals may connote a range of associations that cities are normally keen to disassociate themselves from, including drug use, noise, public disturbances and crime.

One of the reasons why it is difficult for cities to control the connotations disseminated via events is because event images are mainly disseminated through autonomous image formation agents, rather than paid-for advertising. Autonomous agents act independently of official destination marketing and are difficult to control (Gartner, 1997). However, if the imagery disseminated via autonomous agents (such as independent newspaper, television and internet coverage) is positive it may have a more significant effect. As Gartner (1997: 185) states: 'the autonomous image agent, because of its high credibility and high market penetration, may be the only agent capable of changing an area's image in a short period of time'.

Branding and co-branding

Attempts to improve city image are now often discussed with reference to the concept of brands and the practice of branding. Branding can be understood as a management model and mode of communication that aims to position products relative to their competition and by their personality. The aims of branding are to invoke functional attributes and symbolic values and change consumer behaviour by encouraging awareness of and loyalty to brands. Ultimately, the aim is to add value by differentiating products from their competition. The relationship between branding and image is contested, but the simplest way to align the two ideas is to suggest that city branding provides a mechanism with which to change and control city images. One of the noted benefits of branding is that it may simultaneously influence internal and external perceptions. As Kavaratzis (2004: 58) states, 'City branding provides, on the one hand, the basis for developing policy to pursue economic development and, at the same time, it serves as a conduit for city residents to identify with their city.' Thus city branding may be justified not only via economic development effects, but via some of the social effects discussed in Chapter 6 (e.g. civic pride and community cohesion).

Just as host cities have used events to accelerate physical development (see Chapter 5), cities have used events to accelerate the development of their brands. This can be attempted in different ways. Some cities have utilised events as a central part of their identity – incorporating event references into their logos and straplines. The most ambitious approach has perhaps been adopted by Melbourne, Australia, a city that now promotes itself as 'the world's event city'. The devolved national capitals within the UK have adopted a slightly more modest approach. Cardiff promotes itself as an 'events capital' and Edinburgh has used the reputation of its international festivals to develop a city brand as a 'festival city' (Jamieson, 2004). Other cities use more subtle references to convey their role as an event host. Interesting examples were developed in association with European Capital of Culture events staged in the UK. Liverpool (2008) used the event as part of its wider campaign: 'It's happening in Liverpool.' Glasgow (1990) famously deployed the slogan 'There's a lot Glasgowing on.' These promotional campaigns publicised the role of the cities as event hosts, but also tried to evoke symbolic connotations associated with events – such as dynamism and vibrancy. Nevertheless, such slogans are notoriously liable to ridicule and subversion. For example, critics of Glasgow's City of Culture strategy promoted their alternative version of the slogan, 'There's a lot of con going on' (Mooney, 2004).

A slightly different approach is to use individual event connotations to push key city brand messages. This is achieved through the process of co-branding. Many events can be considered to be brands and many cities are now heavily branded. Therefore, one way of understanding the re-imaging of cities using events is as a co-branding process in which brand associations are transferred from the event to the city (and vice versa). Drawing upon principles associated with corporate sponsorship, this process is thought to be facilitated when consumers perceive there to be a correspondence between event associations and those in a city's association set. As Brown *et al.* (2004) suggest, the most significant image effects will accrue when consumers perceive a meaningful match between the image of the event and that of the destination. This is known as 'match-up' theory and there are several implications of this idea for practice:

- It is important to know how a city and certain events are perceived – so that relevant connections can be made between the 'brands'.
- Cities should think about what aspects of their brands they want to emphasise or develop and stage events that are associated with those dimensions.
- Cities should ensure that promotional work they undertake in association with events directs consumers towards the aspects of the event and the elements of the destination brand that they want to emphasise.

The effective transfer of associations between events and cities also depends upon the visibility of the links between the event and the destination. Effects will not occur unless people are aware that the event is associated with a particular place. Although events usually receive a lot of media attention, this does not necessarily mean that the host destination is always featured extensively. As Chalip (2005) notes, during coverage of an event, there is no reason to expect that the media will focus on the host destination. This is why we often see destinations promoting themselves (using banners and advertising hoardings) during events. Destination visibility is less of a problem when an event is staged within a recog- nisable city environment. But if the venue is an anonymous one, for example an indoor arena, this restricts imaging effects. In these cases, to ensure that the event media coverage includes destination imagery, cities often stage mini-events

Figure 7.3 *Footballs in Trafalgar Square, London, emphasising the connection between the 2011 UEFA Champions League Finals and the host city*

and/or launch events in city centres or near to landmarks (see Figure 7.3). These augmentations publicise the event, but they also publicise the host destination. Destination emphasis can be achieved by encouraging and assisting media companies to produce introductions to, or features on, event destinations during media coverage. In some cases, city agencies may even be able to influence editorial decisions regarding camera angles and commentary scripts to ensure that event coverage includes the images that destinations want people to see (Smith, 2008).

One of the key problems with the match-up theory for cities seeking regeneration is that it implies that events can help to develop existing images, but it perhaps restricts the capacity for wholesale image transformation. It is also conceivable that event initiatives could be unhelpful because they may detract from, or dilute, other images that the city is attempting to develop. Indeed, negative associations may be transferred if people think these are both characteristic of the event and the destination. For example, Smith's (2008) research into the 2007 Tour de France Grand Depart (staged in London) noted that in the build-up to the race, the media were keen to draw parallels between the dangers of cycling in London and the dangers associated with the Tour de France. This was unhelpful coverage for an event staged to promote cycling in the city. Similarly, Chalip *et al.*'s (2003) research revealed that images of the Gold Coast's natural environment were affected negatively by a motor race staged in the destination. This was because the event reaffirmed images of urbanism, traffic and concrete – images that the region was trying to disassociate itself from (Chalip *et al.*, 2003).

A further example of problematic image effects is provided by Rowe and McGurk (1999) in their evaluation of the relationship between sport and the image of Newcastle, Australia. This city enjoyed widespread media attention after its rugby league team unexpectedly triumphed in a national final. Using a rather patronising metaphor, the media made connections between the determination of the city's victorious team, and that of its blue-collar workforce. The resultant representation of Newcastle as a masculine, working-class city projected an image that was 'heavily reliant on the very properties that urban modernizers are attempting to de-emphasize' (Rowe and McGurk, 1999: 137). The potential for negative effects is also highlighted by Higham's (1999: 84) pessimistic assertion that cities staging major events 'stand to lose more than they can gain in terms of destination image' because of the possibility of detrimental media exposure.

Problems with applying branding to cities and events

Although the idea of city branding is prevalent within urban policy, that does not mean it is something that is universally advocated. Events and places are not conventional products and this means that the application of branding to cities and events is difficult. The key reasons for this are discussed below:

1   *Products and messages are harder to control.* Branding is about control – over product quality, identity and communications. Events and cities are heterogeneous phenomena that cannot be controlled in the same way. These entities are hard to encapsulate within a single message and attempting to do so often causes controversy. Most of the information we receive about events and cities is via autonomous media sources and, although this provides useful publicity, the content of the messages disseminated is difficult to control.
2   *Multiple objectives.* Companies who benefit from branding usually have a narrow range of objectives: to sell more of their product in the short-term or to build their image in the longer term. Events and cities exist for a wide range of reasons and 'success' can be measured in multiple ways. This makes it harder to put together a homogenous branding strategy that fulfils the different objectives of an event or city.
3   *Consumers already have a high degree of resonance and loyalty.* The main aims of branding include achieving greater resonance and loyalty

amongst consumers. This is necessary for producers of fast-moving consumer goods because these products are not items that people would normally feel affiliated to. Cities and events may command loyal support and evoke strong emotions without branding. This means branding is less relevant to cities and events.

4   *Consumers don't act rationally.* Emotional attachment is why consumers of events (and, to a lesser extent, cities) can be seen as irrational consumers. People prepared to brave the mud and rain at music festivals or sports fans who continue to follow unsuccessful teams are good examples. This irrationality challenges the logic of branding – as these event and city products cannot be easily understood through conventional consumer behaviour models.

A further limitation of branding and reimaging efforts is that it is not entirely clear whether increased revenues and regeneration inevitably follow from any resultant image enhancement. Conative images (those which relate to behaviour) may be unaffected. For Ritchie and Smith (1991: 9), even if destinations do experience image advancement 'it is not immediately obvious that this will translate into increased visitation levels, tourism receipts and/or other forms of economic development'. It is difficult to justify event-led regeneration via envisaged image effects if enhanced images don't deliver increased investment. However, enhancing images not only assists development by directly stimulating demand. Developing an attractive image can assist urban regeneration in an indirect manner, impressing event organisers and administrators, therefore allowing cities to secure events in the future. Events may also affect levels of investment indirectly, via enhancing the images of key opinion formers.

SUMMARY

This chapter has outlined how major events are used as opportunities to usher in a new era for a city. Events can help to inspire, instigate and/or communicate new directions and they can provide a forum in which the future of a city is keenly debated. Major events have been used to provide the tangible and intangible foundations for new sectors of the urban economy that are linked to events. Of course, there is no guarantee of success and the discussion highlights that cities need to be both patient and persistent if they want to reorient urban economies. Cities also use events to challenge problematic images – this can help to provide the basis for new investment. But the discussion in this chapter highlights that there is always the possibility that events will deliver neutral or even negative effects on city images. Branding is now seen as the mechanism which can be used to secure image change. However, the contents of this chapter emphasise that cities need to be clear how they intend to use events within branding: as a central part of their brands, as co-brands, or merely as brand attributes. Furthermore, there seems to be some incompatibility between the aims of branding and the characteristics of cities and events. This challenges the growing trend of using events to develop city brands.

EXTENDED CASE STUDY 4: SINGAPORE'S IMAGE DEVELOPMENT USING EVENTS

Singapore is a highly industrialised and urbanised nation with a population of over 5 million people. This city state is located on a small island (700 square km) near to Malaysia and it is known as a highly regulated place where the government is unwilling to accept interference. Henderson (2006) feels this reputation is somewhat exaggerated, and there are signs within the new regime of more flexibility and a more relaxed attitude. In the 1990s, a tourism advertising campaign was formulated that posed the question: 'Can a city of efficiency still find time to celebrate?' (Chang, 2006). This highlighted the awareness within Singapore of its image problem. Accordingly, the strategy in recent years has been to replace the city's rather sterile image with a more exciting reputation.

Singapore's desire to be known as a more exciting place is epitomised by a new emphasis on events: in recent years the city state has bid for, and staged, some important sport events, and it has also developed a reputation as a venue for business events. This is in keeping with Singapore's reputation for forward thinking and making the most of its limited resources. The city's event strategy aims to seek global recognition for a place that is already 'deeply embedded in the process of globalisation' (Soh and Yuen, 2011: 3). There are secondary motives too: events have been staged to encourage more participation in sport and the arts. The strategy has been focused on bidding for international events, but there has also been investment in existing events and event venues. The emphasis on hardware is attributed to the government's prioritisation of urban regeneration (Chang and Lee, 2003). This 'regeneration' aims to reclaim land from the sea and to rebuild congested districts and slum areas. It also aims to promote the area around the Marina Bay as Singapore's synecdochical image and as the city's 'stage' for national events (see Figure 7.4).

Using high-profile events to assist urban development is a relatively new direction for Singapore, especially as previous urban policies tended to favour non-ostentation and social integration (Soh and Yuen, 2011). Urbanisation in the city has a very distinct character. Most of the population live in high-rise blocks that have been constructed using government finance. Eighty per cent of the population live in this public housing and quotas have been used to prevent the formation of ethnic enclaves: the allocation of housing is one way the government has tried to promote multiculturalism. Rather than aiming to improve the lives of existing residents, the new event-oriented strategy was conceived as a way to attract and retain the international workers required to maintain Singapore's competitiveness.

Esplanade (also known as Theatres on the Bay)

ArtScience Museum

Outdoor Stadium

Figure 7.4 *Marina Bay in Singapore. Perhaps the most explicit example of developing a city centre as a stage for events*

It was also part of a major tourism drive that aims to attract 15 million visitors by 2012 (Foley *et al.*, 2008).

The origins of the current strategy can be traced back to the period just after Singapore gained independence from British rule (1965). The Singapore Sports Council was created in the 1970s and Singapore hosted the Southest Asian Games in 1973, 1983 and 1993. In recent years, the focus of the events strategy has been to secure fewer, better-quality events. The new approach was given a boost when Singapore won the right to stage the 117th International Olympic Committee meeting in 2005. The government spent $S1.7 million (*c.*£850,000) to stage this four-day meeting at which the host of the 2012 Games was announced. Yuen (2008: 33) suggests that, since hosting the IOC, Singapore 'has worked the marketing power of the Olympic brand'. The IOC meeting seems to have helped to raise the profile of Singapore as an events and/or training venue amongst sports federations. Subsequently, as well as staging regular events (golf events and a marathon), Singapore has hosted the FINA (swimming) World Cup, the Volvo Ocean (Sailing) Race in 2008, and various other international tournaments.

Singapore cemented its Olympic credentials by staging the Youth Olympic Games in 2010 (Judge *et al.*, 2009), and later the same year the city was the surprising winner of the 'world's best sports city' title at the International Sports Event Management awards. This honour was questioned by some, including Davidson (2010), who felt Singapore was an undeserving winner as it had no culture of sport, and very poor sport stadia – especially compared to Western rivals such as Paris, London, Barcelona or Los Angeles. This scepticism is justified by the findings of a TSE Consulting study that aimed to assess international perceptions of Singapore as a sporting destination. TSE's study suggests that sport and Singapore do not have a strong connection and that the city state lacks influence within the sport world to secure major events and sport development (TSE, 2010).

The most high-profile event that Singapore has secured is an annual Formula 1 Grand Prix motor race. This is the only race staged at night (under lights) in the Formula 1 calendar. The distinctive character of the race has helped organisers to promote the event in conjunction with its current marketing campaign that uses the strapline 'Uniquely Singapore'. The combination of lights, technology and glamour complements Singapore's image as a modern city. There seems to be an effective match-up between the image of the race (international, modern, urban) and the image of Singapore (international, modern, urban). Following the logic of the co-branding discussed above, Singapore hopes that some of Formula 1's associations with glamour, excitement and luxury will be transferred to the nation's image. To maximise the effects of the event, a festival has been built around the race, creating a 'season' of events, with the Grand Prix as the pivotal focus. The race is staged through the city's streets rather than on a dedicated track, and this means the recent changes to Singapore's cityscape are publicised. Indeed, the layout was designed to draw attention to key landmarks in Marina Bay (see Figure 7.5) – generating important synecdochical images. These include the enormous Marina Bay Sands complex, the Singapore Flyer (Ferris wheel), a new museum of arts and science, the Esplanade Theatre complex and the Merlion statue – Singapore's national symbol.

Culture

Investment in sport events has been accompanied by efforts to stage cultural events. This strategy dates back to 1984 when a report recommended that the city's Festival of the Arts should be staged on a scale comparable to the Edinburgh Festival (Chang, 2006). Singapore's reputation as a slightly boring, sanitised city (Henderson, 2006) means cultivating an image as a festival destination is difficult. The lack of a domestic audience to support the arts is a further obstacle if the city wants to challenge regional rivals such as Hong Kong and Melbourne. Whereas almost 100 per cent of Melbourne's residents have attended

| Singapore
Flyer | | Grand Prix
Circuit | | Sports Hub
(under construction) |

Figure 7.5 *Singaporean event projects in the waterfront area adjacent to Marina Bay*

an arts/cultural performance, this figure is just 25 per cent in Singapore (research cited by Chang and Lee, 2003). The rationale has been to promote external events alongside indigenous cultural events (e.g. the Chingay, River Hong Bao and Taipusum festivals) – presenting a fusion of Asian heritage with modernity. This is consistent with Singapore's branding, which since the 1990s has aimed to position Singapore as a mixture of Eastern and global influences. The initial focus was to promote Singapore as 'Instant Asia', and more recently as 'New Asia' (Chang, 2006). As Henderson (2006: 267) states, the intention of this branding was to promote Singapore as a stimulating place with a distinctly Asian population who were sophisticated members of a global society and where the visitor would feel safe. Although this can be dismissed as marketing rhetoric, branding Singapore as New Asia drew upon the city's unique demographic profile. Since British colonisation it has been home to multiple ethnicities – the population is made up of mainly Chinese, Malay and Indian residents, as well as multiple other international groups. Using a mix of local and international events contributes to established efforts to promote Singapore as 'the most open and cosmopolitan city in Asia' (Soh and Yuen, 2011: 4). In more recent years the brand was slightly reconfigured to emphasise Singapore's uniqueness. But the message remained largely the same – the city is a unique bridge between East and West, as well as a city 'bursting with exciting events' (Henderson, 2006).

Hardware

To facilitate its events strategy, Singapore has invested large amounts of money in events hardware. A new, integrated sports hub has long been envisaged which will involve a cluster of integrated world-class sports facilities within the city (Foley *et al.*, 2008). The hub will include a 74,000-seat national stadium, and although progress on this project has been slow, construction was underway in 2011 on a site next to Singapore's indoor stadium (see Figure 7.5). Spectacular facilities such as a floating stage and waterside arenas have been developed to draw attention to the Marina Bay area (see Figure 7.4). To facilitate the staging of large-scale cultural events, an iconic new performance space has been developed – the Esplanade (also known as Theatres on the Bay, see Figure 7.6). This complex includes a 2,000-seat theatre, a 1,800-seat concert hall and an outdoor auditorium (see Figure 7.4). The Esplanade (so named because it was built on a site that used to be a beach) means that Marina Bay is literally being turned

Figure 7.6 *The 'Lighter Side of the Arts' at Singapore's extravagant new theatre complex – the Esplanade*

into a stage for major events. Its size means it is unsuited to local productions, so instead it has hosted a series of international events imported from New York's Broadway and London's West End (see Figure 7.6). These are preferred by many residents, as it is often assumed by local people that international performances are inherently superior to local events (Chang and Lee, 2003). This inferiority complex is often a feature of small, postcolonial nations that are struggling to find a coherent national identity.

The outcomes of Singapore's events strategy have been mixed. The city has been successful at attracting events and it has become a much more prominent location. Considering its limitations, the city state has made an impression – particularly within the sports world. However, apart from its reputation as a safe, organised and developed city, the city has few advantages. Singapore's projects have had to be developed from a very low base, with an undeveloped sports/arts culture and few established resources/individual role models. The competition to be an Asian sport event capital is very strong, with Abu Dhabi, Dubai, Doha, Seoul, Hong Kong and Kuala Lumpur all investing heavily. Levels of participation in sport and the arts don't seem to have improved significantly. Just as the new cultural venues have not become incubators for the arts (Chang and Lee, 2003), new sport facilities have failed to deliver a boost to grassroots participation levels.

Singapore may have succeeded in its efforts to become an events and entertainment city, but this seems to be mainly for the benefit of tourists and the large number of non-residents who attend these events. According to Soh and Yuen (2011), new spaces of consumption have been created for local elites and non-residents, but not enough attention has been devoted to the wider urban or social fabric. Although the event strategy is something of a new direction for Singapore, it is still one that involves comprehensive state planning, rather than initiatives driven by popular demand. This top-down approach has delivered hardware and international events but it has not been able to generate the atmosphere, software and local participation envisaged by the authorities. Indeed, there is evidence – particularly from the arts sector – that the stringent planning of space for cultural activity is the opposite of what is required to allow such activity to flourish (Chang and Lee, 2003). Despite more obvious limitations such as its size, it is the lack of cultural engagement that may restrict Singapore from using events to cultivate an urban renaissance. In this sense, the Singapore case raises an important question. Can events help to cultivate a sports and/or arts culture within a city, or is such a culture a prerequisite for a successful events strategy?

Events and tourism development in 8 post-industrial cities

INTRODUCTION

The previous chapter outlined how events have been used to instigate new directions for cities. Tourism is one growth 'industry' that has been particularly prioritised by post-industrial cities and event hosts. The tourism sector is perceived to be one of the sectors that benefits most from improvements to a city's image that may result from staging an event (see Chapter 7). And as transport facilities, hotel capacity and city environments may have been enhanced to stage events, it makes sense for cities to try to attract more tourists (or more revenue from tourists) after the event. The economic and physical effects of related development mean that tourism is seen by many cities as a sector that can deliver urban regeneration. However, the relationship between tourism and regeneration is contested, with authors such as Lewis (2003) and Hatherley (2010) critical of the effects of this approach to regeneration. This chapter analyses how staging events can affect the development of tourism facilities and tourism demand.

Events can assist a city's tourism agenda in different ways. These include short-term and long-term effects. Short-term effects include increasing demand: events can attract tourists before and during events. Events can also incite people to stay longer or spend more in destinations (Chalip, 2004). These effects are not considered here because they are usually temporary effects and this book focuses on a long-term objective – regeneration. Longer-term tourism effects relate to post-event demand, the supply of tourism facilities and the provision of new capacity. Events may provide an incentive to develop new accommodation, new attractions and new amenities. They may also enhance a destination's image and instigate new networks and partnerships between organisations that assist the delivery of tourism services. These different long-term objectives are explored in this chapter.

The chapter begins with a review of the way in which events have helped to shape the contemporary tourism sector. The discussion then moves on to analyse the ways that events can affect the demand for, and supply of, urban tourism. Latter sections discuss the relationship between tourism and urban regeneration more generally.

EVENTS AND TOURISM DEVELOPMENT IN CITIES

Major events have assisted tourism development in both obvious and subtle ways. The idea of tourism in general, and city tourism in particular, is something that major events have helped to establish. As Davis and Marvin (2004) explain, before railways enabled the full potential of tourism to be realised, events like the Venice Carnival represented an early form of mass tourism. Once the railways were built, the World Expos of the nineteenth century provided incentives to travel domestically and helped to establish the formal travel industry. Major events also helped to communicate messages about different parts of the world and this increased the appetite for international travel.

Events have helped to shape the supply structure of urban tourism, as well as providing a direct motivation for travel. In Chapter 7 the role of events in inspiring new forms of urbanism was discussed. In a similar manner, experimental tourism attractions were often developed as part of event projects. Many of these now provide important parts of the urban tourism 'product' today. The Ferris wheel that has become a common feature of many city centres (see Figure 8.1) was first seen at the 1893 Chicago World Expo. The modern theme park is often considered to be a permanent manifestation of an event site. Roche (2000) identifies how Walt Disney was inspired by the 1893 Chicago Expo and by the 1939/40 New York Expo. Roche (2000) notes several Expo features that Disney later utilised and integrated within his theme parks: amusement parks, rides, stage set representations of vernacular architecture, state-of-the-art technologies and physical manifestations of ideal communities. Other Disney projects were also inspired by Expo sites: the EPCOT Center in Orlando, USA was essentially designed as a permanent version of a World Expo and its centrepiece was influenced heavily by the spheres that were exhibited at North American Expos. Disney's company even contributed to the design of later projects such as Seattle's World Expo (Monclús, 2009). Expo sites have been the inspiration for theme parks around the world, but they have also been used to house on-site theme parks in the post-event era. Examples include Prater Park in Vienna, and the Isla Magica in Seville.

Figure 8.1 *A Ferris wheel on Brisbane's South Bank. This was the location for the 1988 World Expo. The site is reminiscent of London's South Bank that also staged a major exhibition (the Festival of Britain in 1951)*

Tourism and event regeneration

Tourism is envisaged by host cities as both an outcome of, and mechanism for, event regeneration schemes. However, the logic chains for tourism-related effects are not usually very well developed and tourism is sometimes lazily used to justify events. Merely citing increased tourism activity as a key objective does not necessarily mean that cities have developed rigorous plans to allow such effects to accrue. The UK city of Sheffield provides an illustrative example. Before, during and after the 1991 World Student Games, Sheffield City Council stated its desire to use the Games to generate and promote tourism. However, despite this commitment, Bramwell (1993: 17) suggests that 'there was no clear view of how the World Student Games facilities could help the city's tourism industry'. As Bramwell recognises, during the planning of the WSG and in the immediate aftermath of the Games, there was no strategic plan that outlined 'specific objectives and precise mechanisms' that would ensure tourism benefits (Bramwell 1997: 170).

Tourism after an event

After major events have been staged, achieving a sustained increase in tourism demand is not guaranteed. Some host cities have experienced disappointing tourism outcomes. For example, the anticipated rises in tourism demand did not materialise after the 2004 Olympic Games in Athens (Kissoudi, 2010). As Preuss (2004) recognises, many cities presume that events mean visitor levels will be raised to a new plane that will be sustained after an event. Unfortunately, many events do not deliver large increases in demand and visitor levels often return to pre-event levels. A number of host cities have experienced large increases in visitor numbers over subsequent years, but it is difficult to isolate the extent to which this is directly caused by the event itself. Not enough research has been published that attempts to isolate the effects of events from other factors. One rare example of such research is that produced by Holmes and Shamsuddin (1997). Allowing for the effects of exchange rates, travel prices and disposable income fluctuations, Holmes and Shamsuddin (1997) estimate that the 1986 Vancouver Expo generated an extra 20,000 visitors per month to the city for seven years after the event. These were generally US visitors travelling by land, as the event seemed to have a negligible effect on air passengers. Olympic host cities such as Seoul and Barcelona have also experienced higher numbers of tourism arrivals for a sustained period after staging the Olympic Games (Roche, 2000). This effect is partly due to increased international exposure and associated image enhancement. Infrastructural improvements, such as investment in airports, railway lines and new organisational capacity also assist long-term tourism prospects.

Positive long-term effects on demand levels are sometimes a function of tourism marketing initiatives that are pursued in parallel with events. Barcelona is one city that has pursued strategic tourism initiatives in association with a major event. Alongside using the 1992 Olympic Games to regenerate urban infrastructure and derelict land, Barcelona used the event to 'launch its tourism strategy for the next century' (Glyptis, 1991: 179). As O'Brien (2007) recognises, leveraging programmes to facilitate tourism development have accompanied most major events since 2000. Australia used the 2000 Olympic Games to enhance its overall market position, to encourage repeat visits and to build new relationships amongst a fragmented tourism sector (Faulkner et al., 2001). Malaysia has also tied major events to the development of its tourism industry (Van der Westhuizen, 2004: 1284). The successful 'Visit Malaysia Year' was timed to coincide with the staging of the 1998 Commonwealth Games in Kuala Lumpur and increased tourism revenue by 190 per cent (Van der Westhuizen, 2004).

It is often unclear whether increases in tourists and tourism revenue are due to the effects of an event, or due to the effects of a wider tourism strategy employed in parallel with an event. Increases in tourism demand may also be explained by other external factors. As Hiller (1998: 53) recognises, a major event 'cannot be seen in isolation from other factors occurring simultaneously and independent of it'. The growth in short breaks and the rise of low-cost air carriers certainly assisted Barcelona's post-Olympic visitor numbers. However, the 105 per cent growth in overnight stays achieved by Barcelona 1990–2000 was so much higher than that experienced by rival cities (who also benefited from a favourable external environment) that the 1992 Games and associated initiatives must have played a crucial role (Duran, 2002).

Capacity building

One of the more subtle tourism effects of staging a major event is that it can inspire a new institutional framework that can lead subsequent tourism development. As Getz (1999) notes, the main tourism goals of staging a major event can be to establish relevant tourism partnerships and to heighten local interest in tourism opportunities. This can be achieved on a formal or an informal level. Turisme de Barcelona – the Catalan city's well regarded tourism agency – was one of the lesser known outcomes of the 1992 Olympic Games. The agency was established in 1993 by the City Council in conjunction with the Chamber of Commerce and the Foundation for the International Promotion of Barcelona. According to Pearce (1997: 87) the establishment of Turisme de Barcelona marked 'an important step forward in a city where the role of tourism had previously been rather neglected'. Athens's not for profit Tourism Development Agency was also a by-product of staging the Olympic Games (Kissoudi, 2010). More informal partnerships can also result from the co-operation that is involved in staging major events. Different parts of the sector (tour operators, hotels, transport providers) may work together to develop packages to satisfy the demands of event tourists. Organisations that would normally compete with each other (e.g. hotels) may also be required to collaborate to facilitate an event. On a more symbolic level, the goodwill and common objectives associated with staging an event can also encourage good relations between industry members.

As well as institutional capacity building, major events have been used to develop the intangible capacity of city destinations in other ways. One common strategy is to encourage language development amongst workers who may come into contact with international tourists during an event. This can help the city's long-term tourism ambitions. Similarly, other service skills can be nurtured prior to the event.

IMPROVEMENTS TO URBAN TOURISM RESOURCES

Host cities often assume that staging an event will make them automatically more attractive to tourists. In reality, higher levels of demand only usually follow

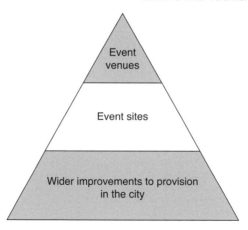

Figure 8.2 *The different spatial scales at which event projects can be used to develop urban tourism attractions*

from an event if a city can demonstrate an improved tourism offer. Major events can influence the provision of tourist attractions at three different spatial scales (see Figure 8.2). New venues and events facilities can act as attractions in themselves; event sites can act as new destination zones in the post-event era; and wider improvements can be made to tourism provision in other parts of the city. These three aspects are discussed further in the sections below.

Venues as new tourism attractions

Major events often help to establish new attractions; these can advance the long-term fortunes of a city's tourism sector. At an obvious level, attractions have sometimes been developed as part of an event site. Barcelona's 1929 World Expo provides a good example. A model village, exhibition spaces, fountains and a palace were built on the Montjuic site for the event and these remain popular attractions today. This approach is also pursued in the contemporary era. Some of the exhibits built for Zaragoza's 2008 World Expo have been retained as permanent attractions – including an innovative river aquarium. Cultural attractions are also bequeathed by events. Many European Capital of Culture hosts have opened new museums and galleries to coincide with the event. These provide the basis for an improved post-event tourism offer. In other examples, event venues have been converted into visitor attractions. For example, Montreal's Olympic velodrome was converted into an ecological museum; venues in other cities have been converted into galleries, theatres, shopping centres and convention halls. Events can also be used to draw attention to existing attractions and landmarks (Richards and Wilson, 2004). For example, Valencia has used major events such

Figure 8.3 *The City of Arts and Sciences in Valencia designed by Santiago Calatrava. The 'Agora' building in the centre hosts an annual ATP tennis event*

as the Open 500 ATP tennis tournament and showjumping tournaments to show-case the development of a new City of Arts and Sciences that includes multiple tourist attractions (see Figure 8.3).

Structures that function as iconic visitor attractions have also been developed in association with events. In some instances, these become symbols of the host city, as well as symbols of the event they are associated with. Towers are often developed using iconic designs, so that they can fulfil functional (points for viewing event sites) and symbolic effects (image development). The Eiffel Tower (developed for the 1889 Paris World Expo) is the obvious example, but the Atomium in Brussels (developed for the 1958 Expo) and Seattle's Space Needle (developed for the 1962 Expo) are also famous city icons developed as part of event projects. Towers have been developed by Olympic hosts such as Amsterdam, Helsinki, Munich and London. Similarly, Doha's Sport City developed for the 2006 Asian Games features an iconic viewing tower (Smith, 2010).

It is perhaps worth remembering that the Eiffel Tower evolved from a controversial structure into a much admired icon. Deliberately trying to create iconic event structures is much more difficult. The efforts of some event hosts have proved that there is a fine line between a destination icon and a futile folly. The Sunsphere in Knoxville, USA – developed as the centrepiece of the 1982 World Expo – is perhaps a good example of the latter. The 1982 Expo was relatively successful, but its legacy was mired in controversy (Monclús, 2009). The Sunsphere survived demolition but it is not well known outside the USA. The structure was later satirised in an episode of *The Simpsons* when Bart and his friends opted for an underwhelming visit to the Knoxville World Expo site rather than going to Disneyland.

The Sunsphere's dramatic collapse in *The Simpsons* is pure fiction, but other icons developed as part of event projects have actually disintegrated. Manchester's 'The B of the Bang' sculpture, designed by Thomas Heatherwick, was developed in conjunction with the 2002 Commonwealth Games. It was inspired by Olympic sprint gold medallist Linford Christie's famous quote about the timing of his starts; and at the time of its construction it was the UK's largest sculpture. Unfortunately, 'The B of the Bang' had to be removed several years after the event when its spikes began to become loose, rendering it a safety hazard. The latest example of an extravagant event icon is the AncelorMittal Tower developed next to London's Olympic Stadium. During preparations for the 2012 Games, legacy planners drew parallels between this structure and the Eiffel Tower to justify its development and the envisaged role it would play (Brown, 2011). Time will tell whether this comparison is justified.

As the discussion above highlights, major event projects often involve the development of iconic monuments and sculptures. These are deliberately built to enhance the image effects of events by generating new synecdochical images that will represent the city as a whole (see Chapter 7). They are also built as structures that can facilitate visitor experiences. Placing the emphasis on iconic visitor attractions is a strategy that extends beyond event projects: it is now very common practice within urban regeneration strategies in general. The idea of using new iconic architecture to generate visitors and to present a new image of the city was reinvigorated by the success of Bilbao, Spain. A new Guggenheim Museum opened here in 1997 and other improvements were made to the city's infrastructure. The new museum was designed in an extravagant style by Frank Gehry and the city received a large amount of publicity and related visits (Plaza, 2000). Many cities have since tried to emulate Bilbao's success, and some of these strategies have been pursued in conjunction with events. When Zaragoza staged its World Expo in 2008, the city's mayor announced that 'vamos a tener seis Guggenheim junto al Ebro' (we are going to have six Guggenheims by the Ebro) (Rollin, 2008). Zaragoza employed superstar architects to design towers, bridges and pavilions in order to achieve 'international renown through innovative and iconic structures' (Rollin, 2008: 267). However, Zaragoza's failure to capture the public imagination suggests that an 'iconic buildings fatigue' now

BOX 8.1 DURBAN

Durban was one of the cities that hosted matches during the 2010 FIFA World Cup. The Moses Mabhida Stadium was built with an innovative design that symbolised the flag of the host nation (see Figure 8.4). The stadium was a 'statement' by the city authorities who wanted to ensure more publicity for Durban and to increase the chances of attracting events in the future. Indeed, the city regarded the World Cup as a stepping stone to bids for the Olympic and/or Commonwealth Games (Maennig and du Plessis, 2009: 67). The design of the stadium – one that includes an unusual walkway across the pitch – also invites visits when events are not taking place. As well as a visitor centre and stadium tours, visitors to the stadium can enjoy some innovative attractions. The stadium's walkway is used to facilitate three different experiences. Visitors can ride up the arch in a 'SkyCar', they can walk up the arch using safety equipment, or (for the bravest of them), they can swing from a rope 106 metres above the stadium. This ensures that the design of the stadium facilitates tourist experiences, as well as merely tourist imagery for the city.

Figure 8.4 *The Moses Mabhida Stadium in Durban, built for the 2010 FIFA World Cup. Another arched stadium – although, unlike Wembley Stadium, this arch can be traversed by visitors*

exists which means it is becoming harder to use contemporary architecture to differentiate post-industrial cities.

Event sites as tourist destinations

Although tourists and the tourism sector benefit from the wider infrastructural legacy bequeathed by major events, the tourism potential of event sites is often neglected. Event sites have been designed to accommodate hundreds of thousands of people and too many cities presume that they will be attractive tourist zones even when events are not being staged. Although such spaces are usually well endowed with transport infrastructure, landscaping and public art, they are often in peripheral areas and exposed to the elements. These sites can – symbolically and literally – leave people feeling cold. One of the reasons Montreal's Olympic site is so unloved is because it is seen as cold and unattractive (Roult and Lefebvre, 2010). As event sites can be vast spaces, there are often inconveniently large distances between the different structures that might be of interest to tourists. Such spaces look spectacular when filled with large numbers of spectators, but rather pathetic when events are not being staged. This means they can be underwhelming tourist sites.

Some event sites have become important tourism attractions because of good design, and/or their symbolic associations. Munich's Olympic Park (developed for the 1972 Games) still attracts 4 million paying visitors per year: 2.3 million who are attending events and 1.7 million who use the recreational facilities (2010 figures; from OlympiaPark München GmbH, 2011). This success may be explained by the fact that the Olympic Park 'was clearly oriented towards urban leisure' (Munoz, 2006) and so retains a functional value. In Seoul, the Olympic Park site attracts 6 million visitors annually to view the parklands and the museums and facilities that exist within it (Pitts and Liao, 2009).

There is a considerable market for event nostalgia and this is something event hosts can capitalise on to attract tourists in the post-event period. By providing markers, associated attractions, exhibitions and anniversary celebrations, host cities can effectively extend the life of an event. Even when event sites have been converted to other purposes, cities often leave monuments to the event to remind people about what happened there. For example, New York's Corona Park still contains some of the pavilions and sculptures constructed for the World Expos staged there in 1939–40 and 1964–5. One of these, the Unisphere, has become an important symbol of the borough of Queens. Other cities have developed visitor centres or museums dedicated to a particular event. These attractions help to commemorate an event and they make event spaces more meaningful to post-event visitors. There have also been more unusual ways of commemorating events staged. Until it left the city in 2004, Montreal's basketball team was called the Expos – in honour of the 1967 Expo staged in the city.

WIDER TOURISM PROJECTS

Just as event projects should be incorporated into wider, established urban regeneration objectives (see Chapter 5), event projects can be used to further long-held tourism ambitions. In Athens, host of the 2004 Olympic Games, the unification of the historic core had been a vision for decades. According to Kissoudi (2010) the Olympic Games provided the momentum to achieve this. New walkways were introduced that linked the main historic sites, including the Acropolis, Roman Agora, Library of Adriano and – fittingly – the temple of the Olympian Zeus (Kissoudi, 2010). Streets and squares were upgraded and the façades of many buildings improved. In other examples, events have helped to realise ambitions to regenerate city centre attractions. Barcelona's recovery of its modernista heritage during its preparations for the 1992 Olympic Games is an example of using an event as an opportunity to deliver established tourism/heritage projects (Smith, 2005b). Similarly, the 1994 European Capital of Culture staged in Lisbon provided a good opportunity to rejuvenate the Coliseu dos Recreios – one of the city's most important symbols and the traditional venue for the city's key cultural events (Holton, 1998).

Hotel development

Hotel development is neglected within the urban regeneration literature. It is also under-represented within the emerging literature on events and regeneration. Hotels are significant urban structures that can play a useful role within physical regeneration. They are labour-intensive facilities that can provide employment at various levels, including accessible jobs for people with few skills. There is often a career path through low-level positions to high level positions in many hotels and this offers possibilities to use hotels within economic regeneration. Hotels can be useful additions to disadvantaged areas, as they offer jobs, as well as amenities that may be used by local residents. They can operate as a hybrid of public and private space and certain parts of hotels (such as lobbies) can act as the interface between public and private spaces (McNeill, 2008). This means they can perform social, as well as economic roles within urban areas. The value of hotels in urban regeneration depends on their location, design and management. Unfortunately many hotels are designed as inward-looking institutions that have poor links with surrounding areas (McNeill, 2008). This is a characteristic they share with event venues (see Chapter 4).

Figure 8.5 *The Hotel Arts in Barcelona built at the time the city staged the 1992 Olympic Games. The hoarding is particularly apt considering Monica Degen's (2003) paper on Barcelona is entitled 'Fighting for the Global Catwalk'*

Hotels are often developed in association with major events, either close to new venues or in central locations that are easily accessible by public transport. Events of the past have been responsible for some of the world's most famous hotels. The Strand hotel in Stockholm, the Château Champlain in Montreal, the Cosmos Hotel in Moscow, and the Hotel Arts in Barcelona (see Figure 8.5) were all developed in association with the Olympic Games. These properties play a similar role to major attractions or venues as they provide synecdochical images and flagship projects which can encourage further development. Building new hotels in association with major events continues in the contemporary era. Events can stimulate hotel construction on a large scale. For example, twenty new properties were built in Seville in preparation for the 1992 World Expo (Maddox, 2004). Events have been used to develop large new hotels (a twenty-three-storey hotel was built for the 1986 Vancouver Expo) or more specialised provision: two new boutique hotels (Malmaison and Hard Days Night) were built in Liverpool to coincide with Liverpool's Capital of Culture Event in 2008. Host cities have also developed hotels on event sites in the post-event period. For example, since 2000 two properties – catering for very different segments of the market – have opened in Sydney's Olympic Park.

There are a number of issues with hotel development in association with events. New rooms come 'on stream' simultaneously and this sudden increase in the size of the local hotel sector can lead to over-capacity in the immediate post-event era. Unless further projects are pursued in the aftermath of a major event (other events, new attractions, intense marketing), host cities tend to find it difficult to fill rooms in the period following an event. This leads to a downward pressure on room rates and, ultimately, to the closure of hotels. This was the case after the 1994 Winter Olympic Games in Lillehammer, Norway. Tourism arrivals peaked during the year before the Games and the provision of new hotel accommodation meant a steep decline in occupancy levels immediately after the event. The diminishing returns for hotels meant that approximately 40 per cent of the full service hotels went bankrupt (Tieglund, 1999). A similar situation occurred in Seville, host of the 1992 World Expo. Hotel capacity was 6,673 in 1988, but the twenty new properties meant the city's bed stock rose to 17,282 by 1993 (De Groote, 2005). This led to a very low occupancy rate of 27 per cent in 1993 and, because of related closures, by 1997 bed capacity had fallen to 15,852 (De Groote, 2005). Closures also meant that, by 1982, the number of hotel rooms in downtown Montreal had declined to the levels that existed before the 1976 Olympic Games (Whitson, 2004).

Gold and Gold (2005: 5) express concern about the long-term viability of hotels developed in association with events. They state that 'newly opened large scale hotels, especially those that are part of luxury hotel chains, frequently change hands after the festivals when local management fail to attract either tourists or the anticipated conference trade'. Hotels located in edge city sites near to event venues can seem rather anonymous and bleak places to stay when major events are not being staged. One way of dealing with this problem is to integrate hotels within the venues themselves. This can turn a rather dispiriting experience into a memorable one. Some of these hotels even offer views of event arenas from the rooms. Examples include the Marriott Hotel at the UK's national rugby stadium, Twickenham.

Avoiding over-capacity in the post-event era

Some holders of event rights (e.g. the IOC) stipulate the minimum number of hotel rooms that must be provided in host cities, but most events are more flexible. One way of avoiding building unnecessary new hotel space is to use temporary provision. This can come in various forms including student accommodation, military barracks and campsites. Accommodation like this may seem rather basic, but research from the 2002 FIFA World Cup in South Korea indicates that event tourists often seek cheaper accommodation (Cho, 2005). Hosting event tourists together in specialist accommodation can even help maximise the event experience. Tourists attending the 2002 World Cup may not have liked the Korean-style Yogwans (Cho, 2005), but the campsites opened in public parks for England's 1996 European Football Championships were a great success. If host cities are located by waterfronts, then cruise ships and waterborne accommodation can also be used to provide temporary accommodation. This was a strategy used successfully by Barcelona – it helped to draw attention to the city's new waterfront. Following the logic introduced in Chapter 4, host cities can also build relationships with neighbouring towns and cities to make use of their hotel stock. In some host cities this may solve the problem of an undersupply of accommodation. For example, during the 2010 FIFA World Cup, the agency responsible for co-ordinating ticketing and travel provision (MATCH AG) contracted accommodation throughout South Africa, including some in National Parks, because it was worried about a significant accommodation deficit (Cornelissen, 2010).

One way of increasing capacity during an event is to encourage home owners to rent their properties. Providing homestays can be seen as a rudimentary way of building capacity from the bottom-up in urban areas that are short of hotel rooms. This can lead to a more permanent increase in accommodation supply. During the run-up to the London 2012 Olympic Games there was an initiative by the Borough of Lewisham to assist home owners who were interested in converting their homes into guest house facilities. Large numbers of people expressed an interest, but it remains to be seen how the project will affect the levels of accommodation provision in the borough. These initiatives are notoriously difficult to manage because of licensing requirements for accommodation and the need for adequate safety provision and insurance protection. In the build-up to the 1984 Olympic Games, a large number of people in LA paid to list their homes as available for rent. But after becoming aware of the legal requirements, many removed their homes from the listings (Lawson, 1985). Demand for these types of initiative is often driven by the media, who exaggerate the expectations of local people about the money-making opportunities that may arise from staging a major event. The reality is often very different, and even if opportunities to make money do exist, there are often financial and legal hurdles that prevent local people and small businesses from accessing them.

Hotel plans

To deliver the hotel provision required in the short and long term, host cities often develop hotel plans in association with events. These provide planning guidance to indicate how much provision is required and where it should go. The plan

provides the framework within which hotel developers and local planning authorities operate. In some instances, incentives (e.g. tax breaks, planning exemptions
or extra land) may be offered to hotel companies to build properties in certain
locations. But hotel plans merely guide development, they cannot guarantee it
will take place. Barcelona's hotel plan of 1986 (prepared in advance of the
1992 Olympic Games) aimed to provide 18,000 new rooms in addition to the
12,000 that already existed in the city (Garcia and Claver, 2003). This level was
achieved only in 1994 and the flagship development – the Hotel Arts – was not
completed in time. This property finally opened in 1993 and by 1994 occupancy
rates had fallen to around 54 per cent (Garcia and Claver, 2003). However,
the increased popularity of the city in the post-event era meant that demand for
Barcelona rooms outstripped supply in the late 1990s, vindicating the new developments in the long term. The vast majority of the hotels were locally owned, or
owned by Spanish companies (Garcia and Claver, 2003), and this optimised the
economic development effects.

Rather than using events to deliver overall increases in hotel capacity, it makes
sense for host sites to encourage the development of particular hotel types that the
destination currently lacks; or the development of hotels in locations where insufficient accommodation is provided. If possible, planning permissions should
include stipulations about engaging local employees. Ideally, when regeneration
is the key objective, new hotels should be located on brownfield sites. This isn't
always the case. Barcelona's Federation of Neighbourhood Associations (FAVB)
campaigned against the city's Olympic hotel plan which reclassified areas
originally earmarked as public/green zones as suitable for hotels (Blakeley,
2005). It also objected to the way in which Barcelona's 2004 Universal Forum of
Cultures project involved the development of hotels on public land (Blakeley,
2005). Hotel strategies should not just focus on building new hotels. Events
can be used as a stimulus to improve existing properties to improve service quality and standards. In the run-up to the Athens Olympic Games, big hotel chains
initiated renovation programmes and developed service innovations (Kissoudi,
2010).

A difficult issue with hotel provision during major events is profiteering. When
cities stage popular events there is a danger that hotels will charge exorbitant
rates. This can damage the visitor experience and the long-term image of the
destination. In the run-up to the 2012 Olympic Games London's mayor Boris
Johnson complained that inflated room rates could have an adverse effect on
tourism to London with 'repercussions for decades to come' (Bryant, 2011: 24).
It is difficult to implement interventions to force hotels to charge certain prices,
but several event hosts have adopted voluntary agreements in association with
events. Hotels may agree to set rates that are pegged to amounts charged in
similar periods in previous years. For example, during the 1984 Olympic Games

in LA there was a voluntary pledge programme. Hotels agreed to charge rates that were not significantly different from those charged earlier the same year. Participating properties were given the right to display an official badge to show they were part of the scheme (Lawson, 1985). However, average room rates were still significantly higher during the Games. And even if city authorities or trade associations can co-ordinate voluntary anti-profiteering schemes amongst hotels, these may not prevent tour operators from charging excessive amounts for pack-aged products that involve accommodation.

THE RELATIONSHIP BETWEEN EVENTS, TOURISM AND URBAN REGENERATION

The preceding sections have introduced the way in which events can assist tourism and regeneration. The relationship between events, tourism and regeneration is often conceived as a process in which an event inspires tourism and this leads to regeneration. This is represented by the linear process:

Event → Tourism → Regeneration

Image is conceived as the main mechanism through which this is to be achieved, so the process can be seen more specifically as one where events are supposed to enhance images, leading to tourism and urban regeneration:

Event → Image enhancement → Tourism → Regeneration

This type of process typifies the approach adopted by Atlanta, USA, where the organisers of the 1996 Olympic Games emphasised that 'image, prestige and pride are the real residuals' which would provide a platform for subsequent urban revival (Rutheiser, 1996: 285). The perceived failure of Atlanta's strategy highlights flaws with this model of regeneration.

Each different part of the process outlined above is questionable. The discussion in Chapter 7 highlighted that cities cannot assume that all image effects will be positive, thus casting doubt on the initial part of the envisaged process (Event → Image enhancement). Whether tourism arrivals will always follow image enhancement is also questionable (Ritchie and Smith, 1991; Chalip et al., 2003). Critics have berated the regenerative power of tourism to achieve regeneration. Authors such as Hatherley (2010) are dismissive of the regeneration effects of high-profile tourism projects pursued in post-industrial cities. There are doubts about the viability of projects, the quality of jobs, the seasonality of labour and the suitability of the employment for those who have lost manufacturing jobs. Even when tourism projects work there may be associated problems such as gentrification, urban polarisation and community disenfranchisement.

This doesn't mean that events cannot be used to encourage regeneration. Successful event regeneration may choose to ignore tourism as a mechanism, and even if it is incorporated, there are ways to combine events, tourism and regeneration more successfully. One way is to use regeneration in association with an event to deliver increased tourism receipts (Smith, 2006). In such cases, tourism is an outcome of, rather than a mechanism for, regeneration effects. This characterises the approach taken by Barcelona, generally regarded as the most successful example of urban regeneration involving a major event (the 1992 Olympic Games). Barcelona has not been regenerated through tourism; instead tourism is one of the beneficial outcomes of developing a more attractive environment for city residents. The event was used as a means to generate funding, publicity and widespread support for more fundamental changes to the city (see Chapter 5).

In terms of maximising tourism benefits from events, it is essential that tourism impacts are properly planned. Too many cities simply assume that major events and associated international exposure will guarantee them subsequent tourism receipts. Urban authorities need to think about what tourism benefits an event may bring and how best to capitalise on those benefits. Cities should consider moving beyond a focus on event tourism by using event sites to house a coherent set of attractions that are accessible to tourists regardless of when they travel or whether they can get hold of elusive tickets (Smith, 2006). Durban's stadium precinct, Seoul's Olympic Park and Munich's Olympic Park are good examples. Furthermore, just as event regeneration should involve a diverse range of projects, some of which may be only tenuously linked to the event itself, cities should consider events as an ideal opportunity to launch a series of diverse tourism initiatives. If timed to coincide with major events, such initiatives will benefit from enhanced opportunities for funding, publicity and civic support; and should help to leave a durable legacy for cities long after an event's closing ceremony (Smith, 2006).

SUMMARY

Promoting a city as a tourist destination is perhaps the most common way major events are used to stimulate a new direction for cities. The tourism sector epitomises the service sector future that many post-industrial cities have targeted. However, tourism is not always viewed positively as an urban regeneration tool. This is a sector that privileges outside interests; and tourism facilities are often concentrated in a distinct zone segregated from other urban districts. Even if a city is successful in reinventing itself as a tourist destination, this may create insecure, poor-quality jobs and challenge the ambience and texture of the city (Lewis, 2003). The wider relationship between events, tourism and urban regeneration is also a tenuous one. However, this has not stopped cities trying to use events to assist the development of tourism. Events can be used to help develop new attractions and tourism precincts as well as improving accommodation and wider supply provision. There have been some examples of success. However, there remains a strong possibility of failure and the odds of succeeding are lengthened by the sheer number of cities that are trying to use major events to launch themselves as tourist destinations. More competition between cities makes it both harder to secure major events and harder to make an impression with those events.

EXTENDED CASE STUDY 5: TOURISM, EVENTS AND URBAN REGENERATION IN NEW ORLEANS

The US city of New Orleans is a good example of a city where tourism and events have played a significant part in urban regeneration. Despite the severe problems experienced since 2005 – when Hurricane Katrina caused devastation throughout the city and other parts of the state of Louisiana – New Orleans remains one of the USA's most popular tourist cities. In 2010 the city attracted 8.3 million visitors. This was the first year that visitor numbers had returned to pre-Katrina levels. The city's success as a tourist destination is a relatively recent phenomenon, and one that has been greatly assisted by major events staged there. The range of events staged in New Orleans means it exemplifies a wide range of issues and processes. However, it is perhaps best seen as an example of how a city has used events, and the regeneration associated with events, to build a successful tourism sector.

Like many other cities mentioned in this book New Orleans suffered greatly from severe de-industrialisation in the late 1960s and 1970s. The city's gas and oil sectors collapsed in this period and manufacturing employment declined significantly. These economic problems resulted in a 10 per cent reduction in the number of people living in New Orleans (Gotham, 2011), contributing to a diminishing tax base from which to fund public services. This is a problem that afflicts many cities undergoing de-industrialisation. Part of the city's response to this crisis was to plan a major event that would instigate a service sector led revival. Montreal had staged a successful World Expo in 1967 and city leaders argued that an Expo in New Orleans could 'stimulate and accelerate the construction of a major convention centre, a national park, a science oriented museum [and] the redevelopment of dilapidated neighbourhoods' (Gotham, 2011: 202). A steering committee was established in 1975 and this evolved into a consortium of private interests that organised the (publicly funded) event. In 1981, the BIE granted approval for the 1984 Louisiana World Expo. Reflecting the 'world of rivers' theme, an 33 hectares site adjacent to the Mississippi was designated as the venue (see Figure 8.6). This was a former

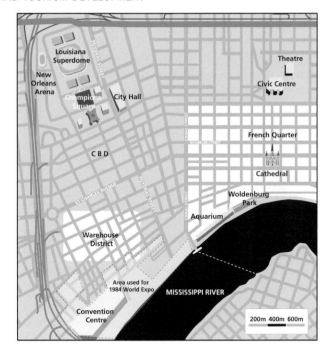

Figure 8.6 *A map of central New Orleans highlighting key event-related sites*

industrial district near to the centre which had largely been forgotten by the city (Lewis, 2003).

The 1984 World Expo

The Louisiana World Expo played an important role in securing long-term tourism resources for New Orleans. But the organisation of the Expo itself was beset with problems. The event was staged in 1984 to coincide with the centenary of a previous World Expo. This event had helped to establish Audabon Park and reinforced uptown New Orleans's reputation as the city's affluent residential district (Lewis, 2003). But the sentimental timing of the 1984 Expo was poorly judged because of competing events. Another US Expo was staged in Knoxville in 1982 and Vancouver had already begun preparing for an Expo in 1986. Furthermore, in 1984 – the year that New Orleans staged the Expo – Los Angeles hosted the Olympic Games. These rival events diverted attention and federal government resources away from Louisiana's event. Soon after its inception, it became clear that the Expo would not receive the federal backing enjoyed by other major events. Indeed, whilst Knoxville's Expo received $350 million from the US federal government, the organisers of Louisiana's World Expo were promised merely $10 million to cover the costs of the US pavilion (Dimanche, 1997). Ticket sales were hindered by high prices, sponsorship revenues were low and organisers had to seek a series of emergency loans from the state government (Gotham, 2011).

Despite the financial problems, the event went ahead as planned, and attracted 7.3 million visitors – mainly from inside the state (Dimanche, 1997). This was less than the 12 million anticipated and the shortfall led to further financial problems. Ultimately, the organisation responsible for managing the event was declared bankrupt in November 1984 with debts of $100 million (Gotham, 2011). The problems arguably led to US cities' loss of faith in World Expos, which contributed to the cancellation of an Expo planned for Chicago in 1992. No US city has staged a World Expo since the New Orleans debacle (Gotham, 2011).

The legacy of the 1984 World Expo

If one merely analyses the short-term impacts of the event, the Louisiana World Expo provides a good example of how not to organise a major event. But viewed retrospectively, the long-term legacy for the city's tourism sector has been extremely positive. Indeed, Dimanche (1997) describes the long-term impact of the event as 'tremendous'. The investments funded and inspired the physical regeneration of the New Orleans waterfront – which is now a key focus for successful tourism and entertainment sectors. As well as providing New Orleans with a 'wonderful new waterfront', Lewis (2003: 109) suggests that the long-term effect of the Expo 'was to help convert a considerable swathe of decaying wharves, warehouses and slums into some of the city's most attractive and vibrant territory'. The result was the regeneration of the warehouse district (see Figure 8.6) – New Orleans's version of New York's Soho. As well as being a successful real-estate venture, new hotels emerged in this district. Lewis (2003) describes the regeneration of this part of the city as an unintended consequence of staging the Expo. However, the regeneration may not have happened without the event, and even if it had, it would have taken substantially longer to come to fruition. As Lewis (2003: 112) recognises, the process of opening the riverfront to the public was already underway, but the World Expo provided 'a sort of municipal steroids' for the project. Improvements to the riverfront continued to be made into the 1990s, benefiting both tourists and residents who could reconnect with a riverfront that had been inaccessible (and invisible) for many years.

The long-term tourism effects of the event were impressive. The 1984 Expo resulted in 10,000 new hotel rooms being built. Major companies opened properties in the city, including Sheraton, Intercontinental, Hilton, Westin, Meridien, Windsor Court and Holiday Inn. This glut of new accommodation encouraged under-occupancy in the years following the event, but it helped to provide a solid foundation for the growth of New Orleans tourism sector in the 1990s. Although hotel occupancy rates fell to 53 per cent in 1985, by 1993 they had recovered to 74 per cent (Dimanche, 1997). During the 1990s there was a 35 per cent increase in employment in hotels, bars and restaurants (Lewis, 2003). The $88 million convention centre used as the great hall for the World Expo has also proved to be a major success (see Figure 8.6). In 1976 the city staged 764 conventions per annum, but by 1992 this had risen to 2,000 (Gotham, 2005b). The convention centre became so successful that it was enlarged in 1991 and expanded again in 2000 (Lewis, 2003). Lewis (2003) suggests that now it has become so big that the riverfront is beginning to be obscured once more! Industrial buildings were converted into leisure facilities and the event spawned one of James Rouse's famed festival marketplaces. Other new facilities were constructed along the riverfront including an aquarium, casino and public park. These facilities helped to encourage a 63 per cent increase in tourism 1990–1998 (Gotham, 2005b).

Other events

The 1984 World Expo is credited with laying the foundations for New Orleans's tourism-led regeneration, but other events have helped to capitalise on this new tourism infrastructure. The city has staged a series of significant events, including the Superbowl, and it has invested in events such as the Jazz and Heritage Festival (650,000 attendees) and the Essence African American Festival (220,000 attendees) (Gotham, 2005b). The event that has played the biggest role in New Orleans's success as a destination is the annual Mardi Gras celebration. As Gotham (2005b: 309) states, 'in the last two decades or so, Mardi Gras has become the lynchpin of a burgeoning tourism industry'. This was confirmed by the mayor's office, which stated in 1995 that 'we build many of our tourism and marketing strategies around Mardi Gras' (cited in Gotham, 2005b: 313).

The New Orleans Mardi Gras involves the twelve days of festivities leading up to Fat Tuesday. Gotham (2005b) estimates that the event can attract up to 6.1 million spectators, with 2.2 million classed as visitors. In 2000, the event generated $1 billion of expenditure for the first time (Gotham, 2005b), but its role as a marketing tool is perhaps even more valuable. The growth of the event has inevitably led to changes, both in the meaning of the festivities and the actual organisation of the parades. In 2000, 70 per cent of the 3,000 residents surveyed felt that the event had become less meaningful for them, because it had evolved into a lewd, tourist-oriented event (Gotham, 2005b). Barricades now separate spectators from the processions, routes have been consolidated in the centre (most follow St Charles Avenue – see Figure 8.6) and commercial interests have begun to infiltrate floats. As Gotham (2005b: 310) argues, the event has reached a level of notoriety that means, whilst it is still a local celebration, 'it is also a marketing slogan to stimulate consumer demand for corporate products'. Thus, while New Orleans may have developed a successful visitor economy, the exploitation of events as tourism resources has come with significant costs.

Major events have undoubtedly helped New Orleans to develop into a successful tourist destination. Investments in events and event spaces have supported the integrated tourism development of the city. Mardi Gras has helped the city to be perceived as a liminal place of festivity; a reputation that has supported the development of events that celebrate marginalised groups including gay events such as Southern Decadence. Events have also delivered year-round tourism. The image of an events city inspires visits and spending on souvenirs even at times when major events are not taking place. New Orleans's events focus has spawned an industry that services events staged in the city, but also those staged elsewhere (Gotham, 2005b). Permanent visitor attractions have been established that draw upon the city's reputation for events: for example, Jazzland – a 57 hectares theme park in the east of the city. The World Expo bequeathed facilities and spaces which could be used by the events that have been staged subsequently. This relationship is reciprocal, in that regular events have helped to publicise the new facilities and venues that were developed. A good example is the development of Lundi Gras – an event that takes place the day before Fat Tuesday. This event was reinstated in 1987 and it was deliberately staged at Rouse's festival marketplace; thus connecting Mardi Gras to the newly developed Expo riverfront.

The Superdome

New Orleans's reputation as one of the world's great event destinations is supplemented by the major sport events that it hosts regularly. In the 1970s, the city constructed the Louisiana Superdome which is used to stage the annual American football event, the Sugar Bowl. The stadium enabled the city to attract an American football NFL franchise – the Saints – and it is also the home to the Essence music festival mentioned above. At the time of its construction the twenty-seven-storey structure created the world's largest room. The size of the stadium seemed out of scale with the rest of the city, and the project cost five times more then expected, but the Superdome helped to revive the downtown area near Poydras Street (see Figure 8.6). This avenue eventually replaced Canal Street as the city's main artery. The Superdome underwent a major refurbishment in 2011 and the facility is now surrounded by the Louisiana Stadium and Exposition district – a collection of venues that includes the New Orleans

Arena (home of NBA franchise, the Hornets) and Champions Square (see Figure 8.6). The latter is a public space adjacent to La Salle Street which hosts celebrations, concerts and pre/post-event festivities.

In recent years the Louisiana Superdome became visible to the world when it provided shelter to thousands of New Orleans residents who were unable to escape from the city when Hurricane Katrina struck in August 2005. The low-lying city was badly affected when levees were breached (80 per cent of New Orleans was covered with water). Many took refuge in the Superdome but the ventilation and sanitation facilities were unable to cope with the influx of people and conditions became unbearable. Schimmel (2006) suggests that this event was highly symbolic in that the TV pictures of people inside New Orleans's tourist zone was a rare representation of urban life outside this bubble. Ironically, this may have been one of the few times many poorer New Orleans residents had ever entered the Superdome or the district that surrounds it.

Images of disadvantaged black people sheltering in the Superdome in the after-math of Hurricane Katrina remind us that New Orleans is a city with a large black population and a history of racial segregation. This is something that can be linked to events in several ways. The 1984 Expo was criticised for the low levels of black employees amongst the workforce. However, Gotham (2011: 207) suggests that the Expo contributed indirectly to campaigns for racial equality because it 'became a medium for the communication of political dissent and a cultural battlefield in which activists manoeuvred and struggled to challenge the racial status quo'. This links to the notion discussed in Chapter 2 that events can facilitate challenges to the establishment. During the aftermath of the Expo, a Black Tourism Network was established that aimed to increase opportunities for African Americans in the industry (Gotham, 2011). In 1996 the State of Louisiana created a multicultural branch of the state tourism office which worked with the Black Tourism Network to identify and promote sites of historical significance for black communities. Gotham (2011) links these initiatives directly to the protests that accompanied the Expo strategy, highlighting the role of events as ways of exposing and opposing injustice.

Postscript

By 2011, the long-term effects of Hurricane Katrina were becoming clear. Figures showed that the city's population had declined by 100,000 in the period 2005–2011 (Pilkington, 2011). This dwarfs the levels of depopulation experienced in the 1970s. The most disadvantaged citizens have suffered most and many black people have moved out of the city and not returned. This, plus the effects of a prolonged recession, meant that over twenty-five years after it staged the Louisiana World Expo, New Orleans is once again searching for ways to instigate regeneration. In a return to the vision of the 1970s, city authorities seem to have chosen the river as the focus of New Orleans's latest regeneration plans. The ambitious 'Reinventing the Crescent' project seeks to redevelop several kilometres of waterfront as parklands – extending the existing promenade from the city centre to the industrial canal.

9 Delivering event regeneration

INTRODUCTION

The preceding chapters in this book have focused on the different aspects of event regeneration initiatives; what they aim to achieve and some brief illustrations of effects. In this chapter the emphasis is on delivery: in other words, how these initiatives are implemented. The delivery of event regeneration projects reflects the delivery of more conventional urban policy. This means it is important to understand some general mechanisms that are used within urban policy, and these are introduced here. However, using a major event within urban regeneration can mean that different agencies are involved and different mechanisms adopted. These exceptional arrangements are also discussed. In some instances major events have actually been responsible for changing the way urban policy is delivered and these changes have been sustained in the post-event era. This trend is also covered in this chapter.

Delivery can be sub-divided into two key elements and these provide the two main sections in this chapter. First, the individuals and agencies involved and the relationships between these agencies. The role of government agencies, partnerships between public agencies, partnerships between public and private agencies and coalitions of private interests are all discussed. Second, the mechanisms used by these agencies to implement projects. The elements of implementation discussed in this section are funding, planning procedures and more specific delivery mechanisms that can be used in conjunction with events.

DELIVERY AGENCIES

As Marcuse (cited in Porter *et al.*, 2009) reminds us, cities do not bid for and implement event projects: governmental leaders do. Accordingly, in this section the aim is to discuss the agencies involved in event regeneration.

The public sector

Event regeneration policy is formulated and implemented by a range of different stakeholders. Government agencies representing different scales are usually involved. Although arrangements differ according to the context under consideration, there are normally three different levels of government involved in event projects:

- Local authorities representing people within individual districts within cities
- Municipal governments representing the populations of cities as a whole
- National governments representing the nation in which a city is located.

In countries where national government is devolved, regional governments are also important stakeholders. And supra-national agencies may also play a role in certain contexts (e.g. in the EU). Event regeneration projects are usually led by city councils with the support of national governments. Many event rights holders often want national governments to be involved to provide financial and political support. Indeed, the availability of this backing is increasingly part of the criteria used to judge candidate cities for World Expos, Olympic Games and other major events. In some examples of event regeneration, the national government is the lead agency. This arrangement tends to occur when the event is deemed to be of great national significance, or in smaller nations where centralisation of political power is more common. Expo '98 in Lisbon is a good example. The project was 'heavily entwined with the national selling of Lisbon' and so it was delivered as a national, rather than a city level, initiative (Nunes Silva and Syrett, 2006: 109). National-level delivery was a less risky option, but one of the negative outcomes was it meant that an opportunity to develop institutional capacity at the city level was missed. As a result, city agencies in Lisbon remain underdeveloped compared to those in other cities (Nunes Silva and Syrett, 2006). The size of major events means that local authorities who represent individual districts within cities do not usually lead on event projects; however, they remain important stakeholders and often retain influence through development control mechanisms (see below).

Events and city governments

At the city level, Lever (2001) suggests that good mayors help to secure event projects and that the strategic use of major events is a key characteristic of good mayors. This is a contentious argument, but it does highlight the influential role of city leaders in event projects. Charismatic city mayors who lead event projects provide a good illustration of the trend for personalisation of city governance. Glasgow's provost Michael Kelly is cited by Lever (2001) as an example of an individual city leader who was responsible for driving a successful event regeneration project (the 1990 European City of Culture). Interestingly, these projects seem to be pursued by city mayors on both the left and right of the political spectrum. This is evidenced by the similarities in the strategies pursued by left-wing (social democratic) mayors in Barcelona during the 1980s/1990s and those of Valencia's (neo-liberal) conservative regime more recently.

The preparations of Barcelona in advance of the 1992 Olympic Games provide a useful illustration of the important role of city mayors in event regeneration. Barcelona's Olympic regeneration is intrinsically associated with the efforts of Mayor Pasqual Maragall (1982–1997). By the time he was elected, Barcelona had already begun to emerge from Spain's dictatorship that ended in 1975, but Maragall was responsible for co-ordinating the latter stages of the city's transformation. Mayor Maragall became the embodiment of Barcelona's Games strategy even though some claim that the most important regeneration work was commissioned before he took office. After the success of the Games, Maragall's efforts were lauded around the world – so much so that cities began to look at the model of governance that had facilitated Barcelona's transformation. London was one city that looked on enviously: the adoption of more powerful mayoral positions in London and other cities is partly due to the perceived success of Barcelona's system of governance in general – and the regime of Maragall in particular.

Major events may be sought and strategically deployed by proactive mayors, but they also provide convenient ways to bolster mayoral power and influence. In this sense, major events can provide significant levers for individuals to shape urban development. London established its new mayoral position in 2000, but until the Olympic Games bid was won (in 2005) the mayor's influence over large-scale regeneration was relatively small. Newman (2007: 260) suggests that, whereas the mayor of London was in a weak position prior to 2005, after London's bid for the 2012 Olympic Games was successful he gained 'substantial authority over large scale renewal'. This observation helps to justify Newman's (2007) prediction that the most significant long-term impact of the 2012 Olympics in London would be its influence on the city's politics and political structure, not necessarily its impact on London's urban development. That is why it is important to examine the effects that event projects have on urban governance, as well as the effects that urban governance arrangements have on event projects.

Multi-level governance

Most major event projects have involvement from different levels of government. This means there are opportunities to employ and develop forms of multi-level governance, where partnerships are forged between government stakeholders at different scales. This may include rare examples of where local authorities and supra-national agencies work in tandem. An arrangement such as this is the epitome of what Swyngedouw (2004) terms glocalisation. Good examples of multi-level governance include Barcelona's Olympic regeneration projects (which involved the city, the region, the state and the EU governments) but also France's 1998 World Cup. The regeneration associated with the Stade de France project in Paris involved different government stakeholders who represented different spatial scales. In France, local districts are organised into communes. The communes surrounding the stadium site were not happy for the state to assume full control of the project – as it had done in other high-profile Parisian urban schemes such as the redevelopment of La Défense (Newman and Thornley, 1996). However, state involvement was needed because locally co-ordinated efforts in the 1990s had been under-funded and unsuccessful (Newman and Thornley, 1996). The site was a former gasworks which had passed to the City of Paris when gas production ceased in 1980 (Newman and Tual, 2002). This meant any project to develop the site had to involve some form of multi-level governance involving the City and the local communes, as well as the state government. The communes were initially reluctant to sanction the stadium project 'fearing distortion of their own planning objectives and the sterilisation of the area' (Newman and Thornley, 1996: 186). Although the state government remained in overall control, local mayors were able to influence the project to prioritise local jobs, transport improvements, better integration of the project with the local area and inclusion of housing projects within the plans (Body-Gendrot, 2003).

Disruption and upheaval

One of the problems with event projects led by the public sector is that elections and associated changes in government can disrupt plans. The long event horizons associated with major events mean that political changes are highly likely. In Greece, there was a change of government at the national level in April 2004, just months before the 2004 Olympic Games began. The change meant that plans prepared by the agency responsible for organising the re-use of Olympic venues were subjected to major revisions (Gospodini, 2009). This may help to explain the sub-optimal use of Games facilities outlined in Chapter 4. Even if the build-up to an event is not disrupted by a change of government, new administrations can disrupt the legacy period. One of Clark's (2008: 178) recommendations for host cities is that they should 'Beware of the event's legacy being susceptible to political changes in the city authorities after the event.' For example, after Porto's European Capital of Culture event (2001), changes in political leadership meant that cultural and regeneration budgets were slashed – and the momentum gained during the event was lost (Clark, 2008). A similar situation occurred in

Glasgow, where progress stalled after the 1990 European City of Culture event because new city leaders adopted a different approach to the more innovative one adopted by the mayor responsible for the event (Lever, 2001). Major event projects are often controversial, and this may mean that events are not merely affected by political upheaval; they can be the causes of it. This increases the chances that event plans will be disrupted by discontinuities in governance arrangements.

Event agencies

The regeneration legacy of an event is often dependent on the management arrangements adopted. Governments establish specialist event agencies to manage event projects on their behalf. These agencies are usually set up as arm's-length companies funded by the public sector, but able to act as commercial enterprises. For example, to deliver the 2008 European Capital of Culture event, Liverpool City Council established a company limited by guarantee (the Liverpool Culture Company). This is a common model for not-for-profit enterprises in the UK. Although the agency had an external board, this 'company' was effectively staffed by Liverpool City Council employees (O'Brien, 2011). For major events that involve substantial capital investment projects two separate agencies may be established: one that focuses on the development of venues/infrastructure and another that focuses on the management/marketing of the event. These agencies are often led by appointed officials who may have been involved in previous events. There are usually elected government representatives on the board, and governments retain direct control over budgets and monitoring functions. However, these agencies can lack accountability and transparency and this challenges democratic principles.

Specialist agencies

As regeneration objectives have emerged as a key priority, specialist legacy agencies have been established. Clark (2008) recommends that host cities should: 'Establish from the start, a structure/organisation with the responsibility for implementing the longer term legacy ambitions.' Dedicated legacy agencies encourage a focus on long-term ambitions and free up delivery agencies to concentrate on meeting the requirements and deadlines for an event. The tasks allocated to legacy organisations include masterplanning the wider functions of event sites in the post-event era, drawing up a business plan for venues and finding tenants for event sites. In the past, host cities have perhaps formed legacy agencies too late in the event horizon. For the 2000 Sydney Olympic Games the legacy authority (the Sydney Olympic Park Authority) was established only after the event (in 2001) to manage the park (and two adjacent parks). This compares unfavourably with arrangements for London's 2012 Olympic Games where a dedicated legacy organisation (the Olympic Park Legacy Company) was established three years before the event was staged.

Having separate delivery and legacy agencies is not necessarily ideal, as it adds to the institutional complexity of event governance. Furthermore, detaching legacy responsibilities from a delivery agency may mean the design of facilities and spaces is too focused on event priorities, at the expense of long-term considerations. Ideally, legacy considerations need to be considered when facilities are planned and delivered, and not merely treated as secondary and separate considerations. There have been several instances where event agencies and legacy agencies have not supported each other's work. Atlanta's Olympic Games in 1996 perhaps provide the most extreme example. The agency with prime responsibility for the delivery of the Games (ACOG) was a private sector entity that was unresponsive to protests from the mayor and city residents about the lack of regeneration assistance. ACOG's co-chair famously stated that the Olympics were a business venture, not a welfare programme (Rutheiser, 1996). Elected officials set up a state body (MAOGA) to ensure that event organisers were accountable to the public sector, but the real authority remained with ACOG. Subsequently, the municipal government established an organisation called CODA, a public–private partnership intended to lead the development of inner-city neighbourhoods. This organisation had few positive impacts because it was under-funded and had such different objectives compared to ACOG (Whitelegg, 2000).

BOX 9.1 LEGACY PLANNING FOR MANCHESTER'S COMMONWEALTH GAMES

The Legacy Programme associated with Manchester's Commonwealth Games raises some interesting issues about appropriate institutional arrangements for co-ordinating regeneration legacy. This programme was established as a separate entity from the Games and it aimed to achieve social and economic benefits for the wider region. Responsibility for this programme changed several times during its lifespan (1999–2004). Although an accountable body, the City Council maintained responsibility throughout, the leadership of the programme was passed from a managing agent back to the Council which then appointed a management team to co-ordinate the programme (Smith and Fox, 2007). These changes resulted in disjointed arrangements and meant systems for management and monitoring were not initially set up (Smith and Fox, 2007). During initial stages, the programme lacked one individual to take responsibility for the development and implementation of systems. The most positive results were obtained from the period during the two and a half years when a permanent Legacy Programme co-ordinator was in post (Smith and Fox, 2007).

It is interesting to note the relationship between Manchester's Legacy Programme and the main Games organisers (M2002). Event regeneration organisations that are too detached from the management of an event may struggle to leave a lasting legacy. In the case of the 2002 Commonwealth Games, links did exist between the Legacy Programme and the agency responsible for organising the Games. The chief executive of M2002 sat on the board of the Legacy Programme and played an active role in steering priorities and activities. There were positive working relationships between key staff and joint working on projects such as the volunteering programme. Links were assisted by locating Legacy Programme staff in M2002's offices for part of the programme's lifespan (Smith and Fox, 2007).

However, there were problems with the relationship between M2002 and the Legacy Programme. M2002's key priorities were infrastructure projects, selling tickets, organising athletes and other complex logistical issues, with legacy issues often relegated down M2002's priority list. Having a small team of individuals based in M2002's offices who managed the Legacy Programme did not ensure that M2002 was properly focused on legacy issues (Smith and Fox, 2007). Instead of simply being the responsibility of those people who delivered the Legacy Programme itself, legacy issues could have been part of the remit of M2002's board, staff, contractors, those constructing facilities and anyone else involved in Games planning and implementation (Smith and Fox, 2007). However, there were certain advantages of divorcing legacy responsibilities from the Games organisers. As Nichols and Ralston's (2011: 11) research suggests, having a legacy programme that was detached from M2002 meant 'there was no possibility of funds being diverted from delivering a legacy to delivering the Games'.

Public–private partnerships

Event regeneration may be delivered through multi-level governance and specialist agencies, but also through public–private partnerships. The increased involvement of private sector agencies has been a noted feature of urban regeneration policy since the 1990s (see Chapter 3). That is why we now talk about governance arrangements as well as government responsibility when discussing regeneration policy. Governance involves two types of arrangements: self-organised networks of non-government agencies; and partnerships that involve governments aligned with other agencies (Davies, 2002). These types of public–private partnerships have been responsible for a new wave of major urban projects in different parts of the world (Orueta and Fainstein, 2008). The basic principle is that the government acts to enable private sector activity, rather than developing land itself. However, there are concerns that these new projects are repeating mistakes of the past by failing to incorporate affordable housing, local benefits and good design (Orueta and Fainstein, 2008).

Partnerships operate at different stages of the regeneration process. Some partnerships are formed to develop policy, whilst others are formed to implement projects. Davies (2002) suggests that policy formation partnerships are usually characterised by weak private sector involvement, usually limited to attending meetings and sitting on committees. However, private sector involvement in delivery is more substantial. Regeneration projects often focus on supply-side deficiencies, so governments have worked with private developers to try to produce environments more conducive to investment from other sources. Development companies tend to be risk averse and focused on profit maximisation, so governments have had to provide incentives for them to work in disadvantaged areas. The role of governments in the development process is usually to assemble land (sometimes through compulsory purchase orders if a large site is required), to deliver key infrastructure, to provide a development framework and/or to offer public land to leverage commitment (Henderson, 2010). Governments may also award grants to private sector companies to build or manage event projects in a manner that will be conducive to regeneration. For example, the UK government offered a large grant to a consortium to buy and manage half of the London 2012 Athletes' Village as affordable housing. One of the dangers of this type of approach is that private sector contributions may be reduced or never materialise because of an unhelpful economic climate. During the build-up to the Athens 2004 Olympic Games, the idea of public–private financing disappeared; leaving responsibility with the public sector (Panagiotopoulou, 2009). London faced similar problems in the run-up to the 2012 Olympic Games.

Political ideologies have provided the stimuli for the new governance arrangements in many host cities. These arrangements can emerge because of the

BOX 9.2 VALENCIA

The Spanish city of Valencia is a good example of a city that has delivered event regeneration initiatives via the establishment of a new approach to urban governance. Despite opposition from some quarters, since the early 1990s the city government has adopted a new entrepreneurial approach that has allocated the business community a privileged role and which has experimented with the private development of public land (Prytherch and Maiques, 2009). A public–private sector agreement was reached to transform the port area into one that was suitable for Grand Prix motor racing. This circuit will stage Formula 1 Grand Prix races 2008–2015.

ineffectual nature of more traditional forms of government. Lever (2001) notes that partnerships often emerge in contexts where the public sector lacks the resources or business acumen required. O'Brien (2011) suggests that this characterised the early stages of the management of the Liverpool 2008 European Capital of Culture event. In this example, an informal public–private partnership 'emerged from the morass of confused and confusing government' (O'Brien, 2011: 57). The lack of established cultural planning allowed space for an alternative form of leadership to emerge. Therefore, in this example, new governance arrangements were an outcome of the event, rather than something that enabled the event to be won and planned. Liverpool's experience seems to fit with Glynn's (2008) notion that the institutional character of a city can change with the significant 'jolt' of a major event.

One of the problems with creating new partnerships in association with events is that they may simply comprise 'marriages of convenience' to help win bids. This leads to superficial partnerships that do not last – something that Davies (2002) sees as a problem with regeneration partnerships in general. The partnership that helped Liverpool to win the 2008 European Capital of Culture event broke up shortly after the city won the bid, leading to organisational problems in the build-up (O'Brien, 2011). Liverpool's main rival in the competition to stage the event was a bid from Newcastle–Gateshead. Even though it lost out to Liverpool, the partnership between agencies that was formed as part of the Newcastle–Gateshead bid was resilient enough to survive. This was because the bid helped to strengthen existing plans and networks, rather than introducing them from scratch.

A number of other examples show that event bids, as well as events, can help effective public–private partnerships to be formed. Manchester's bids for the

1996 and 2000 Olympic Games helped to forge good working relationships between the city council and private sector representatives (Cochrane *et al.*, 1996). The bids helped Manchester to adopt a more entrepreneurial approach to urban governance. Toronto, Canada, is another city where a bid for the Olympic Games led to new governance arrangements (Tufts, 2004). Westerbeek (2009) suggests that Amsterdam's bid for the 1992 Olympic Games was also one that was designed to help to create new partnerships. City councillors had argued that the city needed a project that would encourage more collaboration between the council and businesses (Westerbeek, 2009). Benneworth and Dauncey's (2010) work explores whether major events contribute to the shift from hierarchical government to governance through networks. Their work also focused on a failed event bid – Lyon's bid for the 1968 Olympic Games. The authors state that 'the Olympic bid was a significant moment – a turning point – in the urban govern-ance trajectory of Lyon' (Benneworth and Dauncey, 2010: 1096). A group of actors bought into the vision of a regenerated Lyon and this mobilised a local coalition that did not disappear with the failure of the bid. Indeed, Benneworth and Dauncey (2010) suggest that the regional partnership currently operating locally has it origins in the network that the Olympic bid helped to nurture. These examples highlight the way 'failed' event bids can help to encourage new part-nership working and, ultimately, new ways of delivering urban policy.

Growth coalitions

As well as partnerships involving government, governance for major events can involve autonomous growth coalitions that have interests in a city and seek fur-ther economic growth and investment. These private sector groups emerge in contexts where public authorities do not have the resources or mandate to lead event projects themselves. As Surborg *et al.* (2005) identify, these coalitions are not necessarily limited to local stakeholders; they often involve international companies and professionals who may previously have been involved in events staged elsewhere. Companies with interests in property development are usually prominent. Growth coalitions can influence event bids/event organisation, but also associated urban regeneration projects. Surborg *et al.* (2005) note the central role of property developers in the Bid Corporation that secured the 2010 Vancouver Olympic Games. The relationship between major events and growth coalitions is best understood as a reciprocal one: growth coalitions can help to win and stage events for cities, but events also assist growth coalitions. Major events provide nodes around which these groups coalesce and this explains why these events are often credited with securing the formation, or future influence, of growth coalitions. Major events can also result in changes to the membership of existing growth coalitions. Glynn (2008) notes how the 1996 Atlanta Olympic Games reconfigured the powerful business coalition in this city, extending it beyond the incumbent mix of banks and utility companies. One of the vehicles that facilitated membership was sponsorship of the event (Glynn, 2008). This demonstrates the way events allow commercial interests to access urban decision making.

Community involvement

Although event projects (and event bids) have a noted record of producing and developing partnerships between public and private sector agencies, their record of forging partnerships with local community groups is less impressive. Since the 1990s, regeneration policy in general has included more community involvement. Many of the failures of initiatives in the 1980s and 1990s were blamed on the absence of community input; more recent policies have prioritised partnerships with residents. Indeed, many UK government schemes (e.g. the UK's New Deal for Communities) only fund projects designed to incorporate community involvement (Dargan, 2009). Unfortunately, this progress has not been translated to the field of event regeneration – a practice that remains dominated by top-down, rather than bottom-up initiatives. This is perhaps inevitable if one considers the key characteristics of event regeneration projects. These are projects where the event is usually the priority, with regeneration considerations secondary. If the project was being designed around community priorities, large event venues probably wouldn't figure. The problems integrating communities into decision-making process are exacerbated in event regeneration by the involvement of external stakeholders (see Chapter 4) and the time constraints associated with event projects (see Chapter 5).

Arnstein's (1969) conceptualisation of the different types of community participation is useful in exploring partnerships associated with event regeneration. Arnstein (1969) divides participation modes into eight different types, organised into three categories (citizen power, tokenism, non-participation – see Figure 9.1). Most contemporary event projects are tokenistic projects where local people are merely informed, consulted or placated rather than genuinely involved in some form of collaborative partnership with event organisers. Any 'participation' is usually undertaken after key decisions have been made, meaning that community engagement is a rather routine exercise aimed to fulfil bureaucratic requirements. Unless communities are asked whether they would like their city to stage a major event at the outset, subsequent consultations seem rather tokenistic. Toronto set a good example for future host cities by allocating a large amount of funding to allow community groups to participate in the discussion and evaluation of the city's bid for the 2008 Olympic Games (Olds, 1998). But whilst urban policy in general may have advanced from projects where residents are merely subjects of regeneration (Dargan, 2009), this situation still characterises community involvement in event regeneration projects.

Degrees of citizen power	Community control
	Delegated power
	Partnership
Degrees of tokenism	Placation
	Consultation
	Informing
Non-participation	Therapy
	Manipulation

Figure 9.1 *The ladder of community participation (Arnstein, 1967)*

There have been relatively few instances where communities have actively participated in the planning and implementation of event projects. Even in Barcelona, often lauded as an example of best practice, community involvement was lacking. As Calavita and Ferrer (2000: 804) state:

> It would be tempting to ascribe, at least in part, the success of Barcelona's Olympics to a citywide and neighbourhood participation process in its planning and implementation. But this is not the case.

Barcelona's residents are organised into neighbourhood associations, which should have made their incorporation into decision-making processes easier. Mayor Serra (1979–1982) had responded to the needs of the neighbourhoods but his successor Maragall (1982–1997) had loftier ambitions. This led to controversy. The FAVB (the federation of neighbourhood associations) suggested that the preparations for the Olympics were a private affair between the mayor and the architects of the mayor (Calavita and Ferrer, 2000). This criticism highlights the way local people felt excluded from decisions about event regeneration.

Diversity of stakeholders involved

The involvement of different levels of government, event agencies, private sector enterprises and resident groups in event regeneration is usually supplemented by other stakeholders. Charities, trade unions and other interest groups are usually involved in the policy and delivery partnerships associated with event regeneration. This pluralism can be seen as a strength of event regeneration projects. However, it also makes them very difficult to manage, especially when they come on top of complex existing arrangements. This is illustrated by the example of London. The organisers of the 2012 Olympic Games decided early on that existing organisations were unable to deliver the event or co-ordinate its legacy. Thus new organisations were formed. This created an even more cumbersome institutional framework. As Imrie *et al.* (2009: 17) identified in the build-up to

---

BOX 9.3 THE SYDNEY 2000 OLYMPIC GAMES

Sydney's Olympic Games received plaudits that have subsequently been used as the titles for books about the event: 'The Best Games Ever' (Lenskyj, 2002) and 'The Collaborative Games' (Webb, 2001). But the highly centralised system used to implement initiatives was not one that featured extensive community input (Webb, 2001). Certain developments were 'fast-tracked' and certain procedures (e.g. Environmental Impact Assessments) ignored. This made the Olympic organisers much less accountable to the community than under normal circumstances (Owen, 2002). The Games organisers were also accused of merely encouraging tokenistic input from local government areas (LGAs) and community groups. For example, the general manager of Auburn Council, the LGA in which the main Olympic Park is situated, complained that council representatives were on a lot of 'paper-bag committees … yes, we're on a lot of committees, but I really question the substance or the impact or the effect that any of these have' (Owen, 2002: 301). This reaffirms the rather tokenistic character of attempts to include citizens and their elected representatives within event regeneration projects.

---

the 2012 Games, 'the irony is that every time a "strategic" quango agency is established, London's institutional assemblages become even more complex and disjointed'.

DELIVERY MECHANISMS

The discussion above explores the agencies involved in event regeneration, but it is also important to understand how projects are delivered. One of the main considerations is funding. Event regeneration initiatives are costly and there are different ways of paying for them. Event projects are also delivered using different planning tools that encourage, guide and regulate development. These aspects of delivery are explored further below.

Funding

Funding is perhaps the most controversial aspect of delivering event regeneration. Funding problems have always been a key issue because of the high costs of staging events and high-profile examples of cost-overruns. Flyvbjerg (2005) cites London's Millennium Festival (2000), the Hannover Expo (2000) and the 2000 and 2004 Olympic Games as events with unacceptably high cost overruns. As Flyvbjerg (2005) suggests, the costing of event projects is so often flawed that it is hard to avoid the conclusion that budgets are deliberately underestimated to ensure project approval. In theory events may help to fund themselves and wider regeneration but in practice this model has rarely worked. This highlights the need for more realistic, more innovative and more democratic ways of funding event regeneration. One simple suggestion is that event organisers need to be more honest about the likely cost of events and make this information available to the public earlier in the life-cycle of an event (ideally before the decision to bid is taken).

The first modern mega-events, the nineteenth-century World Expos, were usually funded via four sources: government funds, private sponsorship, lottery revenues and monies from exhibiting companies (Greenlagh, 1989). It is interesting to note that these are almost exactly the same sources that are used to fund twenty-first-century events such as the London 2012 Olympic Games. One of the original motives for staging major events was to generate profits. The Great Exhibition staged in Hyde Park in 1851 provided an early example of how events could be used to fund wider urban development. This event generated enough profit to buy 35 hectares of land in South Kensington, on which several of London's great museums were built (Gold and Gold, 2005). The role of events as fund raisers has continued in the modern era. In post-war Germany, garden festivals have been an established mechanism for funding the development of derelict areas as landscaped parklands (see Chapter 3). The idea that events will somehow fund regeneration is also implicit in many event plans. For example, one of main justifications for Trieste's bid to stage the 2008 World Expo was that the event would provide the funds necessary to develop its half-derelict port (Colombino, 2009).

As event projects have become more ambitious in their aims – and thus more expensive – it is difficult to rely on a model where the event helps to fund wider objectives. Major cultural events are notorious for making losses, with only the largest generating enough revenue to divert proceeds to supplementary projects. However, the commercialisation of major sport events means they can generate funds. The most famous example of a money-making event in the modern era was the 1984 Los Angeles Olympic Games that generated a profit of $225 million (Dyreson and Llewellyn, 2008). This money was distributed to sports federations and the local amateur athletics foundation. The commercial success of the Games laid the foundations for the more commercially oriented major events we see today. Other North American cities have managed to create legacy funds generated through the profits generated by an event. This is especially true of Winter Games hosts, where profits have been used to help maintain expensive facilities in the post-event era. Profits from the 1988 Calgary Games were transferred into a legacy fund that has helped to maintain the Olympic facilities in Alberta Province.

Leveraging external funding

Contemporary events may not earn enough income to pay for urban regeneration projects, but they can help cities to generate funding from external sources. Indeed, major events can be seen as valuable levers for regeneration funds. Many host cities have been successful in using events to secure funding from regional, national and supra-national governments. For example, investment in Barcelona's regeneration associated with the 1992 Olympic Games came from national government (12 per cent of total Olympic investment) and regional government (15 per cent), whereas the city council contributed a much smaller proportion (2 per cent) (Brunet, 2009). Significantly, a large proportion of this funding was not spent on the event venues, but on wider development projects (Brunet, 2009). Similarly, Manchester's 2002 Commonwealth Games were assisted by large amount of UK government money, including capital funding for physical projects, National Lottery funding and funds from a national regeneration programme to assist social and economic objectives (Smith and Fox, 2007). Even though local stakeholders may need to go through conventional procedures to secure such funding, the involvement of a major event helps to secure funds, as it is in the interests of national governments for event projects to be successful.

Major events help to fund urban regeneration in a more indirect manner. Funding for event regeneration is often justified by the speculative assumption that land assembled, reclaimed and redeveloped for the event will be worth more once the event is over. This provides opportunities to generate revenues, either from land sales or property taxes. Post-event, if assets are worth more than the combined costs of acquiring and developing land (and if event management costs are covered by revenues from tickets, TV rights and/or sponsorship), then event regeneration can finance itself. The reality is somewhat different and, in any case, it is unlikely that the lead agency would sell all of a large event site. But if land assets are owned by the government, and if buyers can be found, investments in upgrading urban areas can be offset by any appreciation in the value of specific assets. Although funding urban development through these types of property-led mechanisms is nothing new, it is particularly applicable to events because the publicity and positive associations generated can help to add value to development projects.

There are several problems with the idea of using events as ways of financing the regeneration of sites. The strategy relies on public agencies owning or acquiring large areas of urban land. If acquisition is required, this can involve the purchase of land, businesses and homes from individuals who may not want to move/sell. There are huge ethical, financial, logistical and legal problems involved in compulsory purchase orders. Technical problems may arise too. The viability of the model depends on accurate forecasting regarding the value of land after the event. Future land values are very difficult to predict accurately; and if costs overrun, as they tend to on major event projects, this lessens the likelihood that property sales can balance the books.

It is also hard to estimate land acquisition costs, which makes budgeting for an event funded by property sales very difficult. Assembling different pieces of land with different owners and tenants takes place over an extended period and costs may rise over time. This was something that the organisers of London's 2012 Olympic Games discovered in 2009. As Bernstock (2009: 20) recognises, the 2012 project was 'dependent on increasing land values in order to realise the costs of funding the Olympics'. Between 2005 and 2009 the organisation responsible for land acquisition (the London Development Agency – LDA) spent £750 million on acquiring land for the Olympic Park and work begun on the site. But by 2009, seventy-two of the 193 firms relocated from the area were still negotiating levels of compensation. This resulted in an expanding deficit in the LDA's finances estimated at c.£160 million (KPMG, 2009).

BOX 9.4 LISBON EXPO '98

Lisbon provides a useful example of the difficulties in achieving urban regeneration funded by an event. Property development profits were meant to fund 60 per cent of the site development costs for the massive regeneration project undertaken to stage the World Expo in 1998 (Carrière and Demaziere, 2002). This was part of a wider 'break even' approach which aimed to cover all the costs of event regeneration not paid for by the EU. The strategy was ambitious especially considering the Expo '98 project involved costly land decontamination, the servicing of the land, plus developing iconic venues and facilities. Carrière and Demaziere (2002) highlight the unconventional nature of this 'Anglo-American' funding strategy in what was then a very conservative Portuguese administration. Unsurprisingly, the event did not meet its funding targets. Property sales generated only 51 per cent of the project's income, contributing to a budget deficit of £23 million (Carrière and Demaziere, 2002).

Property prices

The asset sales funding model for event projects relies on the unpredictable property market. It is often assumed that land will rise in value, when it may not – something that was underlined by the global economic crisis 2007–2009. Even if assets do appreciate in value, it may be difficult to justify selling them to private companies. This is why many venues built for events have been leased, rather than sold, to private companies in the post-event era, For example, the Stade de France (the key venue for the 1998 FIFA World Cup) and the ANZ Stadium (the key venue for the 2000 Olympic Games; see Figure 9.2) are currently controlled by private sector organisations but they are due to return to public ownership in 2028 and 2030 respectively (Poynter, 2009). Private ownership is often unpopular amongst citizens who may feel companies have benefited unfairly from public investment (see Chapter 2). This issue was apparent in Athens during preparations for the 2004 Olympic Games. As mentioned in Chapter 4, part of the reason for poor legacy planning was extended wrangling about whether new facilities should be social resources, or whether their commercial value should be exploited (Mangan, 2008). Supplementary projects – media centres and athletes' accommodation for example – may be suited to private sale. But selling swimming

Figure 9.2 The ANZ Stadium (formerly Stadium Australia) in Sydney's Olympic Park

pools, playing fields and specialist indoor areas is both more difficult and more controversial.

If a local property market is too buoyant this may also cause problems. Many event projects involve some form of social provision (social housing, public space), but in a rapidly rising property market, public authorities may be tempted to 'cash in' these assets and reduce the emphasis on accessibility. For example, once it became clear that the high-quality housing in Barcelona's Olympic Village was attractive to private buyers, plans to reserve a large proportion of it for social housing were changed. This helped the organisers to offset the costs of the 1992 Olympic Games. Social and environmental benefits may also be compromised when the profit margins are reduced by a weaker property market. The original innovative eco-design of the Sydney Olympic Village was downgraded to ensure that any investment could be recouped through sales (Kearins and Pavlovich, 2002). A similar problem surfaced during preparations for the 2010 Vancouver Winter Olympic Games. Many of the promises of affordable housing provision were dropped because of unfavourable economic conditions and cost-overruns (see Chapter 5). These problems suggest that clear conditions must be included when developers are awarded planning permissions for event projects. If these are applied and enforced properly, public interests can be protected.

Alternative funding modes

There are alternative ways that land values can be used to fund event developments: for example, the private sector can be involved earlier to reduce public liabilities. Often governments can enter into some form of partnership with private developers to share risks and to provide the necessary expertise to deliver property-led regeneration. When Nanjing, China, hosted the tenth National Sport Games (2005), as well as developing new venues the city authorities used the event to help develop a new city – Nanjing Olympic New Town (Zhang and Wu, 2008). This was achieved via co-operation with private property development companies. Developers coalesced around the event project because they drew confidence from the government's commitment to it. This created a local public–private partnership which was initially very successful; house prices rose by 150 per cent (2003–2005), helping to pay for the project (Zhang and Wu, 2008). However, when market conditions began to deteriorate, the coalition collapsed. To avoid developers pulling out, the government had agreed that companies would not be allowed to suffer losses and this exposed the government to a heavy financial burden. Ultimately, more money was spent on the project for the New Town than was accumulated through land sales (Zhang and Wu, 2008). This meant the property dimension of the event project was a drain on the overall budget, rather than a source of funding.

Another way of funding event projects via private sector finance is by allowing companies to offer shares or bonds prior to construction. A private sector consortium funded the main stadium for the Sydney Olympic Games (see Figure 9.2) via a public flotation on the Australian Stock Exchange. Shares in the stadium were sold with incentives offered such as membership and the guarantee of tickets until 2030 (Poynter, 2009). However, only half the shares were sold because of the uncertainty about the post-event use of the stadium. The discussion in Chapter 4 suggests that investors' scepticism was justified.

Funding via taxation

The traditional model for funding event regeneration is for governments to borrow money to pay for the projects. The problem with this approach is that interest accumulates on these loans and this means that taxpayers pay back far more than was originally envisaged. Residents of Sheffield had to pay an extra £25 a year in tax until 2013 to pay off the debts incurred through the staging of the 1991 World Student Games (Henry and Paramio-Salcines, 1999). In US cities, where there is less tradition of publicly funded event projects, event organisers are often required to ask local businesses and citizens whether they are prepared to pay more tax to fund an event. For example, in Utah, a referendum was held on the issue of diverting $59 million of sales tax revenues to construct facilities for the 1996 Winter Olympic Games (Andranovich et al., 2001). This referendum was staged six years before the IOC made its decision to appoint Salt Lake City as the host (Andranovich et al., 2001). Similarly, the 1984 Games were funded by a local Olympic Tax and a 1.5 per cent surcharge on hotel occupancy tax (Lawson, 1985). If events are justified by local economic development opportunities, then it makes sense that the supposed beneficiaries of those opportunities should help to pay for the event. This approach could be used in other parts of the world and extended to include wider urban regeneration projects, rather than merely funding facilities required to stage the event.

In the future, there may be more use of innovative funding schemes for event developments. For example in the UK there are proposals for Tax Increment Financing (TIF) that allows local governments to finance redevelopment efforts through future increases in property tax revenues. In this model, municipalities are effectively selling off slices of their tax bases which, for the lifetime of the project (normally twenty years), are directed into a fund to pay for regeneration (Weber, 2010). These schemes may not work so well in turbulent market conditions when property values may not increase at the rate expected. There is also a danger that projects may never be completed (Weber, 2010). Various versions of the Business Improvement Districts (BID) model could also be used to help fund regeneration of the districts surrounding event venues. In BIDs, coalitions of business interests and property owners are effectively allowed to create a zone in which they agree to tax themselves in order to fund new facilities – speculating that their contributions will be repaid by future increases in property values. This model differs from normal taxation systems where taxes are collected and distributed centrally (Peel *et al.*, 2009). It represents a further creep of business interests into domains and roles normally reserved for the public sector. This system is usually deployed in town centres, but it could work for event sites, particularly those that need to be transformed in the post-event era.

Planning mechanisms

The successful delivery of event regeneration projects requires funds, but also an effective planning framework. This seems obvious, but event projects have often ignored existing plans and procedures. As Chalkley and Essex (1999: 391) point out, planning for major events often 'sits outside the existing categories of planning'. Similarly, Hall (2000: 21) suggests that many event hosts have adopted a 'boosterist' approach, which he sees as 'a form of non-planning'. This book has repeatedly cited the principle that, ideally, event projects should be used to further existing urban plans. Spatial plans exist at different levels and take different forms. At the macro scale, many cities have broad strategies that outline structural priorities. For example, Barcelona's Olympic initiatives were guided by the 1976 General Metropolitan Plan and London 2012 Games projects were integrated within the 2004 London Plan. These plans indicate long-term aspirations and priorities for different zones. At a smaller scale, cities publish planning documents (known as development frameworks in the UK) that stipulate what different areas should be used for (housing, retail, commerce, etc.) and the infrastructure required to support these uses.

If event venues are dispersed in different sites and/or where there is fragmented ownership of land, they may be guided by an area's development framework. This framework is made up of different plans that guide place shaping at the local level to ensure that new development meets core objectives and key principles. At a smaller scale, cities can formulate masterplans for urban districts that try to unite different elements within a holistic vision. When events venues are concentrated on a particular site, a masterplan will usually be produced. These take different forms. 'Blueprint' masterplans specify all aspects of building design and space configuration. This type of masterplan involves a single architectural project that prescribes what development will take place (Tiesdell and MacFarlane, 2007). 'Coded' masterplans allow some discretion for developers as long as key principles regarding built form are adhered to. At the micro scale, urban authorities/event organisers publish design briefs, which state how large individual buildings should be and what facilities are required to support them.

BOX 9.5 MASTERPLANS FOR HOMEBUSH BAY, SYDNEY

The masterplanning of the main site used for the 2000 Sydney Olympic Games highlights some of the issues with this planning mechanism. New facilities for the 2000 Games were concentrated in a 760 ha site on foreshore land that had been earmarked for renewal since the 1970s (Cashman, 2009). Sydney's population had grown in a westerly direction and although the site was 14 km from the centre, Homebush Bay was still regarded as being in the 'geographical heartland of Sydney's population' (Cashman, 2006: 141). The site was previously used as a brickpit, abbatoir, chemical production site, rubbish dump and munitions centre (Wilson, 1996). The abbatoir closed in the late 1980s, allowing the opportunity for redevelopment (see Figure 9.3). Kearins and Pavlovich (2002) estimate that 20 per cent of the site was contaminated – and therefore land reclamation/ re-use was the main form of regeneration attempted. Before the Games were won, the site had already been earmarked as a leisure destination. A state sport centre was built there in the 1980s and part of the site had been developed for the 1988 Australian Bicentenary celebrations. A development corporation had been set up in 1985 to develop the area over a thirty-year period – and the successful Olympic bid fast-tracked this project. Unlike the Barcelona project(s), this redevelopment was not necessarily integrated into a wider metropolitan strategy, despite the need to reconfigure Sydney – a rapidly growing city.

The first masterplan was produced five years before the Games (Wilson, 1996). The proposal included plans to relocate showgrounds from the inner city to form a space dedicated to sport and exhibitions (Searle, 2002). The masterplan co-ordinated the delivery of large-scale buildings and spaces that were appropriate for mega-events, but not for day-to-day activities. This had been anticipated prior to the event by Wilson (1996: 611): 'Will the 60m wide Olympic Boulevard and the vast building projects produce a useable human space?' Hence, in the post-event period, Lochhead (2005) identifies the need to overlay the rigid structure of the area with smaller buildings.

After the Games (in 2001), a masterplan was published that included proposals for a vibrant town centre not envisaged in the initial plan (Searle, 2002). The plan had shifted from being one dominated

Figure 9.3 *An aerial view of Sydney Olympic Park. The complex in the centre of the picture is the former abbatoir which has been converted into offices and a visitor centre. The station is on the far left of the picture and the multi-storey building next to it houses the new offices of the Commonwealth Bank*

by an event precinct, to one organised around a town centre. Eight key precincts were outlined around a central district, with provision for 3,000 residents and 10,000 workers. Approval was given for a wide range of land uses including leisure, education, retail, hotel and institutional buildings. This plan was criticised by Lochhead (2005) for being too short-term (it covered a timeframe of seven–ten years) and too limited in scale. It was also criticised for the lack of links to local areas and the over-emphasis on commercial potential. Searle (2002) felt that there was a lack of development control – creating a developer's 'tabula rasa'.

'Vision 2025' was then published and replaced the 2002 master-plan. This new plan proposed a denser urban core with a wider variety of uses. The idea was to introduce a range of housing types including affordable housing, hotels and sports hostels and to develop a clear educational role for the site that would differentiate it from surrounding areas (Lochhead, 2005).

Refinement of 'Vision 2025' has resulted in a further masterplan – 'Masterplan 2030'. This proposes a more compact development of the site with new commercial buildings concentrated close to the station. This process has already begun with the construction of the Commonwealth Bank buildings (see Figures 9.3 and 9.4). Other land uses are zoned with community facilities, recreational facilities, residential dwellings confined to specific quarters. The ambitions of the Park have been upsized in the new plan. Rather than merely providing for 3,000 residents and 10,000 workers, the plan is now to host 14,000 residents and 31,500 workers. The idea is to increase footfall in the Park to ensure that it is an active precinct that is used heavily throughout the day and throughout the year.

Overall, the Sydney case shows that, although masterplans are supposedly useful ways of ensuring coherent development, masterplans

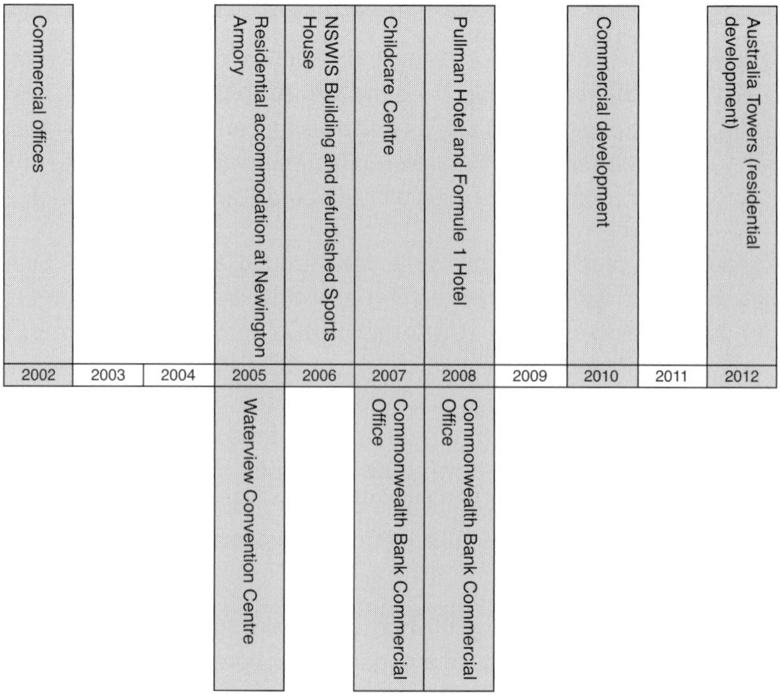

Figure 9.4 Post-event redevelopment in Sydney's Olympic Park

produced in association with event sites are often subject to multiple revisions. In Sydney's case these took place after the Games – suggesting that not enough thought had gone into planning the legacy of the event. Too much attention had been devoted to staging the event itself. The design of the Queen Elizabeth Olympic Park in London was heavily influenced by Sydney's Olympic Park. And it is interesting to note that in advance of the 2012 Games, the legacy masterplan for this site changed several times in the period 2006–2011. This demonstrates the limitations of masterplanning. Whilst masterplans are intended to provide a definitive blueprint to guide development, these plans are often disrupted by the multiple stakeholders and politics involved.

Planning gain

The different types of spatial plans described above provide overall direction for urban development, but they also provide the basis for development control. Planning permissions are normally granted only if proposals fit within the wider plans for the area. The planning process provides opportunities to guarantee that some form of social and economic regeneration takes place. It is now common for governments to require developers to undertake works to secure public benefits from their plans. This is usually known as planning gain. Before planning permission is granted, developers may be required to take action before they commence a project, or they may be asked to ensure provision of social benefits in the long term. In the UK these requirements are known as section 106 agreements. These agreements can stipulate that certain activities be carried out, that land has to be used in a certain way, or that money has to be paid to the local authority to ensure public benefits (Walters, 2005b).

One of the most significant section 106 agreements was implemented in association with a major event venue: the Emirates Stadium in London. A football club wanted to move to a 17 ha site adjacent to railway lines that was used as an industrial estate and location for council services. Several development proposals were submitted before planning permission was finally granted in 2001. As part of the agreement reached, the developer (Arsenal Football Club) was required to contribute £100 million towards regeneration schemes in the immediate vicinity of the stadium (Walters, 2005b). Projects funded through the agreement included affordable homes, a £60 million waste and recycling centre and new community facilities (learning centre, plus nurseries and health centres). The agreement established institutional arrangements to support regeneration ambitions including a partnership between the council and the club, and a liaison committee that helped to minimise negative impacts. The section 106 agreement also required the club to offer season tickets to local people (Walters, 2005b). There have been some complaints about the dominance of the stadium and the limited economic benefits for local businesses, but the project is generally regarded as a success. Rather than simply hoping that some of the positive benefits would trickle down to local communities. The planning system, via the section 106 agreement, ensured that the stadium contributed to urban regeneration.

There are other examples of planning gain instruments throughout the world. In some countries, public–private bargaining systems are used. Under Community Benefit Agreements in the USA, in return for pledges not to file lawsuits against them, developers agree to deliver social benefits from projects (Majoor, 2008). Developers can also be given additional space in exchange for designing facilities in a way that contributes to public goals. These instruments can be used in conjunction with event projects to secure wider regeneration outcomes.

BOX 9.6 THE 2012 OLYMPIC GAMES IN GREENWICH PARK

The problem with relying on planning systems to deliver regeneration benefits from events is that these projects can be treated as exceptional cases. This means event projects can evade scrutiny and/or gain permissions even if they do not meet established criteria. Even if event organisers engage with the existing planning procedures there may be issues because of the exceptionality of major event cases. This was highlighted during the planning process to build a temporary event venue in Greenwich Park for the London 2012 Olympic Equestrian events (see Figure 9.5). The proposal was controversial and a large number of local people objected to the planning application submitted in 2009. Objectors felt the organisers had chosen a location that would generate the most spectacular television pictures rather than one that would result in the lowest environmental and social impacts. The process culminated in a meeting of the Borough of Greenwich Planning Board in March 2010 that lasted almost five hours (attended by the author). This meeting raised various issues regarding the submission of planning applications for major event venues.

Figure 9.5 *The arena for the Olympic equestrian test events being constructed in Greenwich Park, London*

One issue was the conflation of the individual application for the equestrian venue with the justification for staging the event as a whole. Several councillors who voted to grant permission justified their position with reference to their support for Olympic Games in general, rather than the merits of the individual planning application. One asserted that they were 'looking forward to watching the greatest show on earth' as a reason for their position. Another cited the need to have Olympic events in the local borough as the reason to support the application. This shows how normal development control procedures become confused when dealing with an important multi-sport event. The other issue raised by this example was the unenviable position in which members of this committee were placed. Refusing permission would severely disrupt the planning of the Games and this always made it unlikely that councillors would oppose the application. The Borough Council was a key stakeholder in the Games and this made objections by councillors more awkward politically. The application was submitted by the event organisers (LOCOG) and this organisation produced extensive materials to support its case.

> There was an obvious disparity between the power of LOCOG and that of the objectors and the local councillors. This example shows the difficulty of using the existing planning system to scrutinise major event proposals. In this case, the event organisers engaged with the democratic process, but time pressures, political factors and the resources at its disposal meant LOCOG was always likely to secure the outcome it wanted.

Urban development corporations

One way that national governments have tried to avoid complicated goverance arrangements and cumbersome planning restrictions is by establishing urban development corporations. These have been used in many large-scale regeneration projects, including those associated with major events. Urban development corporations are used by governments to develop event sites, assist post-event transformation of those sites and/or to ensure that regeneration extends to areas beyond event venues. These corporations were adopted by the UK government in the 1980s and 1990s to allow national governments to exert more control at the local level and to facilitate private sector drives urban transformation (Raco, 2005). They were often established in zones where local councils were unwilling or unable to lead market-led regeneration. The idea was to invest heavily in infrastructure that could drive regeneration by raising land values. However, urban development corporations were criticised for the way that they ignored the wider planning framework and usurped the existing management of these areas (Raco, 2005). Even in 'successful' examples, they tended to create isolated islands of regeneration that were detached from their surrounding areas. The work of the London Docklands Development Corporation in the 1980s is seen as exemplifying this. This agency helped to create a successful financial district centred at Canary Wharf, but the regenerated zone is physically, socially and economically detached from the disadvantaged districts that surround it.

Several major event projects have been delivered in association with urban development corporations. The National Garden Festivals staged in Liverpool (1984) and Glasgow (1988) discussed in Chapter 3 were co-ordinated by urban development corporations. This model was also adopted by organisers of the 1998 World Expo in Lisbon (see Chapter 3). Urban development corporations are still part of the delivery structure for event projects in the twenty-first century. Newman (2007) suggests that the Olympic Delivery Authority (ODA) that remediated and built London's Olympic Park was a version of an urban development corporation. Stakeholders in East London were used to dealing with these types of institutional arrangements because of the work of the London Docklands Development Corporation (1981–1998) and the London Thames Gateway Development Corporation (2004–2014). The ODA worked within a defined boundary in which it could buy and sell land and act as the local planning authority. This allowed it to deliver projects efficiently. The ODA was funded by, and accountable to, the national government. However, there were often difficult relationships between the ODA and the four local authorities that bordered the Park.

Sydney's Olympic Games were also delivered using an urban development corporation. Homebush Bay was the location for a development corporation that existed fifteen years prior to the 2000 Olympic Games being awarded to the city (Wilson, 1996). In 1995 this agency was superseded by the Olympic Co-ordination Agency (OCA) that built Sydney's Olympic Park. An Act of Parliament provided the OCA with powers to manage and control all the public space and facilities within the perimeter of the Park. Under local government legislation the OCA was also the legal consent authority in respect of all building and planning approvals. In this sense, it also acted as a typical urban development corporation.

In other examples, urban development corporations have been used to help regenerate areas surrounding an events site. This approach was used in Sheffield in association with the 1991 World Student Games and in Manchester as part of the 2002 Commonwealth Games project. In Sheffield, the Sheffield Development Corporation had been founded in 1987 to lead the physical regeneration of the parts of the Don Valley that surrounded the main event venues. However, the World Student Games were not well integrated with the work of the SDC, partly because of the conflict between the locally managed event and the externally driven development corporation. In Manchester, the New East Manchester Company was founded in 1999 to lead the regeneration of a large area including, but not limited to, the main site for the 2002 Commonwealth Games. The company was based on a slightly different model in that it was a partnership between the national government, a regional development agency and the city council. This approach exemplifies a more enlightened version of the urban development corporation instrument that has emerged in recent years. In this revised model, development corporations supplement the work of local stakeholders rather than replace them (Raco, 2005).

Enterprise zones

Alongside urban development corporations, a key delivery mechanism used within property-led urban regeneration policy in the 1980s was giving targeted areas a special status that awarded companies that relocated there certain privileges. In the UK these were established by the Conservative government

(1979–1997) and called Enterprise Zones (EZs). Companies located within EZs benefited from a simplified planning system and exemption from certain taxes (rates and taxes on capital expenditure) and some bureaucratic tasks expected of other companies (Jones, 2006). These zones aimed to attract investment from companies that would build new facilities and create jobs. The idea was based on the success of Hong Kong's free trade zones in the 1950s and 1960s. Jones (2006) suggests that, over time, the core principles of EZs were diluted, and conventional planning requirements gradually crept back into the operation of these areas. However, these mechanisms did demonstrate how taxation could be integrated with planning (Jones, 2006). No new EZs were created after the Labour government was elected to power in 1997. But in 2011, the Conservative–Liberal Democrat government announced that new Enterprise Zones would be created to help deal with effects of the recession. This means they could once again play an important role in UK cities: including in optimising the regeneration legacy of the London 2012 Games.

Other countries have slightly different versions of these zones. The French government has used the ZAC mechanism (Zone d'Aménagement Concerté). Within areas designated as ZACs, authorities can apply special tools such as expropriation (compulsory purchase) and *droits de pre-emption*. The latter ensure a municipality is first in the queue to purchase property when it becomes available to buy (Fraser and Baert, 2003). ZAC status provides an opportunity to masterplan a large urban area. This delivery mechanism was used to assist the redevelopment of St Denis, in association with the 1998 FIFA World Cup. The area around the Stade de France was included in a ZAC (Newman and Tual, 2002) and ZAC status allowed the state to deliver a masterplan and key infrastructure which provided the platform for subsequent private sector investment. A ZAC was also used in a more central area of Paris to deliver another example of regeneration anchored by an events venue. The ZAC de Bercy facilitated the creation of the Palais Omnisports: an indoor arena that hosts the Paris Masters ATP tennis tournament and other major events. The arena was one of the first projects delivered in this zone and it helped to kick-start the ZAC which now boasts a new park, a new residential area, new transport links and a new commercial district. The involvement of different architects within a coherently planned zone means this area is considered as a good example of urban regeneration.

Strategic planning

As well as using spatial planning and statutory mechanisms to co-ordinate event regeneration projects, cities can deliver event regeneration through other forms of strategic planning. Most cities publish economic development strategies, transport strategies, tourism strategies and other strategies to attract other forms of inward investment. These can be updated and synthesised with event projects to maximise positive outcomes. If cities don't have strategic plans, then an event provides a good incentive to produce them. Strategic plans are not regeneration plans, but city-wide strategies that help to support more localised regeneration initiatives. Ideally, these need to be formulated well before an event to ensure that the opportunities presented by the event itself can be maximised. The lack of strategic planning in association with events may be a reason for disappointing outcomes. Bramwell (1997) believes the lack of strategic planning associated with the 1991 World Student Games resulted in missed opportunities for regeneration. Similarly, Deffner and Labrianidis (2005: 257) suggest that the 1997 European Capital of Culture event in Thessaloniki (Greece) should be viewed 'as a series of missed opportunities' because of the lack of associated strategic planning. The authors suggest that the outcomes of this expensive project would have been better if the city had developed an associated tourism policy, a city marketing strategy and a clear policy for the development of flagship projects.

Social and economic mechanisms

Mechanisms for delivering social and economic regeneration are less well developed than spatial/physical mechanisms. As discussed above, the planning system can be used to help deliver social and economic benefits. Majoor (2008: 115) suggests that 'it is certainly possible to connect a progressive planning agenda to a large scale development project with a clear economic motive. However if such an agenda is not linked to adequate planning concepts and tools its execution will be disappointing.' Minimum employment benefits can be secured by the adoption of labour market initiatives such as labour exchange provision discussed in Chapter 5. As the GLLaB example demonstrates, these organisations can also help to ensure that local businesses are able to benefit from the contracts awarded when major events are staged (see Chapter 4). Wider social benefits may result from adopting community focused models of venue and land ownership. Community land trusts and similar models can be used which ensure that buildings are used for community purposes, including supporting social enterprises. These models often transfer the ownership of facilities and land to community groups. Transferring assets may mean that opportunities to secure high returns on investment are lost, but these models can help to ensure community benefits and they may help to secure tenants in the post-event era. Even if ownership of event facilities remains with the public sector, facilities can be managed by social enterprises that reinvest surpluses back into services for the community.

Achieving sustained effects

Sustaining positive effects is one of the great challenges of temporally based urban interventions such as event regeneration. It requires good project design but also effective project implementation. Research by Oc *et al.* (1997) suggests that the longevity of social/economic regeneration programmes relies on two factors: developing a 'forward consciousness' and the chronology of funding arrangements. One of the main obstacles to a 'forward consciousness' is the time expended on meeting bureaucratic requirements such as meetings, documentation and evaluation. A 'forward consciousness' is more likely when there is a continuity of personnel through project design and implementation. It can also be assisted by requiring longer-life agencies to be the major partners in projects. This is particularly relevant to event projects as they often involve limited-life organisations. In terms of funding, Oc *et al.*'s (1997) research found that while front-ended funding ensures an immediate impact, money could often be used to greater effect in the middle and later years. The research concluded that a gradual budget reduction, rather than an abrupt cessation of funding, is a more effective way of ensuring a sustained legacy as it eases the transition to alternate funding sources (Oc *et al.*, 1997). These findings are particularly relevant to event regeneration, where temporal considerations are fundamental because of the transitory nature of events.

SUMMARY

This chapter has outlined the various ways that event projects are delivered. Every example of event regeneration is delivered in a different way, but there are some important trends noted here. Some cities that pioneered event regeneration strategies tried to deliver event projects at the local level (Montreal, Sheffield). Later, more successful, examples showed the value of government involvement at different spatial scales. Major events can help cities to establish, strengthen and utilise government networks – and those involving private sector partners. This can help to deliver event projects, but it can also leave a legacy of better partnership working that can assist a city's prospects in the long term. One aspect of partnership working that has been neglected is how to ensure local people participate in the planning and delivery of event projects. Local groups need to be involved from an early stage to allow these projects to be more community focussed. As well as integrating the needs of local people, the institutional arrangements for a major event should facilitate the integration of events into the wider regeneration plans for an urban area. This means establishing agencies to think about long-term benefits before an event is staged, but it also means properly integrating the event into wider spatial and strategic plans for the city. There have been lots of innovative delivery mechanisms used in association with events. Many of these involve establishing new agencies (e.g. urban development corporations) and arrangements (enterprise zones) that aim to supersede cumbersome planning practices. This may lead to more expedient development but it challenges the accountability of event regeneration. As McCartney *et al.* (2010) recommend, it would be preferable if funding for event initiatives were channelled through existing, elected bodes. Delivery issues are also dominated by concerns over funding; whilst there are lots of innovative ways of paying for event projects, public money is still used to fund projects in which costs are under-estimated and benefits over-estimated. This, alongside displacement, is the most controversial aspect of event regeneration.

EXTENDED CASE STUDY 6: DELIVERING URBAN EVENTS IN GOTHENBURG

Gothenburg is Sweden's second largest city with a population of *c.*500,000 inhabitants. Like many northern European ports its economic base was undermined by the oil crisis in the 1970s and subsequent de-industrialisation (Enhorning, 2010). The demise of many heavy engineering and shipbuilding companies meant the city was forced to turn to retail, tourism and other service sector industries. Authorities in Gothenburg also responded by prioritising events. Indeed, the city now aims to be one of Europe's leading event cities (Göteborg & Co, 2011). Unlike other port cities, new venues and related redevelopment have been focused in the city centre, rather than in waterfront areas (Enhorning, 2010). In the 1980s new exhibition halls and sport arenas were built, and the Scandinavium – a large indoor arena – opened in 1991 (see Figure 9.6). The Scandinavium (mainly used for ice hockey and concerts) became the anchor project for the development of an 'events thoroughfare' (Enhorning, 2010) that now includes the Gamla Ullevi Arena (football stadium), the Nya Ullevi Arena (athletics stadium), the Valhallabadet (swimming pool) and the Swedish Exhibition and Congress Centre (see Figure 9.7). Unlike many other cities, these facilities were not built for one major event but were always designed to host a calendar of events that would support the city's re-imaging as an events capital.

Although Gothenburg has never staged a 'mega-event', two athletics championships have been the pivotal events staged by the city. The World Athletics Championships in 1995 were the launch pad for Gothenburg's focus on events. At the time, this was the largest event ever staged in Sweden (Larson, 2009). The Nya Ullevi Stadium was extended in the run-up to the event to allow the Championships to be staged. As Larson (2009: 397) states, 'the event was so successful that the city decided to focus on strengthening the position of the city as an event destination'. At this time, the city also began making preparations for a second event: the 2006 European Athletics Championships. This event marked

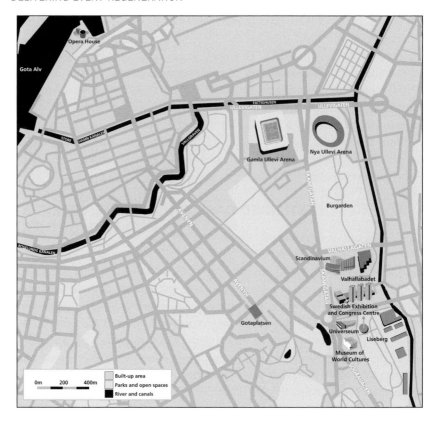

Figure 9.6 *A map of central Gothenburg highlighting key event sites*

the point at which serious efforts to brand Gothenburg as an event capital began. Gothenburg has also hosted numerous large-scale events including the UEFA Cup Final, a Volvo Ocean (Sailing) Race, the Ice Hockey World Championships and World Figure Skating Championships; and it regularly hosts the biggest acts in popular music. The city hosts an annual basketball festival, a youth football championship and the World Youth Games in athletics – regular events that help the city to bid successfully for one-off sport events (Göteborg & Co, 2011). In 2013, Gothenburg will host the European Indoor Athletics Championships – furthering the city's strong links with athletics events.

Sport versus culture

In recent years authorities have been working to develop a city brand that will engage a range of audiences: internal and external. The majority of Gothenburg's investment in events has been allocated to staging sport events; but this is now

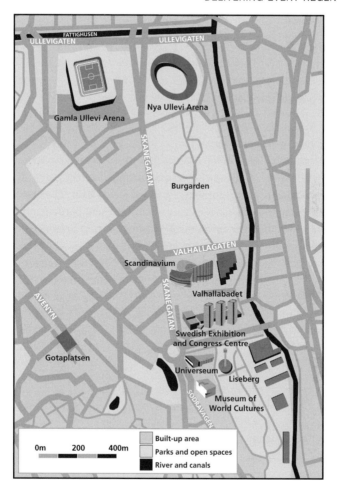

Figure 9.7 *The 'events thoroughfare' in Gothenburg*

changing as the city has decided to balance its portfolio with more emphasis on cultural events. Even though sport events are still a priority they are now promoted in a way that complements a more diverse image of the city. A good example is the 2006 European Athletics Championships which were marketed as 'more than a sport event' (Thörn, 2006). There has also been more investment in a broader range of events, such as the Cultural Festival and Way Out West. The latter is a rock festival that has helped to strengthen the image of Gothenburg as a slightly younger, more exciting city. Staging music festivals corresponds with wider objectives to emphasise Gothenburg's educational qualities – to attract students to the well regarded university. The current strategy is to use events to make Gothenburg a more pleasant and attractive city to live in, work and visit.

The city is generally regarded as open and welcoming, but the aim is to also make it a surprising and interesting city (Göteborg & Co, 2011). Events are afforded a key role in this mission.

Competitive advantage

Gothenburg is one of many cities trying to establish itself as an events city, and it has to contend with much larger metropolises such as Barcelona, London and Madrid. To compete, the city has learned to turn its small size to its advantage. The compact layout of the city's event quarter is very user friendly (see Figure 9.7): the main 'events thoroughfare' is located near the centre of the city and near to the main hotels. This is convenient for event participants and spectators, especially when compared to the complex transport arrangements required to stage events in larger cities. It also appeals to organisers when they are deciding where to stage events. An event may 'disappear' in a bigger city, but in Gothenburg events are more visible and help to animate the city. Gothenburg's compactness and the arrangement of venues also means that the whole central district becomes the hosting arena. The city becomes the stage for events, even when they are principally staged behind closed doors. During the 2006 European Athletics Championships, the opening ceremony was staged in an open square (Gotaplatsen) and a cultural festival was staged that helped to transform Gothenburg's central district for the time the event was being staged (Thörn, 2006). And whilst the city's small size means that it has more limited resources, this is not necessarily a negative thing: it means stakeholders have had to work harder and more imaginatively to attract and stage events (Bjerkne, cited in Nyberg, 2008).

Delivery

There is a long history of public–private co-operation in Gothenburg and this has provided a useful basis for co-operation in the events sphere (Bjerkne, cited in Nyberg, 2008). The small size of the city makes co-operation between stakeholders more straightforward. This co-operation and understanding amongst various organizations and authorities has been critical to Gothenburg's success. There is a strong commitment to the idea of Gothenburg as an 'events capital' amongst a range of organisations. Residents have enjoyed the feeling of being part of something 'big' and they seem positive about the city's role as an event venue. Much of the credit for the effective co-ordination of event stakeholders is attributed to Göteborg & Co – the city's destination marketing organisation. This organisation was established in 1990 and one of its main aims is to be a platform for collaboration between the city, the educational establishments and the private sector (Göteborg & Co, 2011). Göteborg & Co is a not-for-profit company owned by the city council (50 per cent) with the remainder owned by companies and organisations including the regional government (15 per cent), Västsvenska Industri och Handelskammaren (5 per cent), Svenska Mässan (5 per cent), Stena Line AB (5 per cent) and Storhotelgruppen i Göteborg (5 per cent). Göteborg & Co work very closely with other partners such as the city's universities, Volvo, SKF, Skandia, Skanska and Scandinavian Airlines. Of its four main departments, one is a trade and industry group that involves a number of private sector partners. Another is dedicated to events. The aim of the events team is to attract new events, develop new concepts, collaborate with arena owners and manage Göteborg & Co events (Göteborg & Co, 2011).

Many of the events in Gothenburg are organised by Got Event – the city's main event management organisation. This agency is owned by the city government and it manages the events that are staged at the main arenas in the city centre. Control over the main venues allows the city to pursue a co-ordinated event strategy. Event organisers have appreciated the flexibility provided by a highly networked city. Plans can be changed at short notice: for example, the location of the event can be moved easily because the venues, security and transport stakeholders are part of the network of stakeholders committed to the event strategy. This web of stakeholders operates efficiently, but Larson (2009) suggests that one side-effect is that organising events in Gothenburg has become a very closed network. At the beginning of the event strategy, a wide range of organisations was able to access the network, but as relationships have become more embedded it is much more difficult to do so. This privileges some businesses and organisations at the expense of others (Larson, 2009).

This book focuses on one-off events, but the Gothenburg case highlights the useful spin-offs from being a city that regularly stages events. Every time there has been an event in the city, Gothenburg has gained useful experience and learned about the technical challenges of staging large events. The expertise and reputation gained means the city is more likely to be able to attract and deliver events in the future. Furthermore, Gothenburg has benefited from a series of incremental improvements to the cityscape. Every time the city has staged a major event, it has usually improved itself in some way. Indeed, many improvements to the public realm can be linked to events the city has hosted. Events have also assisted Gothenburg's tourism development: in the period up to 2011, the city experienced nineteen years of continuous growth in the number of guest nights recorded (Göteborg & Co, 2011).

10 Conclusions

INTRODUCTION

The preceding chapters of this book have introduced the ways in which major events are linked to urban regeneration. Regeneration has emerged as a key objective for many host cities, with London's 2012 Olympic Games perhaps representing one of the most explicit and ambitious attempts to regenerate a large urban area using an event. Before reading this book you may have assumed that the relationship between events and urban regeneration was straightforward: events are used as tools to help regenerate cities. However, this book has presented a range of different ways that major events can be used – not as forms of urban regeneration, but as agents within urban regeneration strategies. In this concluding section the aims are: to review the key points made in the book; and to draw these together to make some overall observations about event regeneration. In the latter half of the chapter a set of good practice principles is outlined. These ideas help to fulfil one of the secondary aims of the book: to recommend ways that cities engaging in event regeneration can optimise their chances of 'success'.

A NOTE OF CAUTION

Despite the emerging discourse of regeneration that surrounds many major events, it needs to be recognised that major event projects are usually still driven by political motives and/or a commercial rationale. Usually urban regeneration is merely a subsidiary justification for event projects in which other objectives are the main priority. An accompanying discourse of regeneration helps to justify extensive and expensive projects that would be otherwise impossible to justify. In other examples, regeneration is more genuinely sought but that commitment does not necessarily mean positive outcomes. This is because event regeneration is an indirect way of achieving urban policy goals. Imaginative methods can be sought and used to achieve associated regeneration, but in many instances it would be easier to address those objectives directly, rather than through the medium of an event.

It seems important that urban regeneration objectives are pursued vigorously in association with events, or not at all. Sometimes it is appropriate for events to be staged as celebratory occasions – without an associated urban agenda. This suggestion is in line with the conclusions of commentators such as McCartney *et al.* (2010) who advocate recasting major events as simpler, less costly phenomena. In some instances, there may be a great opportunity to lever an event to help regenerate urban areas. Where the potential of an area needs to be unlocked, or where previous efforts to kick-start regeneration have failed, a major event may play a useful role. The danger is that cities fall somewhere in between these options – retro-fitting regeneration initiatives to justify event projects. Ideally, regeneration initiatives should be programmed in from the bidding stage of events – the point at which various commitments are made. Unfortunately, the nuances and unpredictability of the bidding process mean that it is difficult to marry strategic regeneration planning and speculative event projects. Even if bids are successful, staging an event means satisfying a diverse range of internal and external stakeholders. Time and budgetary constraints associated with events often limit what can be achieved. These observations highlight some of the complications introduced by including an event within urban regeneration.

HOW EVENTS CAN ASSIST URBAN REGENERATION

Chapter 2 highlighted various concerns associated with event projects. In subsequent chapters there was evidence of problematic aspects and negative effects. It is easy to be dismissive about the regeneration outcomes of events. However, Chapters 4–8 demonstrated how events can be integrated within projects to encourage positive effects. A summary of these different roles is provided below.

Venue projects

• Anchors for physical regeneration
• New employment centres
• New community hubs.

Parallel physical regeneration

• Providing flagships to stimulate future development
• Overcoming established structural problems

- Accelerating existing plans
- Extending existing plans
- Providing a narrative for wider developments
- Showcasing completed projects.

Social regeneration initiatives

- Enhancing community cohesion
- Encouraging local involvement and civic responsibility
- Increasing employability
- Assisting education engagement
- Encouraging healthier lifestyles
- Assisting persons with disability.

New directions for cities

- Inspiration for new ideas
- Nurturing new sectors: e.g. sport, cultural and ICT industries
- Re-imaging and branding
- The development of tourism.

These different aspects of event regeneration cover a range of physical, social and economic objectives. They are difficult to accomplish, but this book has tried to explain how host cities can achieve some of these effects. Events can play a very obvious role in instigating new venues that, if designed properly, can provide local resources and anchors for regeneration. More subtly, events can provide a theme around which wider projects can be pursued. This includes physical projects where tight deadlines and media exposure help to explain why events can achieve accelerated development. The deadlines associated with events and the idea that an event provides a window of opportunity can encourage development that otherwise may not have happened. Media exposure associated with events acts as an incentive to complete work and it also provides a way of showcasing previous projects that would have been completed anyway. Major events can also be used to theme a range of diverse social regeneration initiatives. Events provide attractive themes because of certain qualities they seem to possess: their popularity, festivity, internationalism and the way in which they engage specific groups of disadvantaged people. Events can also mark a turning point in the lifecycle of a city. They provide opportunities to lay the foundations for new industrial sectors, and to reorient the way they are perceived by those inside and outside the city.

The summary above outlines some of the characteristics of events that allow them to be useful regeneration tools. It is perhaps worth pointing out some other qualities that recur across the preceding chapters. The way that events help to mobilise people, resources and networks is one of their key strengths as regeneration tools. Benneworth and Dauncey (2010) regard events as 'symbolic-emotional' narratives and this is a useful term because it emphasises why events can achieve effects above and beyond those that we could expect to see from more conventional urban interventions. Major events are saturated with imagery and symbolism and they provoke passionate and emotional responses from many people. The aim of many host cities has been to harness these characteristics for the benefit of disadvantaged areas. Unfortunately, this is still a rather speculative process. As Benneworth and Dauncey (2010: 1095) explain, we still 'need to know more about the conditions by which symbolic-emotional narratives become significant in shaping urban development trajectories'.

DIFFERENT TYPES OF EVENTS

This book has intentionally tried to incorporate a range of events into the analysis and the text has attempted to make a series of general observations about events. However, during the course of the discussion it has become obvious that different types of events allow different outcomes to emerge. There are many ways of classifying events (see Chapter 1), but the approach outlined below helps us to understand events according to the opportunities they provide for regeneration

1 *Event projects concentrated on large, purpose-built sites*

Examples: Multi-sport events, World Expos

These events can assist urban regeneration if they are sited on brownfield sites that have the potential to be unlocked using investment associated with an event. To allow regeneration effects to accrue, the site needs to be integrated physically, socially and economically with disadvantaged areas nearby. The danger with this type of approach is that it can produce an under-utilised ghost-town, an artificial space not well integrated with the rest of the city, or a gentrified space that excludes the people it was designed to benefit. This is a very place-based approach to regeneration, but it is one that does not necessarily assist people in need.

2 *Events staged in multiple dispersed venues*

Examples: European Capital of Culture, multi-sport events

These events can assist urban regeneration if the individual venues provide useful resources for local communities, acting as hubs of employment, or community centres. The venues may also act as flagships for further development. They are more likely to assist regeneration if the venues are co-ordinated into a broader strategic plan. A polycentric approach is more likely to assist existing communities and it is less likely that people will be displaced. However, there is a danger that local people will be excluded financially, physically and/or symbolically from poorly planned venues. This is an approach that can deliver people-based and place-based regeneration. But there are usually huge opportunity costs in developing facilities for dispersed major events.

3 *Events staged in public spaces with minimal physical provision*

Examples: Carnivals, music festivals, marathons, cycle races and other street events

Some of the outcomes discussed in this book rely on the festivity associated with events rather than the physical presence of event projects. Organisers of major events have learned to develop social and economic leverage initiatives that can assist objectives such as community cohesion, education, accessibility and employment. This means there is an opportunity – as yet largely unrealised – to use major cultural events and sport events that are staged in public spaces as regeneration tools. The advantages of this approach are the low capital costs and the opportunity to use events that are already well established. Most cities already stage significant events and these could be levered to assist regeneration. The disadvantages of this approach are that there are minimal opportunities for conventional place-based regeneration. However, these events could be used to further a people-based agenda that aims to reduce worklessness, health problems and low educational achievement.

DILEMMAS AND ISSUES

Event regeneration involves a number of stages. The decision whether or not to bid for a major event is usually a contentious one. If cities decide to proceed, this ushers in a whole series of further issues. Indeed, host cities face a number of difficult decisions when planning successful event strategies. Deffner and Labrianidis's (2005) analysis highlights various dilemmas. These include emphasising:

innovation versus tradition;
the global versus the local;
centre versus periphery;
buildings versus networks;
flagships versus modest interventions;
the short term versus the long term;
tourists versus residents;
uniqueness versus the everyday;
isolation versus integration;
ephemera versus endurance.

Formulating event strategies is further complicated by the political and commercial pressures in cities that mean decisions are taken that aren't always in the best interests of disadvantaged citizens. Indeed, various examples cited in the book show that because of the range of stakeholders involved cities are often unable to co-ordinate strategies that allow them to achieve the effects they want.

Preceding chapters have also identified a number of advantages and disadvantages of using major events within urban regeneration. One of the problems in trying to generate policy lessons from these observations is that some of these advantages are also disadvantages. This highlights the problematic and paradoxical nature of major events projects – something that is explored further in the review of key issues below.

Issue 1 *Exceptionality.* The discussion in this book has stressed that major
   events can be powerful agents within urban policy because they are extraordinary opportunities to transform urban areas. This is illustrated by the
   frequent citation of the statement that events provide a 'once in a lifetime'
   chance to improve a city's position. Major events provide unique opportunities to make long planned changes and they can bring together a powerful
   coalition of interests and civic support. However, this exceptionality is a
   characteristic that makes events a problematic component within urban
   regeneration. Exceptionality means that major event projects can introduce
   elements, practices and outcomes that would not normally be tolerated.
   Special laws may be introduced, special exemptions may be made, and they
   may result in negative impacts for certain people and places.

Issue 2 *Distinctive spaces.* There is often a contradiction in event regeneration
   between creating spectacular spaces and creating spaces that are integrated
   into the rest of the city. Cities pursuing event regeneration often try to
   pursue these objectives simultaneously, but they may be mutually exclusive.
   Event projects are often fragmented interventions that are poorly integrated
   with the rest of a city. This is especially true when they are concentrated
   spatially, causing what Monclús (2006) calls investment overdose: poorly
   integrated enclaves or precincts that are excessively themed or banal. Good
   event spaces are not necessarily good urban spaces and this challenges their
   role as regeneration tools. Event spaces have always been designed with a
   fantasy element involved – facilitating a 'separation experience' (Packard
   and Ballantyne, 2010) and allowing people to escape reality. This is not
   necessarily conducive to producing conventional urban districts in the post-
   event era. As Mace *et al.* (2007) have stated with respect to Manchester's
   Commonwealth Games site, host cities need to decide whether to develop
   event sites as 'destinations' or as normalised city zones.

Issue 3   *Time*. Previous chapters have highlighted that the time constraints introduced by including a major event within a regeneration project are both an advantage and disadvantage. Deadlines associated with events are advantageous because they can help to ensure that tentative projects are actually delivered and implemented more quickly than would otherwise be the case. Unfortunately, they also make it harder to incorporate communities within decision making and they can mean that event projects are exempted from time-consuming – but critically important – planning processes. Rushed projects can also affect quality levels and other outcomes. There are also contradictions in the oft cited notion that events help to reduce the time taken to achieve regeneration. Many of the cases reviewed in this book emerged as successes a long time after the event was staged and only after extensive post-event transformations.

Issue 4   *Problematic success.* Event regeneration may or may not lead to successful urban regeneration outcomes. Unfortunately, even if projects succeed, this may lead to sub-optimal outcomes. Success means it may be more difficult for existing residents to continue living there. Displacement – either through forced eviction, social exclusion or the pressures associated with living in a rapidly transforming neighbourhood – is a worrying characteristic of event projects (Porter *et al.*, 2009). As Lawless (2010) states, the way regeneration schemes are now organised and funded, means they usually require private sector investment and the development of housing and other private facilities which local residents may not able to afford. This is particularly applicable to event regeneration projects because of the disjuncture between event venues and disadvantaged communities.

Issue 5   *Urban communities: beneficiaries or bidding pawns?* A common criticism of regeneration projects is that they treat local communities as recipients of projects, rather than active partners. There is a more extreme problem in event projects. Assistance for disadvantaged people and places is often central to the rationale for major event projects, but the wider benefits are often felt by those in other parts of the city, or new residents. There have been a number of examples where urban deprivation was used as a justification for a major event, but very few examples where events have been successfully used to improve levels of deprivation. Disadvantage is used as a way to win event bids, but when the bid is won, disadvantaged people and places are often ignored as other stakeholders and interests rush to capitalise.

Issue 6   *Success of event and success of legacy*. During the build-up to the London 2012 Olympic Games, the chair of the local organising committee was often quoted as saying that the best way to secure a good legacy was to stage a good event. But the preceding chapters suggest that there is not necessarily a direct correlation between the success of an event and the long-term urban regeneration outcomes. There are several examples of events that have been a great success but where the regeneration legacy has been disappointing – for example Sydney's Olympic Games. Conversely, there are examples where the event has been a disappointment, but where long-term urban objectives have been achieved. The 1984 Louisiana World Expo is probably the best example (see Chapter 8). Putting enough emphasis on the event whilst giving sufficient emphasis to legacy is a difficult balance to achieve. In the past, event requirements have dominated, but there is some evidence that priorities are being rebalanced.

Issue 7   *Do events help regeneration, or does regeneration help events?* Whether events can assist regeneration strategies has been a key question posed throughout this book. However, it is possible to turn this question around and ask if regeneration helps event strategies. In the contemporary era, where there is intensive competition for the rights to stage events, major regeneration projects that are underway or complete may help cities to secure major events. For example, Andres (2011) suggests that Marseille's long-term regeneration project to renovate its port area (1995–2020) helped the city to win the right to be European Capital of Culture 2013. The notion of regeneration assisting event strategies does not necessarily contradict the ideas discussed in this book. In Chapter 5 the idea of events as ways of showcasing or extending existing regeneration projects was discussed and these roles can be synthesised with the idea that regeneration projects help cities to stage major events. However, it does challenge the widely held view that events help to regenerate cities. It is hard to avoid the conclusion that events are often merely marketing tools used in conjunction with regeneration projects.

EMERGENT THEMES

During the course of this book various other issues have emerged from the discussion. Many of these are not directly related to the main focus of the book (one-off major events); but they help us to understand the wider relationship between events and urban regeneration. These issues are explored below.

The value of bidding

One of the themes that has emerged from the examples explored in the preceding chapters is the value of bidding for major events, even if those bids are unsuccessful. Bidding for high-profile events can have promotional benefits, but it can also help to deliver outcomes that assist urban regeneration, including:

- Networks and partnerships between key stakeholders within a city
- Discussions about the direction of a city's development

- The production of related plans
- New facilities and spaces planned for an event that are built anyway
- Better chances of securing other major events in the future.

There are lots of examples used in this book that illustrate the benefits of event bidding. According to Benneworth and Dauncey (2010), Lyon's bid for the 1968 Olympic Games was a key moment that facilitated a new era of governance and regional planning. Various cities including Stockholm, Berlin, Manchester, Newcastle/Gateshead and Amsterdam have benefited from plans formulated for events that were never staged. Manchester is perhaps the best example. Manchester's failed bids for the 1996 and 2000 Olympic Games attracted central government funding and inspired important new partnership working in the city. This city is one of several instances where event projects were delivered anyway, despite the failure of the bid. In other examples, failed bids were soon followed by successful ones, that then instigated urban development/regeneration. This suggests that the preparations made, knowledge gained and the relationships forged during a failed bid helped to lay the foundation for future success. Notable examples include:

- South Africa's bid for the 2004 Olympic Games and 2006 World Cup (and South Africa's successful 2010 World Cup bid)
- Qatar's bid for the 2016 Olympic Games (and the successful bid for the 2022 World Cup)
- Manchester's bid for the 1996 and 2000 Olympic Games (and the successful bid for the 2002 Commonwealth Games).

Event bidding can be a costly exercise, so these benefits help to justify this expense. Leveraging event bids is an interesting option for cities, as it seems that cities can benefit from some of the intangible benefits of events (image enhancement, partnership building) without the high cost, risks and controversies associated with actually staging an event. Some unsuccessful event bids have also helped to provide the basis for regeneration pursued in other cities. A good example is the Toronto Olympic bid which demonstrated various elements of good practice that have been integrated within subsequent events staged in Canada and throughout the world.

Staging a series of events

The discussion in this book has highlighted many problems associated with the idea of using major events within urban regeneration. These problems are often related to the size of the event and the way a one-off event disrupts established processes. The re-use of facilities, issues with over-capacity and temporary employment may leave cities with an undesirable 'hangover' effect. Cities are sometimes under-prepared for events, and they may find it difficult to sustain positive effects. One way to address these problems is to stage events in series rather than merely staging a one-off event. This is becoming a common approach. Major event hosts try to stage other events in the pre- and post-event periods. For example, after staging the Winter Olympic Games in 2006, Turin staged the Winter Universiade in 2007, the World Congress of Architects in 2008, the European Diving Championships and Indoor Athletics Championships in 2009, and the World Figure Skating Championships in 2010. Formulating a post-event calendar of events was also an approach pursued by Barcelona after the 1992 Olympic Games: the city organised a series of themed years during which related events were staged.

Strategies involving a portfolio of events are becoming increasingly common. One of the issues associated with this approach is the cocktail of themes promoted. Whereas a select group of cities see themselves as large/diverse enough to use a mixture of culture, sport and business events, other cities have focused on one particular theme. Some cities have adopted strategies that initially focused on one particular type of event, and have then diversified. An example is Gothenburg (see Chapter 9), a city that initially used sport events to promote development, but one that has recently tried to put more emphasis on events such as music festivals and cultural festivals. The gentrification of sport and the popularisation of high culture perhaps allows cities to use a mixture of events without contradicting the key messages they want to send. Indeed, major events are now programmed to include a mixture of sport and cultural events. However, there is still a danger that promoting a city as a host of regular sport events may deter those interested in cultural events. The discussion in Chapter 7 highlights that some images reaffirm existing stereotypes, rather than providing a new direction for cities.

A further issue with the notion of event portfolios concerns the question of whether size matters. The problems associated with mega-events mean that some authors have advocated the use of multiple editions of smaller events, rather than one-off mega-events (Bull, 2005; O'Sullivan and Jackson, 2002). Smaller events are more likely to build on the existing resources of a city; they are more likely to benefit local people and companies; and they do not come with same risks. The positive impacts of smaller events may be smaller, but the negative impacts are smaller too. Cities can build a reputation incrementally, rather than relying on a 'big bang' approach. Places like Cheltenham in the UK and Gothenburg in Sweden have become known as event cities because of their calendar of regular events that make a sustained contribution to local economic development (Bradley and Hall, 2006). This strategy of staging of multiple smaller events, rather than one major event, is something that could be used to assist post-industrial districts. It fits with Balsas's (2004) recommendation that cities should avoid generic 'copy-paste events' and instead focus on developing multiple events that reflect a city's own idiosyncrasies.

RECOMMENDATIONS FOR PRACTICE

The main purpose of this book is to explore the relationship between major events and urban regeneration generally. However, a secondary consideration is to suggest how organisers and other stakeholders can optimise the outcomes of event strategies. Throughout this book, various examples of good practice have been cited and various key principles have been discussed. In this section, an attempt is made to consolidate these into a coherent set of principles that can act as criteria with which to evaluate event regeneration projects.

Developing guidelines for good practice in event projects is something that has been attempted by other authors. Ritchie's (2000) principles for legacy planning (see Table 10.1) include lots of important ideas that remain relevant today. Reflecting the discussion in this book, Ritchie (2000) highlights the need to involve stakeholders and make sure events are relevant to local people. His principles are more oriented to event management than urban regeneration, but his suggestion that events should capitalise on opportunities to develop social understanding/communities corresponds to the social regeneration agenda discussed in this book. His idea to supplement sport events with other types of events has strong parallels with the leverage and festivalisation ideas discussed in Chapter 6.

Pitts and Liao (2009) have also developed a set of good practice criteria for major event projects. Their work is focused on Olympic cities, but many of the ideas are transferable to event regeneration in general. Unlike Ritchie's suggestions, they have operationalised their criteria and used them to evaluate the 2008 Beijing Olympic Games (and to conduct a preliminary assessment of the London

Table 10.1 A summary of Ritchie's (2000) ten-point event legacy plan

1. Involve all stakeholders
2. Build on the values of those stakeholders
3. Supplement sport events with cultural, educational, commercial events
4. Make events as regional as possible
5. Undertake commitment to keep momentum going post-event
6. Train residents to be good hosts
7. Augment events with supporting events, e.g. conferences
8. Capitalise on opportunities to enhance social understanding/ community cohesion
9. Publicise achievements well into the future to maintain effects
10. Tap into another major characteristic of the host city/region

Table 10.2 *A summary of Pitts and Liao's (2009) evaluation criteria for Olympic projects*

---

1. Supports urban containment
2. Optimises urban density
3. Rectifies dispersed urban form
4. Defines community centres
5. Encourages mixed-use development
6. Brownfield development potential
7. Promotes public transport
8. Promotes tourist oriented development
9. Generates inner city renaissance
10. Promotes attractive urban realm
11. Revitalises run-down urban areas
12. Promotes energy efficiency
13. Creates urban landmarks
14. Coherence with IOC policy
15. Implementation feasibility

2012 Games). Their evaluation framework is focused on sustainable development credentials and it is much more detailed than Ritchie's. A summary of the main headings included within their criteria is presented in Table 10.2.

Pitts and Liao's (2009) criteria are focused on the physical qualities of event projects, rather than the social qualities. The social dimensions apparent in Ritchie's criteria are not really addressed. Pitts and Liao's ideas are strongly linked to the principles of sustainable urbanism and sustainable communities: with a focus on containing urban sprawl, energy efficiency and public transport provision. It is not easy to measure the performance of projects according to either of these evaluation frameworks. However, they do help us to identify key principles and priorities.

Ten key principles for event regeneration projects

Using the material in this book it is possible to develop a series of good practice principles that encompass the main lessons highlighted. These ten points are outlined below. This provides a useful set of ideas for future practice, and a way of summarising some of the main ideas considered in the preceding chapters. These principles are designed for those cities that have taken the decision to use events to help regenerate areas. However, as mentioned previously this is not always something that is appropriate for all events.

1 *Embed event projects within wider urban regeneration programmes.* It is important that event regeneration projects build on the existing resources of, and existing plans for, a city rather than overriding them. This includes city-wide plans, plans for specific districts, long-term social policy objectives and more specialised plans such as tourism and economic development strategies. As outlined in Chapter 5, event projects are most successful when used to assist, and to accelerate, the achievement of pre-existing goals. This means ensuring that events and associated initiatives are integrated into broader regeneration programmes. The approach that is most likely to work is one involving a process of urban regeneration that includes an event, rather than hoping that an event will lead to urban regeneration.

2 *Use a major event as an opportunity to deliver parallel initiatives.* Chapter 6 argued that event projects should aim to ensure that regeneration is achieved, rather than simply expecting positive impacts to automatically 'trickle down' to communities. This can be achieved by developing initiatives in association with an event, but making sure that they are not led by the event itself. An 'event themed' approach provides the foundation for sustained benefits, with event associations used to generate publicity, excitement and civic engagement. Uniting a series of local-level initiatives under an event theme achieves a compromise between top-down and bottom-up approaches to regeneration. Numerous smaller initiatives combine to give significant effects, rather than relying on the speculative effects of 'boosterist' schemes.

3 *Ensure that regeneration considerations are incorporated into the initial stages of planning for an event.* Event regeneration projects can be assisted by ensuring that an event is designed to encourage such effects from its inception. Authorities often consider regeneration effects only after key decisions about events have already been made. It is assumed that regeneration objectives are compatible with other objectives, but this is not usually the case. To ensure an optimal relationship between an event and urban regeneration objectives, it is essential that regeneration considerations are addressed as soon as event planning commences. This can allow practical event initiatives to lever regeneration benefits. For example, a volunteering programme is an important part of an event management strategy, but with early planning it can be used as a tool to achieve lasting social regeneration (see Chapter 6).

4 *Promote shared ownership amongst the stakeholders of event regeneration programmes.* It is important that the agencies responsible for an event are fully committed to regeneration considerations and that they represent a range of different interests (see Chapter 9). Although short-term success often relies on key individuals, sustained benefits can be achieved only if

a range of partners lead and support initiatives throughout their duration. It is very difficult for the public sector to take complete control of event/ legacy management. The input of other agencies, including those in the private sector, is crucial to provide key skills, and to provide valuable sources of financial and moral support. This was discussed extensively in Chapter 9. However, when creating public–private partnerships to deliver event projects, it is important to retain central roles for elected authorities, as they provide the representation for disenfranchised groups. Ultimately, shared ownership is achieved by a combination of effective communication between stakeholders, the clear delegation of certain responsibilities and a clear and inclusive institutional framework.

5 *Balance event regeneration and event management priorities.* Host cities will always concentrate on event management and publicity, but regeneration considerations must be given sufficient priority if they are cited as a key justification for staging a major event. Ideally, event regeneration and event management should be fully integrated and self-reinforcing. But in practice, pressures associated with staging events mean that regeneration and event management responsibilities are often divorced. As Chapter 9 outlined, it is useful to have a separate regeneration/legacy agency, but it is important that this agency is not viewed and treated as a 'poor relation' of the event management body. If regeneration is a key objective of an event, then legacy agencies and event management agencies should be given equal priority and their activities should feed into one another. Event management and regeneration organisations often have different agendas, but that does not have to be an obstacle to co-ordinated action.

6 *Allocate resources throughout the lifetime of projects to achieve sustained effects.* It is important for event regeneration initiatives to commence well in advance of an event and to continue once events have ended. Although the focus will inevitably be the event itself, it is important that interest from participants and co-ordinators does not dissipate too quickly in the post-event period. One of the most remarkable features of events is the way attention shifts away from a host city after an event has finished. This can be addressed at the event management level by staging other events and other commemorative activities to keep the event theme visible. It can also be addressed by designing initiatives that are 'owned' by communities and thus championed from within. Event regeneration is a long-term endeavour (see Chapter 5) and host cities need to include post-event development costs into budgets. The chances of sustained benefits are increased by ensuring that event agencies give consistent levels of financial and administrative support throughout the life of projects. This was illustrated by the extended case study in Chapter 6: Manchester's Commonwealth Games Legacy Programme.

7 *Allow the most disadvantaged places and people to benefit.* The engagement, commitment and publicity generated by event regeneration projects should not only be used to encourage community involvement in general. Event projects should be used to target disadvantaged individuals and groups. Sport and cultural events can be used as a 'hook' to engage those who are normally out of reach of regeneration initiatives. Volunteer programmes are one of the best ways to encourage disadvantaged individuals to gain qualifications, work experience and connections to organisations/individuals that can help them. Similarly, other event schemes can provide valuable introductions to more productive, more rewarding and healthier lifestyles (see Chapter 6). Authorities should consider the needs of disadvantaged areas in location decisions (see Chapter 4) and they should ensure that deprived areas are the beneficiaries – not merely the justification for – event projects. Specific measures to protect against displacement also need to be adopted (see Chapter 5).

8 *Ensure community involvement from the outset.* The deadlines and organisational complexities associated with major events often render them incompatible with regeneration best practice (see Chapter 5). Important facets of sustainable urban regeneration – such as embedding initiatives within wider programmes, community collaboration, public accountability, understanding the real needs of an area and maintaining rigorous planning procedures – can be compromised. Wherever possible, events should be accommodated within existing planning procedures rather than treated as exceptional cases. Host cities need to consult with people before event bids are submitted to assess whether this is something that citizens wish to pursue. Subsequently, communities need to be involved in planning events and not merely consulted about key decisions.

9 *Where new venues are required, ensure they are integrated with existing populations, physically; but also social and economically.* The discussion in Chapter 4 emphasised that new venues should be developed only where they are needed. Otherwise, existing, temporary or remote facilities should be used. If new venues are justified, they need to be planned carefully to avoid the artificial separation of venues from local residential areas. This separation can be caused by poor urban design that creates physical barriers, but it can also be caused by symbolic and financial exclusion. This means that venues need to be designed and marketed appropriately. In the contemporary era it is harder to privilege local people (e.g. in employment recruitment), but there are ways that projects can be integrated economically with local companies and residents.

10 *Ensure regeneration promises are not compromised when there is pressure to balance event budgets.* Chapters 4, 5 and 6 highlighted the tendency

to dilute promises or cancel regeneration projects if and when there are budgetary pressures. There is a noted tendency for the costs of event projects to be underestimated for various reasons. When cost savings are required, this often means that associated regeneration initiatives are scaled back. This can be avoided by setting more realistic budgets and by ensuring that planning mechanisms are used to commit developers to certain action. It can also be achieved through institutional arrangements – for example, avoiding the cross-subsidisation of budgets.

VALUE AND LIMITATIONS OF THE BOOK

This book has attempted to explore the relationship between major events and urban regeneration. The aim is to provide an accessible introduction to those who are familiar with events, but may be less familiar with urban regeneration. One of the main objectives is to provide a general overview of key issues rather than a text which is led by individual case studies. This approach means that generalisations and over-simplifications are unavoidable. Obviously, strategies and outcomes vary according to different events and different types of events. The book has pointed out some general patterns to aid understanding, but this is sometimes is at the expense of detailed scrutiny and specific evidence of individual projects.

There are several other useful texts that may be interesting to those who now want to read more specific and more detailed accounts. Roche's *Mega Events and Modernity: Olympics and Expos in the Growth of Global Culture* (Routledge, 2000) is a fascinating text dealing with sociological issues of globalisation and identity – rather than urbanism – as its primary focus. For those more interested in cultural events and cultural policy, Richards and Palmer's *The Eventful City: Cultural Management and Urban Revitalisation* (Elsevier, 2010) and Gold and Gold's *Cities of Culture: Staging International Festivals and the Urban Agenda, 1851–2000* (Ashgate, 2005) provide very useful accounts. There are also a number of texts that focus on the Olympic Games in particular. *Olympic Cities* (Routledge, 2007, 2010), edited by Gold and Gold, is a detailed review of the modern Games and the way in which they have influenced the urban agenda. Liao and Pitts' *Sustainable Olympic Design and Urban Development* (Routledge, 2009) also provides a good review of Olympic projects. Liao and Pitts' work provides a useful complement to this book because it focuses on environmentally friendly design, something that has been covered only briefly in this text. Additionally, there are several special editions of journals that are dedicated to urban event projects. Useful editions include *Urban Studies*, volume 42(5/6); *Urban Forum*, volume 20(10); *Sociological Review*, volume 54; and *Town Planning Review*, volume 82(1).

FINAL SUMMARY

Events and urban regeneration have both risen to prominence in post-industrial urban contexts. In a sometimes desperate search for ways of dealing with de-industrialisation, funding has been allocated to event projects, urban regeneration initiatives and, in some cases, programmes that use events as ways of achieving regeneration. This book has explored these event regeneration projects. Despite some emerging examples of good practice, using events as regeneration tools remains a speculative approach. It is also something that sits awkwardly with recent developments in regeneration policy. Contemporary urban regeneration is usually something pursued at the neighbourhood level, involving bottom-up initiatives and community involvement. Major event projects are often the antithesis of this type of approach. They have more in common with the discredited property-led regeneration initiatives of the 1980s and 1990s. However, if we accept a broader view of regeneration as a discourse that frames varied attempts to reboot, revise and redirect cities, then events seem to have an interesting role to play. The case studies included in this book suggest that events can be used within wider efforts to assist a post-industrial revival. Barcelona, Gothenburg, Manchester and New Orleans are all cities that have used events to reinvent themselves. The critical success factors in these cases seem to be a sustained commitment to using events and incorporating event projects within a broader strategic vision. In this sense, the conclusion of the UK government's review of the National Garden Festival initiative in the 1980s still seems valid (DoE, 1990). This evaluation concluded that a major event may not be powerful in itself but that in some instances events do provide a valuable additional instrument to be included within a regeneration strategy.

Study questions

(Numbers correspond to relevant chapters.)

1 Roche (2000) divides events into two major sub-genres; 'exhibition' and 'performance'. Critically examine the relevance of this categorisation to contemporary major events and evaluate other ways of categorising different events.

2 'Festivals are designed to divert the attention of the masses from "real events" by supplying a carefully regulated diet of synthetic, seemingly inclusive, festivities for popular consumption' (Waterman, 2008: 60). Explain and critically evaluate this theoretical perspective. Compare and contrast it to other theories that can help us to understand the significance of events in contemporary society.

3 With reference to the Olympic Games (from 1896) *or* World Expos *or* European Capitals of Culture, discuss critical moments in the evolution of the event. How does the history of this event illustrate more general changes in the way events are being used strategically by cities?

4 In terms of regeneration legacy, critically discuss whether it is better to place the facilities for a mega-event in one concentrated area, or whether it is better for venues to be spread throughout a city.

5 Several authors have identified a 'Barcelona model' in which 'the use of major events as catalysts for city renewal' is a key element (Garcia, 2004: 321). Critically discuss the idea of a 'Barcelona model' and identify lessons that can be learned from this case study for other cities seeking to use events strategically.

6 Critically discuss the meaning of the term 'leverage' in an events context and critically examine the range of social outcomes that cities can 'lever' from an event.

7 'If a cultural project is going to succeed in leading regeneration it is crucial that is does so as part of a holistic destination brand' (Tibbot, 2002: 73). Critically discuss the implications of this statement for the successful use of events within urban policy.

8 Post-industrial cities with under-performing tourism sectors are often keen to stage events to assist tourism development. Identify how events can encourage different types of destination development. Justify your ideas by referring to specific examples.

9 Critically examine the way that event projects have helped urban governance arrangements to evolve in cities. Evaluate whether these new arrangements represent an opportunity for, or a threat to, disadvantaged urban communities.

10 Some authors have advocated recasting major events as less ambitious projects that should be delivered without large-scale regeneration programmes attached to them. Critically examine the advantages and disadvantages of returning to a more modest version of event projects last seen pre-World War II.

Supporting reading for each of the chapters

CHAPTER 1

Richards, G. and Palmer, R. (2010) *Eventful Cities*. Oxford: Butterworth-Heinemann. (Chapter 1)

Tallon, A. (2010) *Urban Regeneration in the UK*. London: Routledge. (Chapters 1 and 14)

CHAPTER 2

Gotham, K. F. (2005) 'Theorising Urban Spectacles: Festivals, Tourism and the Transformation of Urban Space'. City, 9(2), pp. 225–246.

Hiller, H. (2006) 'Post-Event Outcomes and the Post-Modern Turn: The Olympics and Urban Transformations'. European Sport Management Quarterly, 6(4), pp. 317–332.

CHAPTER 3

Chalkley, B. and Essex, S. (1999) 'Urban Development Through Hosting International Events: A History of the Olympic Games'. Planning Perspectives, 14, pp. 369–394.

Gold, J. and Gold, M. (2005) *Cities of Culture: Staging International Festivals and the Urban Agenda, 1851–2000*. Aldershot: Ashgate. (Chapters 1 and 2)

CHAPTER 4

Balsas, C. (2004) 'City Centre Regeneration in the Context of the 2001 European Capital of Culture in Porto, Portugal'. Local Economy, 19(4), pp. 396–410.

Pitts, A. and Liao, H. (2009) *Sustainable Olympic Design and Urban Development*. Abingdon: Routledge. (Chapters 3 and 4)

CHAPTER 5

Carrière, J. and Demaziere, C. (2002) 'Urban Planning and Flagship Development Projects: Lessons from Expo '98, Lisbon'. Planning Practice and Research, 17(1), pp. 69–79.

Porter, L., Jaconelli, M., Cheyne, J., Eby, D. and Wagenaar, H. (2009) 'Planning Displacement: The Real Legacy of Major Sporting Events'. Planning Theory and Practice, 10(3), pp. 395–418.

CHAPTER 6

Misener, L. and Mason, D. (2006) 'Creating Community Networks: Can Sporting Events Offer Meaningful Sources of Social Capital?' Managing Leisure, 11(1), pp. 39–56.
Waitt, G. (2003) 'Social Impacts of the Sydney Olympics'. Annals of Tourism Research, 30(1), pp. 194–215.

CHAPTER 7

Clark, G. (2008) *Local Development Benefits of Staging Global Events*. Paris: OECD.
Smith, A. (2005) 'Reimaging the City: The Value of Sport Initiatives'. Annals of Tourism Research, 32(1), pp. 229–248.

CHAPTER 8

Getz, D. (1999) 'The Impacts of Mega-Events on Tourism: Strategies for Destinations'. In Andersson, T., Persson, C., Sahlberg, B. and Strom, L.-I. (eds) *The Impact of Mega-Events* (pp. 5–32). Ostersund: European Tourism Research Institute.
Roche, M. (2000) *Mega Events and Modernity: Olympics and Expos in the Growth of Global Culture*. London: Routledge. (Chapter 5)

CHAPTER 9

Benneworth, P. and Dauncey, H. (2010) 'International Urban Festivals as a Catalyst for Governance Capacity Building'. Environment and Planning C, 28, pp. 1083–1100.
Bramwell, B. (1997) 'Strategic Planning Before and After a Mega-Event'. Tourism Management, 18(3), pp. 167–176.

CHAPTER 10

Preuss, H. (2007) 'The Conceptualisation and Measurement of Mega Sport Event Legacies'. Journal of Sport and Tourism, 12(3–4), pp. 207–227.
Ritchie, J. R. B. (2000) 'Turning 16 Days into 16 Years through Olympic Legacies'. Event Management, 6(3), pp. 155–165.

Further research on the internet

SITES OF RIGHTS HOLDERS OF EVENTS

www.olympic.org/
www.bie-paris.org/
http://ec.europa.eu/culture/our-programmes-and-actions/doc413_en.htm
www.thecgf.com/
www.fifa.com/

SITES CONTAINING ARCHIVES OF PREVIOUS EVENTS

www.expomuseum.com/
www.museumoflondon.org.uk/archive/exhibits/festival/

SITES FOR INDIVIDUAL MAJOR EVENTS

www.gardenfestivalwales.co.uk/index.php
www.sydneyolympicpark.com.au/
www.2010legaciesnow.com/
www.gameslegacy.co.uk/cgi-bin/index.cgi

SITES FOR INDIVIDUAL VENUES

www.mosesmabhidastadium.co.za/
www.bcplacestadium.com/
www.superdome.com/site.php
www.donvalleystadium.co.uk/

SITES OF GROUPS CAMPAIGNING AGAINST MAJOR EVENT PROJECTS

www.gamesmonitor.org.uk/
http://web.resist.ca/~orn/blog/

SITES THAT COVER BIDDING FOR MAJOR EVENT PROJECTS

www.gamesbids.com/eng/
www.tseconsulting.com/

SITES OF ORGANISATIONS INVOLVED IN REGENERATION POLICY

www.rics.org/
www.architecture.com/
www.unhabitat.org/categories.asp?catid=9
www.brownfieldbriefing.com/

SITES OF ORGANISATIONS INVOLVED IN URBAN REGENERATION RESEARCH

www.regional-studies-assoc.ac.uk/
www.centreforcities.org/home1.html
www.eura.org/
www.udel.edu/uaa/
www.ecorys.com/

SITES OF URBAN ASSOCIATIONS/PROFESSIONAL NETWORKS

www.fbeonline.co.uk/
www.atcm.org/

SITES FOR INDIVIDUAL CITIES' EVENT ORGANISATIONS

www.goteborg.com/
www.vmec.com.au/

SITES OF KEY INDIVIDUALS WHO HAVE WRITTEN ABOUT EVENT PROJECTS

www.gregclark.net/index.html
www.beatrizgarcia.net/

USEFUL BLOGS

www.estatesgazette.com/blogs/olympics/
http://regenandrenewal.blogspot.com/

USER-GENERATED SITES REGARDING CULTURAL AND SPORT EVENT VENUES

www.skyscrapercity.com/forumdisplay.php?f=218
www.youtube.com/user/WorldExpoBlog

References

AEG (2007) *Sustainability Statement for 'The O2'*. AEG Europe.

Alberts, H. (2009) 'Berlin's Failed Bid to Host the 2000 Summer Olympic Games: Urban Development and the Improvement of Sports Facilities'. International Journal of Urban and Regional Research, 33(2), pp. 502–516.

Amara, M. (2005) '2006 Qatar Asian Games: A Modernization Project From Above'. Sport in Society, 8(3), pp. 493–514.

Anderson, B. and Holden, A. (2008) 'Affective Urbanism and the Event of Hope'. Space and Culture, 11(2), pp. 142–159.

Andranovich, G., Burbank, M. and Heying, C. (2001) 'Olympic Cities: Lessons Learned from Mega-Event Politics'. Journal of Urban Affairs, 23(2), pp. 113–131.

Andres, L. (2011) 'Marseille 2013 or the Final Round of a Long and Complex Regeneration Strategy'. Town Planning Review, 82(1), pp. 61–76.

Arnstein, S. (1969) 'A Ladder of Citizen Participation'. Journal of the American Planning Association, 35(4), pp. 216–224.

Ashworth, G. and Voogd, H. (1990) *Selling the City*. London: Bellhaven.

Atkinson, G., Mourato, S., Szymanski, S. and Ozdemiroglu, E. (2008) 'Are We Willing to Pay Enough to "Back The Bid"? Valuing the Intangible Impacts of London's Bid to Host the 2012 Summer Olympic Games'. Urban Studies, 45(2), pp. 419–444.

Austrian, Z. and Rosentraub, M. (2002) 'Cities, Sport and Economic Change: A Retrospective Analysis'. Journal of Urban Affairs, 24(5), pp. 549–563.

Bakhtin, M. (1984) *Rabelais and His World*. Bloomington: Indiana University Press.

Bale, J. (1993) *Sport, Space and the City*. London: Routledge.

Balibrea, M.-P. (2001) 'Urbanism, Culture and the Post-Industrial City: Challenging the "Barcelona Model"'. Journal of Spanish Cultural Studies, 2(2), pp. 187–210.

Balsas, C. (2004) 'City Centre Regeneration in the Context of the 2001 European Capital of Culture in Porto, Portugal'. Local Economy, 19(4), pp. 396–410.

Barker, M., Page, S. and Meyer, D. (2002) 'Modelling Tourism Crime: The 2000 America's Cup'. Annals of Tourism Research, 29(3), pp. 762–782.

Barthes, R. (1973) *Mythologies*. St Albans: Paladin.

Bathelt, H. and Graf, A. (2008) 'Internal and External Dynamics of the Munich Film and TV Industry Cluster and Limitations to Future Growth'. Environment and Planning A, 40, pp. 1944–1965.

Baudrillard, J. (1993) *The Transparency of Evil: Essays on Extreme Phenomena*. London: Verso.

Beaumont, R. (1985) 'Garden Festivals as Means of Urban Regeneration'. Journal of the Royal Society for the Encouragement of Arts, Manufacture and Commerce, 11, pp. 405–421.

Benedicto, J. and Carrasco, J. (2007) 'Barcelona Universal Forum 2004'. In W. Salet and E. Gualini (eds) *Framing Strategic Urban Projects: Learning from Current Experiences in European Urban Regions* (pp. 84–114). Abingdon: Routledge.

Benneworth, P. and Dauncey, H. (2010) 'International Urban Festivals as a Catalyst for Governance Capacity Building'. Environment and Planning C, 28, pp. 1083–1100.

Beriatos, E. and Gospodini, A. (2004) 'Glocalising Urban Landscapes: Athens and the 2004 Olympics'. Cities, 21(3), pp. 187–202.

Bernstock, P. (2009) 'London 2012 and the Regeneration Game'. In G. Poynter and I. MacRury (eds) *Olympic Cities: 2012 and the Remaking of London* (pp. 201–218). Farnham: Ashgate.

Bianchini, F., Dawson, J. and Evans, R. (1992) 'Flagship Projects in Urban Regeneration'. In P. Healey, S. Davoudi, M. O'Toole, D. Usher and S. Tavsanoglu, *Rebuilding the City* (pp. 245–255). London: E. & F. N. Spon.

Binks, P. and Snape, B. (2006) '"Events, Dear Boy. Events…" Chance, Opportunism and Unpredictability in Pre-Event Planning for Post-Event Function: A Case Study of the Bolton Arena'. LSA Publication number 91, pp. 65–76.

Black, D. (2008) 'Dreaming Big: The Pursuit of "Second Order Games" as a Strategic Response to Globalisation'. Sport in Society, 11(4), pp. 467–480.

Blain, N., Boyle, R. and O'Donnell, H. (1993) *Sport and National Identity in the European Media*. Leicester: Leicester University Press.

Blakeley, G. (2005) 'Local Governance and Local Democracy: The Barcelona Model'. Local Government Studies, 31(2), pp. 149–165.

Blanco, I. (2009) 'Does a Barcelona Model Really Exist? Periods, Territories and Actors in the Process of Urban Transformation'. Local Government Studies, 35(3), pp. 355–369.

Bob, U. and Swart, K. (2009) 'Resident Perceptions of the 2010 FIFA Soccer World: Cup Stadia Development in Cape Town'. Urban Forum, 20, pp. 47–59.

Body-Gendrot, S. (2003) 'City Security and Visitors: Managing Mega-Events in France'. In L. Hoffman, S. Fainstein and D. Judd (eds) *Cities and Visitors: Regulating People, Markets, and City Space*. Oxford: Wiley-Blackwell.

Boyle, M. (1997) 'Civic Boosterism in the Politics of Local Economic Development: Institutional Positions and Strategic Orientations on the Consumption of Hallmark Events'. Environment and Planning A, 29, pp. 1975–1997.

Boyle, M. and Hughes, C. G. (1991) 'The Politics of the Representation of "The Real": Discourses from the Left on Glasgow's Role as European City of Culture, 1990'. Area, 23(3), pp. 217–228.

Bradley, A. and Hall, T. (2006) 'The Urban Hierarchy and Competitive Advantage – The Festival Phenomenon: Festivals, Events and the Promotion of Small Urban Areas'.

In D. Bell and M. Jayne (eds) *Small Cities: Urban Experience Beyond the Metropolis* (pp. 77–90). New York: Routledge.

Bramwell, B. (1993) 'Planning for Tourism in an Industrial City'. Town and Country Planning, 62, 1/2, pp. 17–19.

—— (1997) 'Strategic Planning Before and After a Mega-Event'. Tourism Management, 18(3), pp. 167–176.

Broudehoux, A. (2007) 'Spectacular Beijing: The Conspicuous Construction of an Olympic Metropolis'. Journal of Urban Affairs, 29(4), pp. 383–399.

—— (2010) 'Images of Power: Architectures of the Integrated Spectacle at the Beijing Olympics'. Journal of Architectural Education, 2010, pp. 52–62.

Brown, G., Chalip, L., Jago, L. and Mules, T. (2004) 'Developing Brand Australia'. In N. Morgan, A. Pritchard and R. Pride (eds) *Destination Branding: Creating the Unique Destination Position.* Second edition (pp. 279–305). Oxford: Butterworth-Heinemann.

Brown, R. (2011) *Place Shaping in the Global City: The Social Legacies of London and Rio.* Presentation at Olympic Cities: Social Legacies. 10 March 2011. Toynbee Hall, London.

Brunet, F. (2009) 'The Economy of the Barcelona Olympic Games'. In G. Poynter and I. MacRury (eds) *Olympic Cities: 2012 and the Remaking of London* (pp. 97–120). Farnham: Ashgate.

Bryant, B. (2011) 'No Room at the Inn'. Evening Standard, 28 June 2011, pp. 24–25.

Bull, A. (2005) 'Mega or Multi-Mini? Comparing the Value to a Destination of Different Policies towards Events'. Available at: www.nottingham.ac.uk/ttri/discussion/2005_4. pdf (accessed 1 July 2011).

Burgan, B. and Mules, T. (1992) 'Economic Impact of Sporting Events'. Annals of Tourism Research, 19(4), pp. 700–710.

Busquets, J. (2005) *The Urban Evolution of a Compact City.* Rovereto: Nicolodi.

Calavita, N. and Ferrer, A. (2000) 'Behind Barcelona's Success Story: Citizen Movements and Planners' Power'. Journal of Urban History, 26(6), pp. 793–807.

Carrière, J. and Demaziere, C. (2002) 'Urban Planning and Flagship Development Projects: Lessons from Expo 98, Lisbon'. Planning Practice and Research, 17(1), pp. 69–79.

Cashman, R. (2006) *The Bitter Sweet Awakening: The Legacy of the Sydney 2000 Olympic Games.* NSW, Australia: Walla Press.

—— (2009) 'Regenerating Sydney's West: Framing and Adapting an Olympic Vision'. In G. Poynter and I. MacRury (eds) *Olympic Cities: 2012 and the Remaking of London* (pp. 133–144). Farnham: Ashgate.

Cashman, R. and Darcy, S. (2008) *Benchmark Games: The Sydney 2000 Paralympic Games.* NSW, Australia: Walla Press.

Chalip, L. (2004) 'Beyond Impact: A Generalised Model for Host Community Event Leverage'. In B. Ritchie and S. Adair (eds) *Sports Tourism: Interrelationships, Impacts and Issues* (pp. 226–252). Clevedon: Channel View.

—— (2005) 'Marketing, Media and Place Promotion'. In J. Higham (ed.) *Sport Tourism Destinations* (pp. 162–176). Oxford: Butterworth-Heinemann.

Chalip, L. and Costa, C. (2005) 'Sport Event Tourism and the Destination Brand: Towards a General Theory'. Sport in Society, 8(2), pp. 218–237.

Chalip, L., Green, B. and Hill, B. (2003) 'Effects of Sport Event Media on Destination Image and Intention to Visit'. Journal of Sport Management, 17, pp. 214–234.

Chalkley, B. and Essex, S. (1999) 'Urban Development Through Hosting International Events: A History of the Olympic Games'. Planning Perspectives, 14, pp. 369–394.

Chang, T. (2006) 'Tourism in a Reluctantly Small City-Island Nation: Insights from Singapore'. In D. Bell and M. Jayne (eds) *Small Cities: Urban Experience Beyond the Metropolis* (pp. 59–74) New York: Routledge.

Chang, T. and Lee, W. (2003) 'Renaissance City Singapore: A Study of Arts Spaces'. Area, 35(2), pp. 128–141.

Cho, M. (2005) 'Budget Traveler Accommodation Satisfaction: The Case of Yogwans During the 2002 FIFA World Cup Korea/Japan'. Asia Pacific Journal of Tourism Research, 10(3), pp. 275–287.

City of Melbourne (undated) '2006 Commonwealth Games: Promoting Melbourne'. Available at: www.melbourne.vic.gov.au/aboutmelbourne/history/pages/promotingmelbourne.aspx (accessed 1 July 2011).

City of Vancouver (2010) 'Olympic Village Greenest Neighbourhood in the World'. Available at: http://vancouver.ca/greenestcity/greeninitiatives.htm#village (accessed 1 July 2011).

Clark, G. (2008) *Local Development Benefits of Staging Global Events*. Paris: OECD.

Coalter, F. (1998) 'Leisure Studies, Leisure Policy and Social Citizenship: The Failure of Welfare or the Limits of Welfare?' Leisure Studies, 17(1), pp. 21–36.

—— (2004) 'Stuck in the Blocks? A Sustainable Sporting Legacy'. In A.Vigor, M. Mean and C. Tims (eds) *After the Gold Rush: A Sustainable Olympics for London* (pp. 91–106). London: Institute for Public Policy Research and DEMOS.

—— (2010) 'Sport-for-Development: Going Beyond the Boundary?' Sport in Society, 13(9), pp. 1374–1391.

Cochrane, A., Peck, J. and Tickell, A. (1996) 'Manchester Plays Games: Exploring the Local Politics of Globalisation'. Urban Studies, 33(8), pp. 1319–1336.

Colombino, A. (2009) 'Multiculturalism and Time in Trieste: Place-Marketing Images and Residents' Perceptions of a Multicultural City'. Social and Cultural Geography, 10(3), pp. 279–297.

Connell, J. and Page, S. (2005) 'Evaluating the Economic and Spatial Effects of an Event: The Case of the World Medical and Health Games'. Tourism Geographies, 7(1), pp. 63–85.

Cornelissen, S. (2007) 'Crafting Legacies: The Changing Political Economy of Global Sport and the 2010 FIFA World Cup™. Politikon'. South African Journal of Political Studies, 34(3), pp. 241–259.

—— (2010) 'Football's Tsars: Proprietorship, Corporatism and Politics in the 2010 FIFA World Cup'. Soccer and Society, 11(1/2), pp. 131–143.

Couch, C. and Fraser, C. (2003) 'Introduction: The European Context and Theoretical Framework'. In C. Couch, C. Fraser and S. Percy (eds) *Urban Regeneration in Europe* (pp. 1–16). Oxford: Blackwell.

Dabinett, G. (1991) 'Local Policies Towards Industrial Change: The Case of Sheffield's Lower Don Valley'. Planning Practice and Research, 6(1), pp. 13–18.

Dansero, E. and Puttilli, M. (2010) 'Mega-Event Tourism Legacies: The Case of the Torino 2006 Winter Olympic Games – A Territorialisation Approach'. Leisure Studies, 29(3), pp. 321–341.

Dargan, L. (2009) 'Participation and Local Urban Regeneration: The Case of the New Deal for Communities in the UK'. Regional Studies, 43(2), pp. 305–317.

Dauncey, H. (1999) 'Building the Finals: Facilities and Infrastructure'. In H. Dauncey and G. Hare (eds) *France and the 1998 World Cup* (pp. 98–120). London. Frank Cass.

Davidson, J. (2010) 'Why Singapore's World Best Sport City Award is a Joke'. CNN Go, 8 December 2010. Available at: www.cnngo.com/singapore/life/john-davidson-why-singapores-worlds-best-sports-city-award-is-a-joke-861361 (accessed 1 July 2011).

Davies, J. (2002) 'The Governance of Urban Regeneration: A Critique of the Governing Without Government Thesis'. Public Administration, 80(2), pp. 301–322.

Davies, L. (2006) 'Sporting a New Role? Stadia and the Real Estate Market'. Managing Leisure, 11(4), pp. 231–244.

Davis, R. and Marvin, G. (2004) *Venice, the Tourist Maze: A Cultural Critique of the World's Most Touristed City*. Berkeley: University of California Press.

Davison, G. (1997) 'Welcoming the World: The 1956 Olympic Games and the Re-Presentation of Melbourne'. Australian Historical Studies, 27, pp. 64–76.

DCMS (2001) *Creative Industries: Mapping Document*. London: Department of Culture, Media and Sport.

Debord, G. (1994) *The Society of the Spectacle*. New York: Zone Books.

Deffner, A. and Labrianidis, L. (2005) 'Planning Culture and Time in a Mega-Event: Thessaloniki as the European City of Culture in 1997'. International Planning Studies, 10(3/4), pp. 241–264.

Degen, M. (2003) 'Fighting for the Global Catwalk: Formalizing Public Life in Castlefield (Manchester) and Diluting Public Life in el Raval (Barcelona)'. International Journal of Urban and Regional Research, 27(4), pp. 867–880.

De Groote, P. (2005) 'A Multidisciplinary Analysis of World's Fairs (Expos) and Their Effects. Tourism Review, 60(1), pp. 12–19.

Dickens, C. (1995) *Sketches by Boz*. London: Penguin.

Diez, J. R. (2003) 'Hannover after the World Exhibition EXPO 2000: An Attempt to Establish an ICT-Cluster'. European Planning Studies, 11(4), pp. 379–394.

Dimanche, F. (1997) 'Special Events Legacy: The 1984 Louisiana World's Fair in New Orleans'. In P. E. Murphy (ed.) *Quality Management in Urban Tourism* (pp. 67–74). Chichester: John Wiley & Sons.

Dodouras, S. and James, P. (2007) 'Fuzzy Cognitive Mapping to Appraise Complex Situations'. Journal of Environmental Planning and Management, 50(6), pp. 823–852.

DoE (Department of the Environment) (1990) *An Evaluation of Garden Festivals*. London: HMSO.

Duffy, R. (2002) *A Trip Too Far: Ecotourism, Politics and Exploitation*. London: Earthscan.

Duran, P. (2002) 'The Impact of the Olympic Games on Tourism.' In M. Moragas and M. Botella (eds) *Barcelona: l'herència dels Jocs 1992–2002*. Barcelona: Centre d'Estudis Olímpics UAB.

Dyreson, M. and Llewellyn, M. (2008) 'Los Angeles Is the Olympic City: Legacies of the 1932 and 1984 Olympic Games'. International Journal of the History of Sport, 25(14), pp. 1991–2018.

Eagleton, T. (1981) *Walter Benjamin: Towards a Revolutionary Criticism*. London: NLB.

Edensor, T., Christie, C. and Lloyd, B. (2008) 'Obliterating Informal Space: The London Olympics and the Lea Valley: A Photo Essay'. Space and Culture, 11, pp. 285–293.

Edgar, A. and Sedgewick, P. (1999) *Key Concepts in Cultural Theory*. London: Routledge.

Ehrenreich, B. (2007) *Dancing in the Streets: A History of Collective Joy*. London: Granta.

Ellis, C. (2005) 'Lewis Mumford and Normal Bel Geddes: The Highway, the City and the Future'. Planning Perspectives, 20(1), pp. 51–68.

Enhorning, G. (2010) 'City Profile: Gothenburg'. Cities, 27(3), pp. 182–194.

Environmental Partnership (2006) *Proposed Re-development of Green Point Stadium and Associated Infrastructure*. Draft EIA Report, July 2006.

Essex, S. and Chalkley, B. (2004) 'Mega-Sporting Events in Urban and Regional Policy: A History of the Winter Olympics'. Planning Perspectives, 19(2), pp. 201–204.

Euchner, C. (1999) 'Tourism and Sports: The Serious Competition for Play'. In D. Judd and S. Fainstein (eds) *The Tourist City* (pp. 215–232). New Haven, CT: Yale University Press.

Evans, B. (2007) 'The Politics of Partnership: Urban Regeneration in New East Manchester'. Public Policy and Administration, 22, pp. 201–215.

Farley, P. and Roberts, M. (2011) *Edgelands: Journeys into England's True Wilderness*. London: Jonathan Cape.

Faulkner, B., Chalip, L., Brown, G., Jago, L., March, R. and Woodside, A. (2001) 'Monitoring the Tourism Impacts of the Sydney 2000 Olympics'. Event Management, 6, pp. 231–246.

Finkel, R. (2009) 'A Picture of the Contemporary Combined Arts Festival Landscape'. Cultural Trends, 18(1), pp. 3–21.

Florida, R. (2002) *The Rise of the Creative Class: And How It Is Transforming Work, Leisure, Community, and Everyday Life*. New York: Basic Books.

Flyvbjerg, B. (2005) *Design by Deception: The Politics of Megaproject Approval*. Harvard Design Magazine, Spring/Summer, pp. 50–59.

Foley, M., McPherson, G. and McGillivray, D. (2008) 'Establishing Singapore as the Events and Entertainment Capital of Asia'. In J. Ali-Knight, M. Robertson, A. Fyall and A. Ladkin (eds) *International Perspectives of Festivals and Events*. Oxford: Butterworth-Heinemann.

Fraser, C. and Baert, T. (2003) 'Lille: From Textile Giant to Tertiary Turbine'. In C. Couch, C. Fraser and S. Percy (eds) *Urban Regeneration in Europe* (pp. 85–108). Oxford: Blackwell.

Furbey, R. (1999) 'Urban "Regeneration": Reflections on a Metaphor'. Critical Social Policy, 19(4), pp. 419–445.

Ganau, J. (2008) 'Reinventing Memories: The Origin and Development of Barcelona's *Barri Gòtic*, 1880–1950'. Journal of Urban History, 34(5), pp. 795–832.

Garcia, B. (2004) 'Cultural Policy and Urban Regeneration in Western European Cities: Lessons from Experience, Prospects for the Future'. Local Economy, 19(4), pp. 312–326.

Garcia, B., Melville, R. and Cox, T. (2010) 'Impacts 08: Liverpool's Experience as European Capital of Culture'. University of Liverpool. Available at: www.liv.ac.uk/impacts08/papers/creating_an_impact–web.pdf (accessed 1 July 2011).

Garcia, M. and Claver, N. (2003) 'Barcelona Governing Coalitions, Visitors and the Changing City Centre'. In L. Hoffman, S. Fainstein and D. Judd (eds) *Cities and Visitors: Regulating People, Markets and City Space* (pp. 113–125). Oxford: Wiley Blackwell.

Garcia-Espuche, A., Guardia, M., Monclús, F. and Oyon, J. (1991) 'Modernization and Urban Beautification: The 1888 Barcelona World's Fair'. Planning Perspectives, 6, pp. 139–159.

Gartner, W. (1997) 'Image and Sustainable Tourism Systems'. In S. A. Wahab and J. Pigram (eds) *Tourism Development and Growth* (pp. 177–198). London: Routledge.

Getz, D. (1997) *Event Management and Event Tourism*. New York: Cognizant Communications.

—— (1999) 'The Impacts of Mega-Events on Tourism: Strategies for Destinations'. In T. Andersson, C. Persson, B. Sahlberg, and L.-I. Strom (eds) *The Impact of Mega-Events* (pp. 5–32). Ostersund, Sweden: European Tourism Research Institute.

Gibson, O. (2011) 'Olympic Basketball Arena's Design Hailed as "Template for Future"'. Guardian, 8 June 2011. Available at: www.guardian.co.uk/sport/2011/jun/08/olympic-basketball-arena-template-future (accessed 1 July 2011).

Glancey, J. (2001) *London: Bread and Circuses*. London: Verso.

Glynn, M. (2008) 'Configuring the Field of Play: How Hosting the Olympic Games Impacts Civic Community'. Journal of Management Studies, 45(6), pp. 1117–1146.

Glyptis, S. (1991) 'Sport and Tourism'. In C. Cooper (ed.) *Progress in Tourism, Recreation and Hospitality Management 3*. London: Bellhaven.

Goffman, E. (1967) *Interaction Ritual: Essays on Face-to-Face Behaviour*. London: Allen Lane, the Penguin Press.

Gold, J. and Gold, M. (2005) *Cities of Culture: Staging International Festivals and the Urban Agenda, 1851–2000*. Aldershot: Ashgate.

—— (2007a) 'Access for All: The Rise of the Paralympic Games'. Journal of the Royal Society for the Promotion of Health, 127, pp. 133–141.

—— (2007b) 'The Paralympic Games'. In J. Gold and M. Gold (eds) *Olympic Cities: City Agendas, Planning and the World's Games, 1896–2012* (pp. 84–99). London: Routledge.

—— (2009) 'Future Indefinite? London 2012, the Spectre of Retrenchment and the Challenge of Olympic Sports Legacy'. The London Journal, 34(2), pp. 179–196.

Gospodini, A. (2009) 'Post-Industrial Trajectories of Mediterranean European Cities: The Case of Post-Olympic Athens'. Urban Studies, 45(5/6), pp. 1157–1186.

Göteborg & Co (2011) 'Annual Report 2010'. Available at: http://www2.goteborg.com/templates/Page.aspx?id=7960 (accessed 1 July 2011).

Gotham, K. F. (2005a) 'Theorising Urban Spectacles: Festivals, Tourism and the Transformation of Urban Space'. City, 9(2), pp. 225–246.

—— (2005b) 'Tourism from Above and Below: Globalization, Localization and New Orleans's Mardi Gras'. International Journal of Urban and Regional Research, 29, pp. 309–326.

—— (2011) 'Resisting Urban Spectacle: The 1984 Louisiana World Exposition and the Contradictions of Mega Events'. Urban Studies, 48(1), pp. 197–214.

Grammatikopoulos, V., Papacharisis, V., Koustelios, A., Tsigilis, N. and Theodorakis, Y. (2004) 'Evaluation of the Training Program for Greek Olympic Education'. The International Journal of Educational Management, 18(1), pp. 66–73.

Greene, S. (2003) 'Staged Cities: Mega-Events, Slum Clearance, and Global Capital'. Yale Human Rights and Development Law Journal, 6, January, pp. 161–187.

Greenlagh, P. (1989) Ephemeral Vistas: Great Exhibitions, Expositions Universelles and World's Fairs, 1851–1939. Manchester: Manchester University Press.

Gursoy, G. and Kendall, K. (2006) 'Hosting Mega Events: Modeling Locals' Support'. Annals of Tourism Research, 33(3), pp. 603–623.

GVA Grimley (2006) 'Urban Design, Heritage and Character Analysis Report for Gateshead Council'. March 2006.

Hall, C. M. (1992) Hallmark Tourist Events: Impact, Management and Planning. London: Bellhaven.

—— (2000) Tourism Planning: Policies, Processes, and Relationships. Harlow: Pearson Education.

—— (2006) 'Urban Entrepreneurship, Corporate Interests and Sports Mega-Events: The Thin Policies of Competitiveness within the Hard Outcomes of Neoliberalism'. The Sociological Review, 54(2), pp. 59–70.

Harcup, T. (2000) 'Re-Imaging a Post-Industrial City: The Leeds St Valentine's Fair as a Civic Spectacle'. City, 4(2), pp. 215–231.

Harvey, D. (1989) The Condition of Postmodernity. Blackwell: Oxford.

Hatherley, O. (2010) A Guide to the New Ruins of Great Britain. London: Verso.

Helleman, G. and Wassenberg, F. (2004) 'The Renewal of What Was Tomorrow's Idealistic City: Amsterdam's Bijlemermeer High Rise'. Cities, 21(1), pp. 3–17.

Hemphill, L., McGreal, S. and Berry, J. (2004) 'An Indicator-Based Approach for Evaluating Sustainable Urban Regeneration Performance. Part 2, Empirical Evaluation and Case-Study Analysis'. Urban Studies, 41(4), pp. 757–772.

Henderson, J. (2006) 'Uniquely Singapore? A Case Study in Destination Branding'. Journal of Vacation Marketing, 13(3), pp. 261–274.

Henderson, S. (2010) 'Developer Collaboration in Urban Land Development: Partnership Working in Paddington, London'. Environment and Planning C, 28, pp. 165–185.

Henry, I. and Paramio-Salcines, J. (1999) 'Sport and the Analysis of Symbolic Regimes: A Case Study of the City of Sheffield'. Urban Affairs Review, 34(5), pp. 641–666.

Higham, J. (1999) 'Sport as an Avenue of Tourism Development: An Analysis of the Positive and Negative Impacts of Sports Tourism'. Current Issues in Tourism, 2(1), pp. 82–89.

Hiller, H. (1998) 'Assessing the Impact of Mega-Events: A Linkage Model'. Current Issues in Tourism, 1(1), pp. 47–57.

—— (2000) 'Mega-Events, Urban Boosterism and Growth Strategies: An Analysis of the Objectives and Legitimations of the Cape Town 2004 Olympic Bid'. International Journal of Urban and Regional Research, 24, pp. 439–458.

—— (2006) 'Post-Event Outcomes and the Post-Modern Turn: The Olympics and Urban Transformations'. European Sport Management Quarterly, 6(4), pp. 317–332.

Hjalager, A.-M. (2009) 'Cultural Tourism Innovation Systems: The Roskilde Festival'. Scandinavian Journal of Hospitality and Tourism, 9(2), pp. 266–287.

Holden, R. (1989) 'British Garden Festivals: The First Eight Years'. Landscape and Urban Planning, 18(1), pp. 17–35.

Holmes, R. and Shamsuddin, A. (1997) 'Short and Long-Term Effects of World Exposition 1986 on US Demand for British Columbia Tourism'. Tourism Economics, 3(2), pp. 137–160.

Holton, K. (1998) 'Dressing for Success: Lisbon as European Cultural Capital'. Journal of American Folklore, 111, pp. 173–196.

Horne, J. and Manzenreiter, W. (2004) 'Accounting for Mega Events'. International Review for the Sociology of Sport, 39(2), pp. 187–203.

Hughes, G. (1999) 'Urban Revitalization: The Use of Festive Time Strategies'. Leisure Studies, 18(2), pp. 119–135.

Hughes, R. (1999) Barcelona. London: Verso.

Imrie, R., Lees, L. and Raco, M. (2009) 'London's Regeneration'. In R. Imrie, L. Lees and M. Raco (eds) Regenerating London (pp. 3–23). Abingdon: Routledge.

Inglis, S. (2004) Played in Manchester. London: English Heritage.

Insight Economics (2006) Triple Bottom Line Assessment of the XVIII Commonwealth Games. Report to the OCGC. October.

Jamieson, K. (2004) 'Edinburgh: The Festival Gaze and Its Boundaries'. Space and Culture, 7(1), pp. 64–75.

Jansson, A. (2005) 'Re-Encoding the Spectacle: Urban Fatefulness and Mediated Stigmatisation in the "City Of Tomorrow"'. Urban Studies, 42(10), pp. 1671–1691.

Jenkins, R. (2002) Twelve Cities: A Personal Memoir. London: Macmillan.

Jenkins, S. (2007) 'Coe and Jowell Have Been Duped by the Biggest Overselling Scam in History'. Guardian, 2 March, p. 36.

Johnson, L. (2009) Cultural Capitals: Revaluing the Arts, Remaking Urban Spaces. Farnham: Ashgate.

Jones, C. (2004) Paris: Biography of a City. London: Penguin.

—— (2006) 'Verdict on the British Enterprise Zone Experiment'. International Planning Studies, 11(2), pp. 109–123.

Jones, P. and Gripaios, P. (2000) 'A Review of the BURA Awards for Best Practice in Urban Regeneration'. Property Management, 18(4), pp. 218–229.

Judge, L., Petersen, J. and Lydum, M. (2009) 'The Best Kept Secret in Sports: The 2010 Youth Olympic Games'. International Review for the Sociology of Sport, 44(2/3), pp. 173–191.

Kavaratzis, M. (2004) From City Marketing to City Branding: Towards a Theoretical Framework for Developing City Brands. Place Branding, 1, pp. 58–73.

Kearins, K. and Pavlovich, K. (2002) 'The Role of Stakeholders in Sydney's Green Games'. Corporate Social Responsibility and Environmental Management, 9, pp. 157–169.

Kellett, P., Hede, A.-M. and Chalip, L. (2008) 'Social Policy for Sport Events: Leveraging (Relationships with) Teams from Other Nations for Community Benefit'. European Sport Management Quarterly, 8(2), pp. 101–121.

Khakee, A. (2007) 'From Olympic Village to Middle Class Waterfront Housing Project: Ethics in Stockholm's Development Planning'. Planning Practice and Research, 22(2), pp. 235–251.

Kissoudi, P. (2010) 'Athens' Post Olympic Aspirations and the Extent of Their Realisation'. International Journal of the History of Sport, 27(16–18), pp. 2780–2797.

Köhring, A. (2010) '"Sporting Moscow": Stadia Buildings and the Challenging of Public Space in the Post-War Soviet Union'. Urban History, 37, pp. 253–271.

KPMG (2009) 'Olympic Land Development: Findings and Recommendations. 8 September 2009'. Available at: www.lda.gov.uk/documents/board-and-commmittee-papers/board-papers/2009/16-september-2009/public_item_02.3(1)_appendix_1,_kpmg_report.pdf (accessed 1 July 2011).

Larson, M. (2009) 'Joint Event Production in the Jungle, the Park, and the Garden: Metaphors of Event Networks'. Tourism Management, 30(3), pp. 393–399.

Laurier, E. (1993) 'Tackintosh: Glasgow's Supplementary Gloss'. In G. Kearns and C. Philo (eds) Selling Places: The City as Cultural Capital, Past and Present (pp. 267–289). Oxford: Pergamon.

Lawless, P. (2010) '"Urban Regeneration: Is there a Future?" People, Place and Policy Online', 4(1), pp. 24–28.

Lawless, P. and Ramsden, P. (1990) 'Land Use Planning and the Inner Cities: The Case of the Lower Don Valley, Sheffield'. Local Government Studies, 16(1), pp. 33–47.

Lawson, C. (1985) Intergovernmental Challenges of the 1984 Olympic Games. Publius, Summer, pp. 127–141.

LDA (London Development Agency) (2007) 'London 2012 Opportunities. Fund Projects Funded by Opportunities Fund "Opportunities for Engagement in London 2012"'. Available at: legacy.london.gov.uk/news/docs/opportunities_fund_apr07.rtf (accessed 1 July 2011).

Lee, P. (2002) 'The Economic and Social Justification for Publicly Financed Stadia: The Case of Vancouver's BC Place Stadium'. European Planning Studies, 10(7), pp. 861–873.

Leeds, M. (2008) 'Do Good Olympics Make Good Neighbours?' Contemporary Economic Policy, 26(3), pp. 460–467.

Lenskyj, H. (2002) Best Olympics Ever? The Social Impacts of Sydney 2000. New York: SUNY Press.

Lesjo, J. (2000) 'Lillehammer 1994: Planning, Figuration and the Green Winter Games'. International Review for the Sociology of Sport, 35(3), pp. 282–293.

Lever, W. (2001) 'Charismatic Urban Leaders and Economic Development: Good Mayors and Bad Mayors in Europe'. Space and Polity, 5(2), pp. 113–126.

Lewis, P. (2003) New Orleans: The Making of an Urban Landscape. Sante Fe, NM: Center for American Places.

Liao, H. and Pitts, A. (2006) 'A Brief Historical Review of Olympic Urbanism'. International Journal of the History of Sport, 23(7), pp. 1232–1252.

Lim, S. and Lee, J. (2006) 'Host Population Perceptions of the Impacts of Mega-Events'. Asia Pacific Journal of Tourism Research, 11(4), pp. 407–415.

Lochhead, H. (2005) 'A New Vision for Sydney Olympic Park'. Urban Design International, 10, pp. 215–222.

Lockyer, A. (2007) 'The Logic of Spectacle c. 1970'. *Art History*, 30(4), pp. 571–589.

Lowes, M. (2002) *Indy Dreams and Urban Nightmares*. Toronto: Toronto University Press.

MacAloon, J. (2008) 'Legacy as Managerial/Magical Discourse in Contemporary Olympic Affairs'. International Journal of the History of Sport, 25(14), pp. 2060–2071.

Mace, A., Hall, P. and Gallent, N. (2007) 'New East Manchester: Urban Renaissance or Urban Opportunism?' European Planning Studies, 15(1), pp. 51–65.

MacRury, I. and Poynter, G. (2008) 'The Regeneration Games: Commodities, Gifts and the Economics of London 2012'. International Journal of the History of Sport, 25(14), pp. 2072–2090.

Maddox, R. (2004) *The Best of all Possible Islands*. Albany, NY: SUNY Press.

Madsen, H. (1992) 'Place Marketing in Liverpool: A Review'. International Journal of Urban and Regional Research, 16(4), pp. 633–40.

Maennig, W. and du Plessis, S. (2009) 'Sport Stadia, Sporting Events and Urban Development: International Experience and the Ambitions of Durban'. Urban Forum, 20(10), pp. 61–76.

Majoor, S. (2008) 'Progressive Planning Ideals in a Neo-liberal Context: The Case of Orestad Copenhagen'. International Planning Studies, 13(2), pp. 101–117.

Mangan, J. (2008) 'Prologue: Guarantees of Global Goodwill: Post-Olympic Legacies – Too Many Limping White Elephants?' International Journal of the History of Sport, 25(14), pp. 1869–1883.

Marshall, T. (1996) 'Barcelona – Fast Forward? City Entrepreneurialism in the 1980s and 1990s'. European Planning Studies, 4(2), pp. 147–165.

Mayor of London (2011) 'The O2 Named World's Most Popular Music Venue'. Available at: http://blog.visitlondon.com/2011/01/the-o2-named-worlds-most-popular-music-venue/ (accessed 1 July 2011).

McCartney, G., Thomas, S., Thomson, H., Scott, J., Hamilton, V., Hanlon, P., Morrison, D. and Bond, S. (2010) 'The Health and Socioeconomic Impacts of Major Multi-Sport Events: Systematic Review (1978–2008)'. British Medical Journal 2010; 340: C2369.

McCully, M. (1985) 'Introduction'. In M. Raeburn (ed.) *Homage to Barcelona* (pp. 15–78). London: Arts Council of Great Britain.

McGuigan, J. (2005) 'Neo-Liberalism, Culture and Policy'. International Journal of Cultural Policy, 11(3), pp. 229–241.

McManus, P. (2004) 'Writing the Palimpsest, Again: Rozelle Bay and the Sydney 2000 Olympic Games'. Urban Policy and Research, 22(2), pp. 157–167.

McNab, T. (2010) 'Taking Part in Sport is Vital to Our Society, but It Will not Come for Free'. Guardian, 22 December.

McNeill, D. (1999) *Urban Change and the European Left: Tales from the New Barcelona*. New York: Routledge.

—— (2003) 'Mapping the European Left: The Barcelona Experience'. Antipode, 35(1), pp. 74–94.

—— (2008) 'The Hotel and the City'. Progress in Human Geography, 32(3), pp. 383–398.

Melbourne City Council (2002) *Melbourne City Plan 2010*. June.

Mihalik, B. and Simonetta, L. (1998) 'Host Perceptions of the 1996 Atlanta Olympic Games – Year II'. Festival Management and Event Tourism, 5, pp. 9–19.

Misener, L. and Mason, D. (2006) 'Creating Community Networks: Can Sporting Events Offer Meaningful Sources of Social Capital?' Managing Leisure, 11(1), pp. 39–56.

Modrey, E. (2008) 'Architecture as a Mode of Self Representation at the Olympic Games in Rome (1960) and Munich (1972)'. European Review of History, 15(6), pp. 691–706.

Mohan, G. and Mohan, J. (2002) 'Placing Social Capital'. Progress in Human Geography, 26(2), pp. 191–210.

Monclús, F.-J. (2003) 'The Barcelona Model: An Original Formula? From Reconstruction to Strategic Urban Projects (1979–2004)'. Planning Perspectives, 18(4), pp. 399–421.

—— (2006) 'International Exhibitions and Planning: Hosting Large-Scale Events as Place Promotion and as Catalysts of Urban Regeneration'. In F.-J. Monclús and M. Guardia (eds) *Culture, Urbanism and Planning* (pp. 215–239). Aldershot: Ashgate.

—— (2007) 'Barcelona 1992'. In J. Gold and M. Gold (eds) *Olympic Cities: City Agendas, Planning and the World's Games, 1896–2012* (pp. 218–235). London: Routledge.

—— (2009) *International Exhibitions and Urbanism: The Zaragoza Expo 2008 Project*. Farnham: Ashgate.

Mooney, G. (2004) 'Cultural Policy as Urban Transformation? Critical Reflections on Glasgow, European City of Culture 1990'. Local Economy, 19(4), pp. 327–340.

MORI (2004) 'The Sports Development Impact of the Commonwealth Games 2002'. Post-Games Research Final Report. London: MORI.

Morris, P. (2004) *The Bakhtin Reader: Selected Writings of Bakhtin, Medvedev, Voloshinov*. London: Edward Arnold.

Mumford, L. (1961) *The City in History: Its Origins, Its Transformations, and Its Prospects*. London: Secker & Warburg.

Munoz, F. (2006) 'Olympic Urbanism and Olympic Villages: Planning Strategies in Olympic Host Cities, London 1908 to London 2012'. Sociological Review, 54, pp. 175–187.

Murukami-Wood, D. and Coaffee, J. (2007) 'Lockdown! Resistance, Resurgence and the Stage Set City'. In R. Atkinson and G. Helms (eds) *Securing an Urban Renaissance: Crime, Community, and British Urban Policy* (pp. 91–106). Bristol: Policy Press.

Museum of London (2011) 'Outliving the Festival'. Available at: www.museumoflondon.org.uk/archive/exhibits/festival/permanence.htm (accessed 1 July 2011).

Nappi-Choulet, I. (2006) 'The Role and Behaviour of Commercial Property Investors and Developers in French Urban Regeneration: The Experience of the Paris Region'. Urban Studies, 43(9), pp. 1511–1535.

Newby, L. (2003) *To What Extent Have the Commonwealth Games Accelerated the Physical, Social, and Economic Regeneration of East Manchester?* Glasgow: University of Glasgow Press.

Newman, H. (1999) 'Neighborhood Impacts of Atlanta's Olympic Games'. Community Development Journal, 34, pp. 151–159.

—— (2002) 'Race and the Tourist Bubble in Downtown Atlanta'. Urban Affairs Review, 37(3), pp. 301–321.

Newman, P. (2007) '"Back the Bid": The 2012 Summer Olympics and the Governance of London'. Journal of Urban Affairs, 29(3), pp. 255–267.

Newman, P. and Thornley, A. (1996) *Urban Planning in Europe: International Competition, National Systems, and Planning Projects*. London: Routledge.

Newman, P. and Tual, M. (2002) 'The Stade de France. The Last Expression of French Centralism?' European Planning Studies, 10(7), pp. 831–84.

Newsome, T. and Comer, J. (2000) 'Changing Intra-Urban Location Patterns of Major League Sports Facilities'. Professional Geographer, 52(1), pp. 105–120.

Newton, C. (2009) 'The Reverse Side of the Medal: About the 2010 FIFA World Cup and the Beautification of the N2 in Cape Town'. Urban Forum, 20, pp. 93–10.

Nichols, G. and Ralston, R. (2011) *Lessons from the Volunteering Legacy of the 2002 Commonwealth Games*. Urban Studies, published online 31 March 2011.

Nielsen, N. (1995) 'The Stadium in the City: A Modern Story'. In J. Bale and O. Moen (eds) *The Stadium and the City* (pp. 21–44). Keele: Keele University Press.

Nordin, S. (2003) *Tourism Clustering and Innovation: Paths to Economic Growth and Development*. Oestersund: European Tourism Research Institute.

Nunes Silva, C. and Syrett, S. (2006) 'Governing Lisbon: Evolving Forms of City Governance'. International Journal of Urban and Regional Research, 30(1), pp. 98–119.

Nyberg, M. (2008) 'Sports Events Put Gothenburg on the Map'. Available at: www.sweden.se/eng/Home/Lifestyle/Sport-leisure/Reading/figure-skating-gothenburg-sweden/ (accessed 1 July 2011).

Nylund, M. (2006) 'Sporting Mega-Events and the Residents: Assessing the IAAF World Championships 2005'. Helsinki Quarterly, 4, pp. 12–17.

O'Brien, D. (2006) 'Event Business Leveraging: The Sydney 2000 Olympic Games'. Annals of Tourism Research, 33(1), pp. 240–261.

—— (2007) 'Points of Leverage: Maximising Host Community Benefit from a Regional Surfing Festival'. European Sport Management Quarterly, 7(2), pp. 141–165.

—— (2011) 'Who is in Charge? Liverpool, European Capital of Culture 2008 and the Governance of Cultural Planning'. Town Planning Review, 82(1), pp. 49–59.

O'Callaghan, C. and Linehan, D. (2007) 'Identity, Politics and Conflict in Dockland Development in Cork, Ireland: European Capital of Culture 2005'. Cities, 24(4), pp. 311–323.

O'Sullivan, D. and Jackson, M. (2002) 'Festival Tourism: A Contributor to Sustainable Local Economic Development?' Journal of Sustainable Tourism, 10(4), pp. 325–342.

Oatley, N. (1998) 'Restructuring Urban Policy: The Single Regeneration Budget and the Challenge Fund'. In N. Oatley (ed.) *Cities, Economic Competition and Urban Policy* (pp. 146–162). London: Paul Chapman.

Oc, T., Tiesdell, S. and Moynihan, D. (1997) 'The Death and Life of City Challenge: The Potential for Lasting Impacts in a Limited-Life Urban Regeneration Initiative'. Planning Practice and Research, 12(4), pp. 367–381.

ODPM (2003) *Sustainable Communities: Building for the Future*. Wetherby: Office of the Deputy Prime Minister.

Ohmann, S., Jones, I. and Wilkes, K. (2006) 'The Perceived Social Impacts of the 2006 Football World Cup on Munich Residents'. Journal of Sport and Tourism, 11(2), pp. 129–152.

Olds, K. (1998) 'Urban Mega-Events, Eviction and Housing Rights: The Canadian Case'. Current Issues in Tourism, 1(1), pp. 1–47.

OlympiaPark München GmbH (2011) 'Die Olympiapark München GmbH: World Record in Events'. Available at: www.olympiapark.de/en/home/olympic-park/olympiapark-muenchen-gmbh/ (accessed 1 July 2011).

Orueta, F. and Fainstein, S. (2008) 'The New Mega-Projects: Genesis and Impacts'. International Journal of Urban and Regional Research, 32, pp. 759–767.

Owen, K. (2002) 'The Sydney Olympics and Urban Entrepreneurialism'. Australian Geographical Studies, 40(3), pp. 323–336.

Packard, J. and Ballantyne, J. (2010) 'The Impact of Music Festival Attendance on Young People's Psychological and Social Well-Being'. Psychology of Music, 39, pp. 1–18.

Panagiotopoulou, R. (2009) 'The 28th Olympic Games in Athens 2004'. In G. Poynter and I. MacRury (eds) *Olympic Cities: 2012 and the Remaking of London* (pp. 145–162). Farnham: Ashgate.

Pappalepore, I. (2011) *The Olympics Cultural Programme and Its Role in Fostering Local Creativity*. Unpublished Paper for IOC. January.

Parker, S. (2004) *Urban Theory and the Urban Experience*. Abingdon: Routledge.

Pearce, D. (1997) 'Tourist Organisations in Catalonia: Regional and Local Structures and Issues'. In C. Cooper and S. Wanhill (eds) *Tourism Development: Environmental and Community Issues* (pp. 75–88). Chichester. John Wiley & Sons.

Peel, D., Lloyd, G. and Lord, A. (2009) 'Business Improvement Districts and the Discourse of Contractualism'. European Planning Studies, 17(3), pp. 401–422.

Pilkington, E. (2011) 'New Orleans Population Falls 30% in 10 years'. Guardian, 4 February.

Pillay, U. and Bass, O. (2008) 'Mega-Events as a Response to Poverty Reduction: The 2010 FIFA World Cup and Its Urban Development Implications'. Urban Forum, 19, pp. 329–346.

Pine, B. and Gilmore, J. (1998) 'Welcome to the Experience Economy'. Harvard Business Review, 76(4), pp. 97–105.

Pitts, A. and Liao, H. (2009) *Sustainable Olympic Design and Urban Development*. Abingdon: Routledge.

Plaza, B. (2000) 'Evaluating the Influence of a Large Cultural Artefact in the Attraction of Tourism: The Guggenheim Museum Bilbao Case Study'. Urban Affairs Review, 36(2), pp. 264–274.

Porter, L., Jaconelli, M., Cheyne, J., Eby, D. and Wagenaar, H. (2009) 'Planning Displacement: The Real Legacy of Major Sporting Events'. Planning Theory and Practice, 10(3), pp. 395–418.

Potter, K. (2009) 'Using the Power of a Major Sporting Event as a Catalyst for Community Regeneration: A Case Study of the 2005 UEFA Women's Championships'. In J. Magee (ed.) *Women, Football and Europe: Contemporary Perspectives, 2*. London: Meyer & Meyer.

Poynter, G. (2009) *Literature Review: Olympic Legacy Governance Arrangements*. Report for London Assembly. London: LERC/UEL.

Preuss, H. (2004) *The Economics of Staging the Olympics*. Northampton: Edward Elgar.

—— (2007) 'The Conceptualisation and Measurement of Mega Sport Event Legacies'. Journal of Sport and Tourism, 12(3–4), pp. 207–227.

Prytherch, D. and Maiques, J. V. B. (2009) 'City Profile: Valencia'. Cities, 26(2), pp. 103–115.

Putnam, R. (2000) *Bowling Alone: The Collapse and Revival of American Community*. New York: Simon & Schuster.

Quinn, B. (2005) 'Arts Festivals and the City'. Urban Studies, 42(5/6), pp. 927–943.

Raco, M. (2004) 'Whose Gold Rush? The Social Legacy of a London Olympics'. In A. Vigor., M. Mean and C. Timms. (eds) *After the Gold Rush: A Sustainable Olympics for London* (pp. 31–50). London: IPPR/DEMOS.

—— (2005) 'A Step Change or a Step Back: The Thames Gateway and the Re-birth of the Urban Development Corporations'. Local Economy, 20(2), pp. 141–153.

Raitz, K. B. (1987) 'Perception of Sport Landscapes and Gratification in the Sport Experience'. Sport Place, Winter, pp. 4–19.

Ralston, R., Lumsdon, L. and Downward, P. (2005) 'The Third Force in Events Tourism: Volunteers at the XVII Commonwealth Games'. Journal of Sustainable Tourism, 13(5), pp. 504–519.

Ray, N. and Ryder, M. (2003) '"Ebilities" Tourism: An Exploratory Discussion of the Travel Needs and Motivations of the Mobility-Disabled'. Tourism Management, 24, pp. 57–77.

Reid, G. (2007) 'Showcasing Scotland? A Case Study of the MTV Europe Music Awards Edinburgh 03'. Leisure Studies, 26(4), pp. 479–494.

Reiss, S. (1981) 'Power Without Authority: Los Angeles' Elites and the Construction of the Coliseum'. Journal of Sport History, 8(1), pp. 50–65.

Ren, X. (2009) 'Olympic Beijing: Reflections on Urban Space and Global Connectivity'. International Journal of the History of Sport, 26(8), pp. 1011–1039.

Renzaho, A. (2008) 'Re-Visioning Cultural Competence in Community Health Services in Victoria'. Australian Health Review, 32(2), pp. 223–235.

Richards, G. and Palmer, R. (2010) *Eventful Cities*. Oxford: Butterworth-Heinemann.

Richards, G. and Wilson, J. (2004) 'The Impact of Cultural Events on City Image: Rotterdam, Cultural Capital of Europe 2001'. Urban Studies, 41(10), pp. 1931–1951.

—— (2007) 'Developing Creativity in Tourist Experiences: A Solution to the Serial Reproduction of Culture?' Tourism Management, 27(6), pp. 1209–1223.

Ritchie, J. R. B. (2000) 'Turning 16 Days into 16 Years through Olympic Legacies'. Event Management, 6(3), pp. 155–165.

Ritchie, J. R. B. and Aitken, C. E. (1984) 'Olympulse I: The Research Program and Initial Results'. Journal of Travel Research, 22, pp. 17–25.

—— (1985) 'Olympulse II: Evolving Resident Attitudes toward the 1988 Olympic Winter Games'. Journal of Travel Research, 23, pp. 28–33.

Ritchie, J. R. B. and Lyons, M. (1987) 'Olympulse III/IV: A Mid-Term Report on Resident Attitudes Concerning the 1988 Olympic Winter Games'. Journal of Travel Research, 26, pp. 18–26.

—— (1990) 'Olympulse VI: A Post-Event Assessment of Resident Reaction to the XV Olympic Winter Games'. Journal of Travel Research, 28(3), pp. 14–23.

Ritchie, J. R. B. and Smith, B. H. (1991) 'The Impact of a Mega Event on Host Region Awareness: A Longitudinal Study'. Journal of Travel Research 30, pp. 3–9.

Roberts, D. (2010) 'Durban's Future? Rebranding through the Production/Policing of Event Specific Spaces at the 2010 World Cup'. Sport in Society, 13(10), pp. 1486–1497.

Roberts, P. (2000) 'The Evolution, Definition and Purpose of Urban Regeneration'. In P. Roberts and H. Sykes (eds) *Urban Regeneration: A Handbook* (pp. 9–36). London: Sage.

Roca, F. (1985) 'From Montjuic to the World'. In M. Raeburn (ed.) *Homage to Barcelona* (pp. 133–140). London: Arts Council of Great Britain.

Roche, M. (1994) 'Mega Events and Urban Policy'. Annals of Tourism Research, 21(1), pp. 1–19.

—— (2000) *Mega Events and Modernity: Olympics and Expos in the Growth of Global Culture.* London: Routledge.

Rohrer, J. (1985) 'The Universal Exhibition of 1888'. In M. Raeburn (ed.) *Homage to Barcelona* (pp. 97–100). London: Arts Council of Great Britain.

Rollin, H. (2008) 'International Exhibitions and Urban Renewal: Zaragoza Expo 2008 on Water and Sustainable Development'. International Journal of Iberian Studies, 21(3), pp. 263–273.

Rosentraub, M. (2003) 'Indianapolis: A Sports Strategy and the Redefinition of Downtown Redevelopment'. In D. Judd (ed.) *The Infrastructure of Play* (pp. 104–124). New York: M. E. Sharpe.

Roult, R. and Lefebvre, S. (2010) 'Planning and Reconversion of Olympic Heritages: The Montreal Olympic Stadium'. International Journal of the History of Sport, 27(16–18), pp. 2731–2747.

Rowe, D. (1995) *Popular Cultures: Rock Music, Sport and the Politics of Pleasure.* London: Sage.

Rowe, D. and McGurk, P. (1999) 'Drunk for Three Weeks: Sporting Success and City Image'. International Review for the Sociology of Sport, 34(2), pp. 125–141.

Rowe, P. (2006) *Building Barcelona: A Second Renaixenca.* Barcelona: Actar.

Runciman, D. (2010) *The Politics of the London Olympic Games: 1908, 1948, 2012.* Lecture, 23 February 2010, Queen Mary's College, London.

Rutheiser, C. (1996) *Imagineering Atlanta.* New York: Verso.

Sandercock, L. and Dovey, K. (2002) 'Pleasure, Politics, and the Public Interest: Melbourne's Riverscape Revitalization'. Journal of the American Planning Association, 68(2), pp. 151–164.

Schimmel, K. S. (1995) 'Growth Politics, Urban Development, and Sports Stadium Construction in the US: A Case Study'. In J. Bale and O. Moen (eds) *The Stadium and the City* (pp. 111–156). Keele: Keele University Press.

—— (2006) 'Deep Play: Sports Mega-Events and Urban Social Conditions in the USA'. Sociological Review, 54, pp. 160–174.

Scott, A. (1999) 'The Cultural Economy: Geography and the Creative Field'. Media, Culture and Society, 21, pp. 807–817.

Searle, G. (2002) 'Uncertain Legacy: Sydney's Olympic Stadium'. European Planning Studies, 10(7), pp. 845–860.

Searle, G. and Bounds, M. (1999) 'State Powers, State Land and Competition for Global Entertainment: The Case of Sydney'. International Journal of Urban and Regional Research, 23(1), pp. 165–172.

Shaw, S. (2009) 'It Was All "Smile for Dunedin!" Event Volunteer Experiences at the 2006 New Zealand Masters Games'. Sport Management Review, 12, pp. 26–33.

Silk, M. (2002) '"Bangsa Malaysia": Global Sport, the City and the Mediated Refurbishment of Local Identities'. Media, Culture and Society, 24, pp. 775–794.

Silk, M. and Amis, J. (2005) 'Sport Tourism, Cityscapes and Cultural Politics'. Sport in Society, 8(2), pp. 280–301.

Sjøholt, P. (1999) 'Culture as a Strategic Development Device: The Role of "European Cities of Culture" with Particular Reference to Bergen'. European Urban and Regional Studies, 6(4), pp. 339–347.

Smith, A. (2005a) 'Reimaging the City: The Value of Sport Initiatives'. Annals of Tourism Research, 32(1), pp. 229–248.

—— (2005b) 'Conceptualizing Image Change: The Reimaging of Barcelona'. Tourism Geographies, 7(4), pp. 398–423.

—— (2006) 'After the Circus Leaves Town: The Relationship Between Sport Events, Tourism and Urban Regeneration'. In M. Smith (ed.) *Tourism, Culture and Regeneration* (pp. 85–110). Wallingford: CABI.

—— (2007) 'Large-Scale Events and Sustainable Urban Regeneration: Key Principles for Host Cities'. Journal of Urban Regeneration and Renewal, 1(2), pp. 178–190.

—— (2008) 'Using Major Events to Promote Peripheral Urban Areas: Deptford and the 2007 Tour de France'. In J. Ali-Knight, M. Robertson, A. Fyall and A. Ladkin (eds) *International Perspectives of Festivals and Events* (pp. 3–19). Oxford: Butterworth-Heinemann/Elsevier.

—— (2009) 'Spreading the Positive Effects of Major Events to Peripheral Areas'. Journal of Policy Research in Tourism, Leisure and Events, 1(3), pp. 231–246.

—— (2010) 'The Development of "Sports-City" Zones and Their Potential Value as Tourism Resources for Urban Areas'. European Planning Studies, 18(3), pp. 385–410.

Smith, A. and Fox, T. (2007) 'From "Event-Led" to "Event-Themed" Regeneration: The 2002 Commonwealth Games Legacy Scheme'. Urban Studies, 44(5/6), pp. 1125–1143.

Smith, A. and Stevenson, N. (2009) 'A Review of Tourism Policy for the 2012 Olympic Games'. Cultural Trends, 18(1), pp. 97–102.

Smith, A. and Strand, I. (2011) 'Cultural Flagship, Regeneration Tool or Destination Icon? Exploring the Rationale for Oslo's New Opera House'. European Journal of Urban and Regional Research, 18(10), pp. 93–110.

Smith, A. and Thomas, N. (2005) 'The "Inclusion" of Elite Athletes with Disabilities in the 2002 Manchester Commonwealth Games: An Exploratory Analysis of British Newspaper Coverage'. Sport, Education and Society, 10(1), pp. 49–67.

Smith, Y. (1991) 'The World Student Games: An Initial Appraisal'. The Regional Review, 1(3), pp. 8–19.

Smyth, H. (1994) *Marketing the City: The Role of Flagship Development in Urban Regeneration*. London: E. & F. N. Spon.

Soderstrom, O. (2001) 'Expo. 02: Exhibiting Swiss Identity'. Ecumene, 8(4), pp. 497–451.

Soh, E. and Yuen, B. (2011) 'Singapore's Changing Spaces'. Cities, 28, pp. 3–10.

Solù-Morales, I. (1995) 'Terrain Vague' in C. Davidson (ed.) *Anyplace*. Cambridge: MIT Press.

Stevens, T. and Wootton, G. (1997) 'Sports Stadia and Arenas: Realising their Full Potential'. Tourism Recreation Research, 22(2), pp. 49–56.

Stevenson, D., Rowe, D. and Markwell, K. (2005) 'Explorations in Event Ecology: The Case of the International Gay Games'. Identities, 11(5), pp. 447–465.

Surborg, B., Van Wynsberghe, R. and Wyly, E. (2005) 'Mapping the Olympic Growth Machine'. City, 12(3), pp. 341–355.

Swart, K. and Bob, U. (2009) 'Venue Selection and the 2010 World Cup: A Case Study of Cape Town in Development and Dreams'. In U. Pillay, R. Tomlinson and O. Bass (eds) The Urban Legacy of the 2010 World Cup (pp. 111–140). Cape Town: HSRC.

Swyngedouw, E. (2004) 'Globalisation or "Glocalisation"? Networks, Territories and Rescaling'. Cambridge Review of International Affairs, 17(1), pp. 25–48.

Swyngedouw, E., Moulaert, F. and Rodriguez, A. (2002) 'Neoliberal Urbanization in Europe: Large-Scale Urban Development Projects and the New Urban Policy'. Antipode, 34(3), pp. 542–577.

Tallon, A. (2010) Urban Regeneration in the UK. London: Routledge.

Taylor, I., Evans, K. and Fraser, P. (1996) A Tale of Two Cities: A Study in Manchester and Sheffield. London: Routledge.

Thamnopoulos, Y. and Gargalianos, D. (2002) 'Ticketing of Large Scale Events: The Case of Sydney 2000 Olympic Games'. Facilities, 20(1/2), pp. 22–33.

Thörn, C. (2006) '"Dressed for Success" Entrepreneurial Cities, Sports and Public Space'. Paper presented at the ESF-LiU Conference, Vadstena, Sweden, 25–29 October. Linköping: Linköping University Electronic Press.

Thornley, A. (2002) 'Urban Regeneration and Sport Stadia'. European Planning Studies, 10(7), pp. 813–818.

Tibbot, R. (2002) 'Culture Club: Can Culture Lead Urban Regeneration?' Locum Destination Review, 9, pp. 71–73.

Tieglund, J. (1999) 'Mega-Events and Impacts on Tourism: The Predictions and Realities of the Lillehammer Olympics'. Impact Assessment and Project Appraisal, 17(4), pp. 305–317.

Tiesdell, S. and MacFarlane, G. (2007) 'The Part and the Whole: Implementing Masterplans in Glasgow's Gorbals'. Journal of Urban Design, 12(3), pp. 407–433.

Tranter, P. and Keefe, T. (2004) 'Motor Racing in Australia's Parliamentary Zone: Successful Event Tourism or the Emperor's New Clothes?' Urban Policy and Research, 22(2), pp. 169–187.

Tranter, P. and Lowes, M. (2009) 'Life in the Fast Lane: Environmental, Economic and Public Health Outcomes of Motorsport Spectacles in Australia'. Journal of Sport and Social Issues, 33(2), pp. 150–168.

Truno, E. (1995) 'Barcelona: City of Sport'. In M. de Moragas and M. Botella (eds) The Keys to Success: The Social, Sporting, Economic and Communications Impact of Barcelona '92. Barcelona: CEO-UAB.

TSE (2010) Developing a Winning Sports Event Strategy. Switzerland: TSE Consulting Publishing.

Tuan, Y. (1977) Space and Place: The Perspective of Experience. London: Edward Arnold.

Tufts, S. (2004) 'Building the "Competitive City": Labour and Toronto's Bid to Host the Olympic Games'. Geoforum, 35(1), pp. 47–58.

Turner, R. and Rosentraub, M. (2002) 'Tourism, Sports and the Centrality of Cities'. Journal of Urban Affairs, 24(5), pp. 487–492.

Turok, I. (2003) 'Cities, Clusters and Creative Industries: The Case of Film and Television in Scotland'. European Planning Studies, 11(5), pp. 549–565.

UEL (2007) *A Lasting Legacy for London? Assessing the Legacy of the Olympic Games and Paralympic Games*. May 2007. London: LERI.

United Nations (2011) 'Right to Housing at Risk as Brazil Prepares for World Cup and Olympics – UN expert'. Available at: www.un.org/wcm/content/site/sport/home/sport/template/news_item.jsp?cid=26117 (accessed 1 July 2011).

Valera, S. and Guardia, J. (2002) 'Urban Social Identity and Sustainability'. Environment and Behaviour, 34(1), pp. 54–66.

Van der Westhuizen, J. (2004) 'Marketing Malaysia as a Model Modern Muslim State: The Significance of the 16th Commonwealth Games'. Third World Quarterly, 25(7), pp. 1277–1291.

VANOC (2010a) 'Legacies of North American Olympic Winter Games. Volume 4: Vancouver 2010'. Available at: www.linkbc.ca/torc/downs1/legacies_of_the_2010_vancouver_olympic_and_paralympic_games_report_june_2010_final.pdf (accessed 1 July 2011).

—— (2010b) 'Sustainability Report 2009–10'. Available at: www.2010legaciesnow.com/vanoc_sustainability/ (accessed 1 July 2011).

Vanolo, A. (2007) 'The Image of the Creative City: Some Reflections on the Branding of Turin'. Cities, 25(6), pp. 370–381.

van Vrijaldenhoven, T. (2007) *Reaching Beyond the Gold: The Impact of Global Events on Urban Development*. Rotterdam: 010 Publishers.

Villette, S. and Hardill, I. (2007) 'Spatial Peripheries, Social Peripheries: Reflections on the "Suburbs" of Paris'. International Journal of Sociology and Social Policy, 27(1/2), pp. 51–64.

Waitt, G. (2003) 'Social Impacts of the Sydney Olympics'. Annals of Tourism Research, 30(1), pp. 194–215.

Walters, G. (2005a) 'Bidding for International Sport Events: How Governments Support and Undermine National Governing Bodies of Sport'. Sport in Society, 14(2), pp. 208–222.

—— (2005b) 'The Implementation of a Stakeholder Management Strategy During Stadium Development: A Case Study of Arsenal Football Club and the Emirates Stadium'. Managing Leisure, 16, pp. 49–64.

Walton, H., Longo, A. and Dawson, P. (2008) 'A Contingent Valuation of the 2012 London Olympic Games: A Regional Perspective'. Journal of Sports Economics, 9(3), pp. 304–317.

Wang, W. and Theodoraki, E. (2007) 'Mass Sport Policy Development in the Olympic City: The Case of Qingdao'. Journal of the Royal Society for the Promotion of Health, 127(3), pp. 125–132.

Waterman, S. (2008) 'Carnivals for Elites? The Cultural Politics of Arts Festivals'. Progress in Human Geography, 22, pp. 54–74.

Webb, T. (2001) *The Collaborative Games*. Sydney: Pluto.

Weber, R. (2010) 'Selling City Futures: The Financialisation of Urban Redevelopment Policy'. Economic Geography, 86(3), pp. 251–274.

Weed, M., Coren, E., Fiore, J., Mansfield, L., Wellard, I. and Chatziefstathiou, D. (2009) *A Systematic Review of the Evidence Base for Developing a Physical Activity and Health Legacy from the London 2012 Olympic and Paralympic Games*. London: Department of Health.

Weiner, J. (2000) *Stadium Games*. Minneapolis: Minnesota University Press.

Westerbeek, H. (2009) 'The Amsterdam Olympic Games of 1928 and 2028: Will City Heritage Inform Legacy Intent?' Sport in Society, 12(6), pp. 776–791.

Whitelegg, D. (2000) 'Going for Gold: Atlanta's Bid for Fame'. International Journal of Urban and Regional Research, 24, pp. 801−817.

Whitson, D. (2004) 'Bringing the World to Canada: "The Periphery of the Centre"'. Third World Quarterly, 25(7), pp. 1215–1232.

Wilson, H. (1996) 'What is an Olympic City? Visions of Sydney 2000'. Media, Culture and Society, 18, pp. 603–618.

Wood, E. (2006) 'Measuring the Social Impacts of Local Authority Events: A Pilot Study for a Civic Pride Scale'. International Journal of Nonprofit Voluntary Sector Marketing, 11, pp. 165–179.

Woodward, C. (1992) *Buildings of Europe: Barcelona*. Manchester: Manchester University Press.

Yoon, H. (2009) 'The Legacy of the 1988 Seoul Olympic Games'. In G. Poynter and I. MacRury (eds) *Olympic Cities: 2012 and the Remaking of London* (pp. 87–96). Farnham: Ashgate.

Yuen, S. (2008) 'Sport and Urban Development in Singapore'. Cities, 25, pp. 29–36.

Zhang, J. and Wu, F. (2008) 'Mega-Event Marketing and Urban Growth Coalitions'. Town Planning Review, 79(2–3), pp. 209–226.

Zhou, Y. and Ap, J. (2009) 'Residents' Perceptions Towards the Impacts of the Beijing 2008 Olympic Games'. Journal of Travel Research, 48(1), pp. 78–91.

Author Index

Page numbers in *italics* refer to figures and tables, those in **bold** indicate case studies.

Subject Index

Page numbers in *italics* refer to figures and tables, those in **bold** indicate case studies.